Dear Su:

Hannah

Handmaid of the Highest

We hope you have a very happy birthday! God bless + keep you.

With our love in the Lord
bro Terry + sis. Pat
xx

Hannah
Handmaid of the Highest

Roger Lewis

The Christadelphian
404 Shaftmoor Lane, Hall Green, Birmingham B28 8SZ, UK

2020

First published 2020

© 2020 The Christadelphian Magazine and Publishing Association

ISBN 978 0 85189 435 5 (print edition)
ISBN 978 0 85189 436 2 (electronic edition)

Printed and bound in the UK by
CMP (UK) Limited

Scripture quotations are from the Authorised Version of the Bible (The King James Bible) unless otherwise stated, the rights in which are vested in the Crown, and reproduced by permission of the Crown's Patentee, Cambridge University Press.

Scripture quotations marked (GLT) are from the Literal Translation of the Holy Bible (LITV), copyright © 1976-2000, by Jay P. Green, Sr. Used by permission of the copyright holder.

Scripture quotations marked (RSV) are from the Revised Standard Version Bible, copyright © 1946, 1952 and 1971 the Division of Christian Education of the National Council of the Churches of Christ in the United States of America. Used by permission. All rights reserved.

Contents

Prologue 1
1. Hannah and her grief 7
2. Hannah and her vow 31
3. Hannah and her loan 55
4. Hannah and her song 79
5. Hannah and her child 103
6. Hannah and her hope 127
7. Hannah and her priest 151
8. Hannah and her Lord 175
Epilogue 200

Appendices
1. What was the setting for Hannah's troublous times? 206
2. Who were the enemies of Hannah's holy cause? 212
3. What was the source of Hannah's great adversity? 216
4. What was the import of Hannah's special song? 221
5. What was the lesson of Hannah's little coat? 225
6. Who was the guardian of Hannah's firstborn son? 228
7. What was the story of Hannah's faithful priest? 232
Scripture index 235

Prologue

CAPTURING the likeness of a person is no easy task. Yet the skilled painter can evoke with a single image, the sum of a person's whole. Every portrait has a context which provides its vital focus, a distinct impression formed by the careful symmetry of the details. We observe the tilt of the face, the folding of the hands, the shape of the smile. We notice the colour of the hair, the texture of the robe, the light of the eyes. These are all clues which conspire to tell us who the person was, though their life was captured in but an instant of time. That single moment however, invites the deepest reflection as to what their circumstances might have been, and what that moment in their life really told. A picture tells a tale, and when the seeing eye is turned upon it, the viewer not only delights in the details to be discovered, but departs with a deeper understanding, enriched with lessons learned from the story that lies behind the likeness.

The Bible, with similar clarity exhibits men and women whose lives the Father was pleased to outline. In every generation of the saints, such individuals have loomed large upon the landscape of their times. Their inclusion in the divine narrative comes because they reveal an aspect of the ways of God, which can inform us in our own journey of faith. They march in procession across the canvas of scripture, each profile an illustration of an attitude and a disposition that can encourage us in similar circumstances. We witness the integrity of Joseph, and the faith of Rahab. We see the bravery of Jonathan, and the courage of Esther. We observe the wisdom of John, and the care of Lydia.

In many of these Bible cameos, the Spirit draws attention to one outstanding aspect. The painting of their life is shot through with one colour above all others, the one tone that made their life so memorable. Thoughtful contemplation is needed before our sight becomes insight, and that tone is seen. But with awareness comes appreciation. When we grasp the key to their lives, the men and women of scripture provide us with inspiration. Their portraits, painted so long ago, and in times so different from our own, still portray characters to whom we are drawn, and from whom we can take both comfort and counsel. Godly Bible characters are the best of role models. They bear the mark of God, for their lives otherwise would not have been recorded at all. It is our privilege and burden to discover their secret, and use it for good in our own walk before God. The best of Bible study is to be found in Bible meditation, for the message that lies beyond the words can only be discovered by that thoughtful contemplation which neither dictionary nor device can reveal. The thinking of the Spirit is the only means by which we can discern the deeper message of God, concealed in holy writ. That thinking is God's gift to all His people, and in its exercise, the lessons we discern are granted that our lives might be changed to magnify His name.

The story that follows is one such picture of the Spirit, the account of a sister so special, that her life has been preserved in a portrait of particular intensity. Her prominence came not because of ambition or pride, for her deepest passion lay not in her own importance at all. She was made famous by what she accomplished in the purpose of God, and by her commitment to the advancing of that purpose with single-minded devotion. It is but a picture of the pen, and yet it captures the very likeness of this woman of God, that we might feel we have come to know and to understand her. The lines of her life are drawn with the unerring brushstrokes that only the Spirit could draw, shaded in the chiaroscuro of good and evil that light and dark have always conveyed, and coloured in the tone of her most remarkable quality. The result is a portrait so vivid and real, that we know it to be wholly true.

How often is life painted in the intermingled shades of weeping and laughter.[1] And yet, the experience of these things varies with the individual. Some, set alight with the divine fire, feel the Truth with greater intensity, and rejoice in a hope so sublime as to fill them with "joy unspeakable and full of glory". Their strongest yearnings are satisfied in those moments of meditation, prayer and praise, where to their wonder, heaven is opened and the visions of God are seen. In those special and precious times, they know what it is like to draw nigh into His sacred presence, a moment which others might never have felt. But the converse is also true. Those who have known the brightness of such transcendent heights, are also susceptible to the darkness of despair. Their capacity to rise toward the light is the very thing that makes them vulnerable to its opposite. They possess a tendency to fall into the depths, and to feel "the day of grief and of desperate sorrow", to a degree which others might mercifully escape. Their weeping and their laughter are alike intense, and rare is such a person who knows only the weal, but none of the woe.

That Hannah was of this disposition, her story would plainly show. Her sense of joy was so deep, that it was as honey to the mouth for its sweetness. But she would also feel a sorrow so sharp, that she could taste its bitterness as myrrh, as she wept tears which flowed unabated to be stored in the bottle of God's remembrance. She would know both the abundance of her grief, and the exaltation of her joy, the misery of being brought low, and the jubilation of being lifted up. There was nothing of the colourless in Hannah.

In truth, weeping and laughter are the common themes of all human life. There is of course a place for them both, for God

---

[1] Luke 6:21.

in His wisdom, brings each in its time upon us. [2] Through them, He shapes us for His purpose. Without the sorrow of the former, we would never realise the joy of the latter. Hannah, so certain in hope and exalted in thought, could not escape the anguish of doubt and pain of distress that were their very antithesis. For her, sadness and gladness were never far apart. The light and the dark would always be present, [3] the good and the evil would never cease. [4] Yet, so authentic is the story, that in her picture we see our own triumph and tragedy, and know our own despair and delight. We look upon her portrait and are moved, for in her tears we find a kinship, and with her joys we feel a bond.

For this Hannah would become one of the most remarkable of all Bible characters. Her life would reveal the highest of godly principles, and an example of triumph through submission that would inspire Mary, the mother of Messiah herself. The spirit of this amazing woman would be seen in her passion for the Truth which set her apart from others, in a disposition to prayer that brought her close to God, and in her ability to set the heart of her child alight with her own spiritual fervency. But the brightest colour would be seen in a powerful sense of purpose which directed her life. That strong and guiding principle coloured her whole being with its tone, and so completely did that purpose envelop her, that her entire life shone with its lustre. It will be our task to discover why it filled her so, and how it made her who she was.

We may be certain from her portrait that her purpose was never simply to bear a child, but rather to become God's agent for the outworking of His plan. Her desire to be this, in an age when every man did that which was right in his own eyes, is the lesson of her life that inspires brother and sister alike. In a time so like Hannah's, when the spirit of humanism advances every evil against the holiness of the Truth, living lives of purpose on God's

---

[2] Ecclesiastes 3:4.
[3] Daniel 2:22.
[4] Job 2:10.

behalf is the very thing that all God's people must seek to do. But Hannah's purpose, kept deep within her heart, would demand such commitment to its cause, that a lesser person would have quailed at the task. Her vision was of such magnitude, that the Lord alone could fulfil it. How then might her strong desire be bound with His involvement? "Do not forget thine handmaid" was her prayer.

That request, so deceptive in its simplicity, lay at the heart of all that she was, and at the centre of all that she did. To be the Handmaid of God was not just a declaration of submission to His will. It was a cry that she might be used by the Deity for His own sovereign purpose, and in the accomplishment of His purpose, Hannah found the outworking of her own. Wherever it might lead, and whatever it might mean, she would not be deterred from her vow to be the Handmaid of the Highest. Here then is a Bible meditation on the Spirit's portrait of Hannah, and the wonderful character that was revealed in the glow of her commitment.

Roger Lewis
Christchurch, New Zealand
November 2020

1 |

Hannah and her grief

(1 Samuel 1:1-8)

THE closing episode of the book of Judges, and the opening event of the book of Samuel would start with strangely similar cameos. [1] The first would begin with a certain man of Zorah, whose name was Manoah, and whose wife was barren, that she bare not. [2] There must have been sadness in his household owing to the childless state of his wife, rendered the more painful by the fact that as a woman of spiritual discernment, her capacity for motherhood was so real, yet so unfulfilled.

The beginning of the book of Samuel, portrayed in almost identical tones, would be so like its antecedent as to strike the reader with the sense of having seen the picture before. Yet again there was a certain man, this time of Ramathaim-zophim, whose name was Elkanah, and whose wife had no children, since the Lord had closed her womb. [3] There would be sadness in this household as well, the sadness of a couple without children, and the sadness of another woman whose spiritual ability to nurture godly offspring was undoubted.

---

1 See Appendix 1 – "What was the setting for Hannah's troublous times?" on page 206. The final chapters of the book of Judges (Judges 17-21) form a series of appendices to the book, making the story of Samson (Judges 13-16) the final episode in the book chronologically.
2 Judges 13:2.
3 1 Samuel 1:1,2,5.

It was evident that the Spirit intended to draw a parallel between the two. A certain man and a barren wife. Not only would the women be compared, but the subsequent history of their respective sons would be linked, both in time and significance. Scripture thereby advanced from one epoch in the divine purpose to the next, with a sense of continuity that every age rested under the hand of God, who would accomplish His will through those whom He chose. But this time, the woman of His choosing would be identified. Her name was Hannah, and her life and times would be the focus of the first narrative recorded in the book that would bear her son's name.

Long before Hannah was born, Moses had spoken the word of the Lord that every man should keep himself to the inheritance of the tribe of his fathers.[4] Elkanah in observing this rule, sought a woman of Levi in marriage, and found her in Hannah, whose own parents were Levites. She stood related to the things of the house of God, which the Levites attended upon.[5] Her earliest memory at the sanctuary had been of the priesthood of Eli, who had presided in Shiloh since she was a babe.[6] Hannah's early years were shaped by the influence of a priest, under whose lax control the sanctity of the Truth had steadily declined in Israel. As a member of the priestly tribe, it was this circumstance, coupled with the increasing evil of her times, that fanned the flame of yearning within her for a spiritual leader in the nation.

It was a difficult time in which to live a godly life. In an age where every man did that which was right in his own eyes, the

---

[4] Numbers 36:7-9.

[5] The law was occasioned by the petition of the daughters of Zelophehad concerning their father's inheritance. It was granted to them, but on condition that they must marry within their tribe. This they did, as all five daughters married men of the tribe of Manasseh that the tribe's inheritance not be lost (Numbers 36:10-12). The same provision would make it customary for Levites to marry within their own tribe. Given that Elkanah was a Levite, it is most likely that he married a woman of Levi, and hence this suggestion of Hannah's own Levitical origin.

[6] Estimating Hannah's age at thirty at the birth of Samuel, and Samuel's age at twelve – fifteen at the death of Eli, would mean that Hannah was approximately two when Eli assumed the role of priest and judge.

spirit of the Truth was first compromised and then abandoned. In most generations, the Truth was not lost through wholesale apostasy. Instead it declined through a thousand small changes, each so small, so incremental, so gradual, that no one protested. The spirit of gradualism proceeded in its work of spiritual erosion, until in the end the Truth was unrecognisable.

The challenge for every generation is to distinguish between changes which arise, but which will not compromise the ways of God, and those alterations of thinking and conduct which will undermine the foundations of the Truth. Most are insensibly affected by the passage of time and change, and gradually adjust to new realities, accepting the decline in spiritual standards that come with them. A few see far enough ahead to discern that certain trends will bring spiritual catastrophe that could extinguish the Truth. Part of the uniqueness of Hannah's spirit, was that she saw those trends and recognised their danger. What made her distinctive however, was her readiness to uphold the right, and to eschew the wrong, in an age when it was easier to tolerate it.

Elkanah and his family lineage in Israel

> "Now there was a certain man of Ramathaim-zophim, of mount Ephraim, and his name was Elkanah, the son of Jeroham, the son of Elihu, the son of Tohu, the son of Zuph, an Ephrathite. And he had two wives; the name of the one was Hannah, and the name of the other Peninnah: and Peninnah had children, but Hannah had no children." (1 Samuel 1:1,2)

Elkanah was a man of faith, whose forebears, a distinguished and respected family of Levites, had long lived in Mount Ephraim. His genealogy gave proof of his descent, not just from the tribe of Levi, but from the line of Kohath, Levi's second son.[7] The Levites were granted cities and suburbs among the other tribes, and so were counted as belonging to that tribe by location. Kohath

---

[7] Elkanah's genealogy (1 Samuel 1:1), traced to his great-great grandfather, Zuph, establishes his link to Kohath (1 Chronicles 6:33-38).

received cities in Ephraim, Dan and Manasseh, [8] besides those already granted to the children of Aaron. Elkanah's family had settled in Mount Ephraim, and he was therefore an Ephraimite [9] by settlement, but a Levite by descent.

Many towns in ancient Israel were named because of the physical attributes of their location, whether it was on a fertile plain, within a sheltered valley, or atop a commanding elevation. [10] In the case of Ramathaim, it was distinguished by two adjacent hills which afforded expansive views of the region, and perhaps fortified watchtowers for the guardianship of the town. No doubt, its suitable terrain permitted its early settlement, and there may have already been an established town in that place when the children of Israel settled the land under Joshua. But Ramathaim was not one of the cities in Ephraim allotted to Kohath, when they first took their place among that tribe. Evidently, a family of Kohath had moved there subsequently, either as pioneers or settlers, and no doubt for good reason. And its more complete name of Ramathaim-zophim suggested that the key to its growth and importance lay in the vigorous labours of Elkanah's great-great grandfather.

Zophai, [11] whose name was lent to the town, [12] must have migrated from one of the main Kohathite cities in Ephraim to establish a new centre from which the voice of the 'teaching priest' might be heard. He had chosen carefully, for the town which he established, or in which he settled, was close enough for regular pilgrimage to Shiloh, and yet was still in an area which did

---

8   Ten cities in all, four from Ephraim, four from Dan, two from Manasseh (Joshua 21:20-26).
9   The phrase "an Ephrathite" (*ephrathiy* – 1 Samuel 1:1) could mean either 'of Ephrath' or 'of Ephraim', as determined by context. It is rendered here as "an Ephraimite" by ASV, Rotherham, RSV and others, and this is correct, since Elkanah lived in Ephraim not Benjamin. There are other instances where the word *ephrathiy* also means 'an Ephraimite' (Judges 12:5, 1 Kings 11:26).
10 Such towns as Ramah, Geba, Gibeah, Gibeon, Mizpeh and close derivatives were so named to reflect the physical aspects of the land around them.
11 His name is given as both Zophai and Zuph (1 Chronicles 6:26,35).
12 Ramathaim-zophim referring to 'the twin heights of the Zophites'.

not encroach on existing Kohathite towns. [13] His proselytising zeal had reached beyond the city's own environs, [14] until the whole area came to be known as the land of Zuph. [15]

Ever since, the presence of Levite influence in Ramathaim was so marked that its role as a priestly city continued throughout many, many generations, reaching to the time of Christ himself. [16] Elkanah certainly came from an illustrious line, and as a member of the most prominent and influential family in that place, he was a notable man of his times.

Even his name was a celebration of the unique relationship that his tribe held before the God of Israel, a name that was common in his own family. [17] His was a special lineage for he belonged to the Kohathites, the family of the Levites with responsibility for the charge of the tabernacle of the congregation, including the guardianship of the ark of God. When the tabernacle was set up in Shiloh, [18] the work of the Levites changed, since the Kohathites would no longer be needed to carry the ark and other items on their journeys. But that concern for the ark, which they had borne throughout the wilderness, remained the spiritual focus of the family. Even in later times, they never forgot the charge, and were there to act when the sacredness of the ark was under threat. [19]

---

13   Those towns in Ephraim were Shechem, Gezer, Jokmeam, Beth-horon, Aijalon, and Gath-rimmon (1 Chronicles 6:66-69). Ramathaim-zophim was situated almost equidistant between several of these, suggesting its choice by Zophai as a suitable place in which to extend Levitical influence.

14   A similar view of Zophai's activity is suggested by Michael Ashton (*Samuel the Seer*, page 8).

15   Given that both town (1 Samuel 1:1) and territory (1 Samuel 9:5) carried his name, Zophai was clearly a man of great spiritual influence indeed.

16   Significantly, only Luke's Gospel will record that Arimathaea, where Joseph came from, was "a city of the Jews" (Luke 23:51), the phrase here indicating that even then, it was known as a priestly city.

17   Elkanah means 'God has possessed' (from *qanah* to acquire or purchase). His name celebrated the unique role of the Levites whom God counted as belonging to Him (Numbers 3:6-12,45). The name was found several times in his own family (1 Chronicles 6:34-36).

18   Joshua 18:1.

19   Both the tragedy of Uzzah in David's time (1 Chronicles 15:2,3,15,26), and the idolatry of Manasseh (2 Chronicles 33:4,7) before Josiah's reign (2 Chronicles

At such times, it was clear that their role was distinctly more than ceremonial. But with the tabernacle settled in its own place, there came other responsibilities for a more permanent system of worship. There were many tasks which needed to be fulfilled, as the spiritual calendar of the nation, codified in the Law of Moses, began its yearly rhythm. The Kohathites were responsible for matters which all stood related to the holiness of the sanctuary and the worship of God. Such was the importance of their labour that the Kohathites came under the direct supervision of the High Priest elect, who superintended their work. [20]

Many and varied were the tasks which fell to the family of Kohath. Some had charge of all the temple vessels, caring for them in their use, and accounting for their tally. Others were involved with the instruments of the sanctuary to ensure that they were always on hand. Some within the family were responsible for all the holy ingredients to be used in the holy offerings. The fine flour, the oil, the wine, the frankincense, the spices all came under the watchful eye of Kohathite ministers. The cooking of the meal offerings, and even the weekly shewbread was theirs to prepare. [21] Each branch of the house of Levi provided singers for the sanctuary, and there was a Kohathite choir who offered praise in subsequent generations. [22]

The family were evidently faithful in their execution of these tasks. So dedicated was their spirit, that David [23] would

---

35:2,3), gave evidence that Kohath had stepped forward to fulfil their ancient role, when occasion required.

[20] Eleazar presided over their charge from the outset of the tabernacle service (Numbers 3:30-32).

[21] This catalogue of duties evidently fell to their lot from the earliest of times (1 Chronicles 9:23-33).

[22] Kohathite singers were seen in the times of several later kings: David (1 Chronicles 15:16,17), Jehoshaphat (2 Chronicles 20:19), and Josiah (2 Chronicles 34:12). But the offering of praise to God must have begun much earlier in the nation's history as an essential part of worship. The Levites would always have been to the forefront of this matter of sanctuary service.

[23] David's confirmation of these to continue in the offices they had previously held, was presumably because of the faithful discharge of their duties (1 Chronicles 23:26-29). The context of the passage clearly refers to Kohathite Levites in particular.

confirm them in their duties for the much greater tasks of the temple worship which began in Solomon's day. But the greatest charge of the Kohathites lay in being made the guardians of the thresholds of the tabernacle. [24] Their appointment to this role came long before the days of David and even of Elkanah, dating back to the time when Eleazar, the son of Aaron, was High Priest and Phinehas his son was the High Priest elect. As their most illustrious preceptor, Phinehas imbued them with a strong sense of responsibility, and what it truly meant to be the guardians of the house. Under his tutelage, they learned to be zealous for God's honour, to be faithful guardians of the Lord's holiness, and the dedicated upholders of the purity of His sanctuary. [25]

Samuel and David would later determine that these Kohathite guardians of the thresholds should continue to fulfil their role in the temple service. [26] So devoted were they to this charge, that they chose to lodge round about the house, to be on hand at all times to attend to the opening and the closing of the doors. It was the highest honour to which they would be appointed, and the standard of their household ever after. [27]

From the beginning of this family's history then, to be a Kohathite was to be focused upon the ark of the presence, to be aware of a calling to guardianship, and to be devoted to the holiness

---

[24] The record in Chronicles (which concerns those returning from the captivity), indicated that the task of being keepers of the thresholds belonged to Kohathites. But the record was careful to note that this appointment came, not in the days of Solomon's temple, but during the earlier period of tabernacle worship (1 Chronicles 9:19,21).

[25] Phinehas himself was zealous for God's honour and holiness at the door of the tabernacle of the congregation (Numbers 25:6-13). There was no better example of guardianship to inspire the Kohathites. His charge over Kohath (1 Chronicles 9:20) is rendered the more remarkable by the fact that he is the only High Priest elect singled out as having been over them. Clearly, his example inspired the household through their future generations.

[26] Kohathite doorkeepers were established in their office by Samuel because of their continued faithfulness (1 Chronicles 9:22). Given his own outstanding example of being a diligent guardian of the door (1 Samuel 3:15), this was an affirmation of the high regard in which they were held.

[27] The spirit of being the guardians of the threshold was the essence of one of their most famous family psalms (Psalm 84:10).

of God's sanctuary. By Elkanah's time, that rich legacy of spiritual excellence was already imbedded in the family. As a Kohathite, Elkanah may well have felt the fulness of this heritage, and yet there was no indication, no sign that he held any special duty in the tabernacle service. His family was well known, but his only contribution was to visit the house of the LORD, since attendance there for worship was also enjoined upon the Levites. It was perhaps, strange that such a man did not hold some office. But then Elkanah, despite his background was not to be at the centre of this story. That honour would belong to his wife, and the details which placed Elkanah in his home town and his own tribe would but serve as an introduction to the true heroine of the story – Hannah.

Married to a Levite, and probably a Levite herself, she entered fully into the legacy of her tribe, as later events would show. The place where God dwelt among His people, the ark of the covenant where He inhabited the cherubim, was the place where Hannah found her focal point and the centre of her spiritual life. This was her calling, and her passion for things divine was real, personal and individual. Ramah might have been her home town, but Hannah in her spirit belonged to the house of God.

Hannah and her spirit in the Truth

For what Elkanah stood related to in principle, Hannah was bound to in practice. She would never minister in the sanctuary as a temple servant, but in her heart she entered its gates and came into its courts. The ark which betokened the presence of the Lord among His people, and the temple where one might meet with Him were never far from her mind. Her vow of dedication was uttered at the temple. Her child of promise was given at the temple. Her song of thanksgiving was offered at the temple. Her stand for purity was taken at the temple. This was where her calling was.

In an age so given over to the expression of the individual, Hannah stood out as uniquely different for her unwavering focus on higher things which stood beyond herself. She was so aware of God and so mindful of Him each day, that to draw near to

Him was a conscious act of regular occurrence. Coming into the presence of God was not reserved for a visit to the sanctuary, but was an attitude that permeated her daily experience. The substance of her prayers, whether in petition or praise, revealed a woman who walked with God. But, for one whose disposition was so finely attuned to His supremacy, to come and eat her peace offering in the place where He met with His people, was truly a spiritual climax. To partake of a meal that had been shared with God brought a sense of fellowship so special, a feeling of honour so high, that it was a privilege beyond compare.

Perhaps her attachment to the temple had been formed at an early age, when visiting with her parents. It would certainly seem that her visits with Elkanah had commenced at the start of their marriage. However it had begun, there was no doubt that Hannah loved the sanctuary and all that it spoke of. Her heart was in that place, for the great milestones of her life were to be measured in the moments when she stood at the door of the tabernacle of the congregation. [28] Whatever her own family line might have been, Hannah was a Levite in spirit, and a Kohathite in fervour. It was through her that this story would be unfolded, and in her that this story would have meaning. [29]

Hannah was evidently Elkanah's first wife, his companion and the wife of his covenant. [30] He did not take a second out of dissatisfaction with the first, for he loved her dearly, as she did him. [31] But Hannah was barren. She had no children. Elkanah would have been better to wait upon his God, for there were other

---

28 The idea, once noticed, is marked (1 Samuel 1:7,9,24; 2:1,19). Her life revolved around incidents at the 'temple', the door of the tabernacle being the closest she could usually come.

29 That the story of 1 Samuel 1,2 is centred on Hannah is evident from the record itself. A survey of all references to Elkanah and Hannah by name or personal pronoun in 1 Samuel 1,2 reveals almost four times the number of references to Hannah (approximately eighty), compared to Elkanah (approximately twenty). Hannah is undoubtedly the focus of the narrative.

30 The phrase "the name of the other", in describing Peninnah means literally, 'the name of the second', making Hannah his first wife (1 Samuel 1:2).

31 1 Samuel 1:5.

examples of faithful but barren couples who had gone before, and who had eventually experienced God's blessing of a family. But, so strong was the need for children in those times, both for the continuation of the family, and to preserve its God appointed inheritance, [32] that it was felt with an urgency and a force which other generations have not known. Elkanah, deciding not to wait upon God, took him another wife. [33]

Hannah, already caught in the turmoil of love for her husband and grief for her barrenness, was placed in a situation made infinitely more complex by the addition of another. Others looking on, saw in Hannah's grief the understandable feelings of sorrow and loss which every barren woman in Israel felt, for to be barren was to experience the reproach of others. [34] They sympathised with Hannah entirely, for in an age when the blessing of children was the very mark of womanhood, their absence chafed the soul and wounded the heart. What they did not see however, was a woman whose sorrow was immeasurably greater than they could have known. Hannah's reason for wanting a child lay beyond the yearning of maternal instinct that is God's endowment to womankind. She felt that as well, but in her case, there was something more.

Her mind was focused on higher things that transcended self and exalted God, and her desire for a child related to His purpose and not her own. And because the purpose of the Lord was at work in the life of this woman who walked with Him, that most mysterious of all mysteries, would be set forth in blessing Hannah with the fruit of the womb. It would require the power

---

[32] Even Levites, within their allocated cities, had houses, suburbs, fields and flocks which represented "the inheritance of their possession" (Leviticus 25:32-34; Numbers 35:1-5).

[33] In the case of both Sarah (Genesis 16:1,2), and Rachel (Genesis 30:1-3), the suggestion of taking another wife was at their prompting. But the record is silent here as to any such suggestion on Hannah's part, inferring that this was Elkanah's initiative.

[34] This was a far more powerful reality in Biblical times, than our own age permits us fully to comprehend. A wife who could not bear felt the shame of her inadequacy in a society where the fruit of the womb was counted as God's blessing (Genesis 30:23; Isaiah 4:1; Luke 1:25).

of the Highest to overshadow her. But His strength would be made perfect in her weakness, and her weakness would become the basis for her triumph. How that triumph occurred, and to what end, is the burden of the story which follows.

The yearly worship of a faithful family

> "And this man went up out of his city yearly to worship and to sacrifice unto the LORD of hosts in Shiloh. And the two sons of Eli, Hophni and Phinehas, the priests of the LORD, were there." (1 Samuel 1:3)

At a time when most of the nation had forgotten what true worship was all about, this man and woman came every year to the sanctuary in Shiloh. [35] Elkanah and Hannah were consistent in their cycle of worship, so much so, that their annual pilgrimage became the very measurement by which the seasons of their life were marked off as complete. Most of the nation did not visit the tabernacle at all, and those who did made their appearance less frequently than the law had required. [36] By the time of Hannah, the established practice was to make a yearly visitation, [37] and hers was one of the families in Israel that upheld this annual routine. Even so, it took commitment to make such a journey each year, despite the promise of divine protection for their homes and possessions whilst they were absent from them. [38] Work was needed to organise the provisions of food and raiment required for the journey and return. Suitable animals and produce needed to be gathered for their offerings at the sanctuary. To worship at God's altar meant planning and preparation. It always has.

---

[35] The record is pronounced in marking this yearly cycle in their lives (1 Samuel 1:3,7,21; 2:19), and it is evident that their annual pilgrimage involved Hannah every bit as much as Elkanah.

[36] The law prescribed the attendance of all males three times a year (Exodus 34:23), and later identified those occasions as relating to the three great feasts of Passover, Pentecost and Tabernacles (Deuteronomy 16:16).

[37] The only references to assembling for worship in the epoch of the Judges suggest this (Judges 11:40; 21:19).

[38] Exodus 34:24.

Hannah's influence was one of the key reasons why they went. She wanted to draw near to God in a spirit of purity and dedication. She desired to worship the Lord of hosts in spirit and in truth. She yearned for the joy of being at peace with God in the place of His sanctuary. She was a driving force behind this annual journey northwards to the temple, such was her need for that spiritual exaltation. For Hannah especially, this passage year by year was truly an ascent, [39] a going up in heart and mind to the place where the Lord dwelt among His people. And every year the ritual of the offerings would be the same. First the sin offering, that confession of sin might be made as the prerequisite of all mercy that might follow. Then the burnt offering, that a fresh vow of dedication might be made to serve the Lord with all the heart and mind and strength. Finally, the peace offering, that the offerer might know the joy of fellowship with their God. This is what Hannah wanted. This is what she came for. She came to find fellowship with God, and to eat her thanksgiving offering with Him. But in coming to the sanctuary, Hannah found that the very place where the tabernacle, and the altar, and the ark of God were to be found, was the last place where fellowship could be had.

Eli was already too old to attend to the offering of the sacrifices, [40] and so his two sons had now assumed that responsibility, as officiating priests. They were not just present at the tabernacle. Hophni and Phinehas were in control. [41] Their very names were indicative of their attitudes, for the one concerned the spirit of pugilism, and the other the spirit of arrogance. These two were aggressive in their deeds (Hophni – the man of the clenched fist), [42] and arrogant in their words (Phinehas – the

---

[39] The word 'went up' (1 Samuel 1:3) is *alah* – to ascend, with all the spiritual overtones that such a word suggests.

[40] Even his being seated (1 Samuel 1:9; 4:18) is suggestive of the idea that he no longer had the physical capacity to complete the demanding labours of the priest in attending to the sacrificial offerings.

[41] Cp. Rotherham – "And there, the two sons of Eli, Hophni and Phinehas, were priests to the LORD". The force of the verse is not just that they were present, but that they were in charge.

[42] Hophni means 'pugilist', but is derived from *chophen* – the fist.

man of the brazen mouth). **43** Here at the place of God's sanctuary were two men who debased the role of priesthood, who defiled the principle of holiness, and who destroyed the joy of fellowship with God. Hophni and Phinehas disgraced the place of worship, and lived scandalous lives in Shiloh, in contempt of both God and the nation.

When Hannah came to find fellowship with God, the centre of iniquity in the land was at the sanctuary itself. Her contact with these two, sent her away determined to seek the Lord's power upon her to break the cycle of the age, when every man did that which was right in his own eyes. But this was Hannah's thought, not Elkanah's. He was a good man, a loving husband, a godly Levite. But he lacked Hannah's breadth of vision and intensity of purpose. She wanted a strong deliverer to redeem the nation from this yoke of bondage to evil. She wanted a faithful priest who could restore the nation to fellowship with God. And she dared, she dared to dream of a son who could be both. If only she could become the Lord's instrument to that end. After all, what could she alone accomplish? She was but one woman in all Israel, insignificant and invisible. How could she overcome the evil of Hophni and Phinehas? She could not. But if God would use her, if God might direct her, then the task might be encompassed.

When this woman in her passion and her purity met these two men in their evil and iniquity, they were set on a collision course concerning the purpose of God with His people, and it was Hannah who would set that contest in motion. This would be her controversy, and God through His Handmaid would work a wondrous work indeed. The battle was joined here and now, for in these two Hannah found her real enemies, **44** and the episodes in this story would resound to the clash of the contest until God's will had triumphed, and the work of His Handmaid was complete.

---

43 Phinehas means 'mouth of brass', and is derived from *peh* – the mouth, and a variation of *nachash* – serpent (not unlike *nehushatan* – a thing of brass).
44 See Appendix 2 – "Who were the enemies of Hannah's holy cause?" on page 212.

Ever since Elkanah and his family had begun their annual journey to offer sacrifice, Hannah had been shocked by the conduct of Eli's sons. Their brazen effrontery in robbing the people of the best of their own portions, left her feeling that her spiritual offering to God had been profaned. No one was exempt from their reach,[45] and Hannah knew first-hand how the desecration of her sacrificial meal left her feeling sick at heart. The moment that should have been Hannah's greatest joy, had become the reason for her greatest sorrow. How many visits were needed before she determined in her heart that she would seek a way to overthrow them? How many prayers were offered that she might be granted a child for that work, even though her womb had been shut by the Lord?

Year by year, as she came to worship, this was her experience with these men, and she could not leave this evil unchallenged. Her love of the Truth was too strong to permit it. But from the moment she decided in her heart to make this request, every further visit without God's answer only aggravated her spirit further. Every subsequent experience of their robbery pierced Hannah's heart with sorrow, until her pilgrimage became an agony. It was a mark of her astounding faith that she did not stop. Both pilgrimage and prayer continued in her life, as it must in ours. The answers to our deepest woes will only be found in our continual prayers and by our continued presence at the place of meeting.

A generous portion but a closed womb

> "And when the time was that Elkanah offered, he gave to Peninnah his wife, and to all her sons and daughters, portions: but unto Hannah he gave a worthy portion; for he loved Hannah: but the LORD had shut up her womb."
>
> (1 Samuel 1:4,5)

---

[45] See Chapter 5 – "Hannah and her child" on page 103 for more detailed comments on the actions of the priests against the people. The statement, "So they did in Shiloh unto all the Israelites that came thither" (1 Samuel 2:14), may be taken as sufficient evidence to indicate that Hannah and her family had more than once experienced this gross violation of their own fellowship meal.

Alone among the altar sacrifices, the peace offering was unique in granting a portion to the offerer. Although the law specified an offering for an individual, Elkanah's offering did not pertain to himself alone, but to his family who were all bound with him in its partaking. After both God and the priests had received their parts, that which remained was his to divide severally as he willed. [46] Elkanah, a just man in all his dealings, was equitable in distributing the portions of the peace offering. He was anxious for all his household to partake, and since Peninnah had several children he ensured that both she and they all had their rightful part. There would be no deprivation here, for after all, they were his children as well. Each one was given a share, and the very task of these apportionments, and the sight of several children all gathered around their mother, only emphasised Hannah's solitary state. How could it do otherwise?

Peninnah's family being provided for, Elkanah turned his attention to Hannah's part. Although she had no children, he still gave her a portion that reflected his love for her, and her honoured status in his eyes. [47] Perhaps a larger share than usual, it was placed in front of her as the mark of Elkanah's unchanging esteem. He loved her, and wanted her to know that her state of barrenness would never change that. But to Hannah, already distressed by her situation, this yearly bestowal from Elkanah only made her condition worse. How could she explain that this special share, this extra portion was more painful than she could bear? Its generosity only emphasized the absence of children beside her, and the very gift that Elkanah gave to comfort only

---

[46] See Chapter 5 – "Hannah and her child" on page 103 for further detail on how the peace offering was apportioned under the law.

[47] The phrase – *yitten manah achath appayim* is unusual, and (despite the KJV margin) is not the same expression for the "double portion" of the firstborn (Deuteronomy 21:17). It has been translated – "one portion of two faces or two nostrils". It may suggest a portion sufficient for two persons, but it might indicate a larger, but still single portion only, given Hannah's lack of children. In either case, the record is clear however that it reflected her husband's love, despite her barren state. The KJV has endeavoured to express the Hebrew term by translating it as "a worthy portion".

added to her pain. The table was filled with a father, a mother, and their numerous children each one with their portions, and finally with Hannah. She no doubt was seated close to Elkanah, but the setting of the table told its own story.

All Elkanah's liberality and kindness could not disguise the sad reality. Hannah had no children, and all her household knew it. She had lived with the pain of being childless for years, and knew the affect it had upon her life. Yet there was a reason why she remained in a state of barrenness. The truth was that the Lord had closed her womb, [48] but He could also open it. That there was deliberate intention here on God's part was evident, but it was the nature of His intention that Hannah needed to understand. The Lord was directly at work in her life, and in control of the very thing that was dearest to her heart, her ability to bear children. The closing of her womb was not a punishment, but neither was it a mistake. For some reason, the Lord Himself had prevented her from bearing.

Until now His purpose in doing so had not been disclosed, but it was about to be, and in its revelation Hannah would learn a powerful truth. What is seen on earth is often not the view of heaven. What she construed as the pain of delay, God considered to be the wisdom of sequence and timing. She needed to learn that God would graciously open her womb, but not until her petition was coincident with His purpose. When those two met, His answer would be heard, and His power would be seen. Even now, the Lord was at work to arrange the convergence of circumstance and people that were needed for the accomplishment of His plan.

---

[48] The phrase – "the LORD had shut up her womb" was repeated for emphasis (1 Samuel 1:5,6). The primary meaning of the term *cagar* (to shut doors or dam streams) suggests something more than barrenness, since other women were described as being barren, but without any suggestion that the Lord had specifically closed their wombs to prevent bearing (Genesis 25:21; Judges 13:3; Luke 1:7). It does however mention it of Hannah. But He who could fast close wombs, could also certainly open them (Genesis 20:17,18). A moment of miracle was to occur in Hannah's life, for to enable the birth of her firstborn son, the Lord would need to open her womb. Samuel was to be a special child, born by divine intervention.

Hannah's role was but a part, and she would yet marvel at how her part would intersect with others. She would bear a child at the exact moment of God's choosing, but only time would reveal how perfect that moment was.

It is a lesson which all the faithful must learn in their dealings with God, for the same principle is at work in our lives. Our belief in the work of providence must extend to accepting that God's timetable is paramount, and not our own. How vital it is then, that the focus of our prayers should be on the performance of His will and on the accomplishment of His purpose, rather than the mere fulfilment of our requests. It was to her credit that Hannah's urgency in prayer sprang not from selfish interest, but from a burning sense of the injustice being done to God. Rarely had a woman of faith been afflicted to the degree of anguish that Hannah felt. Her overwhelming desire was to right that wrong, and her adversity was related to that great cause.

The matter of Hannah's adversity

> "And her adversary also provoked her sore, for to make her fret, because the LORD had shut up her womb. And as he did so year by year, when she went up to the house of the LORD, so she provoked her; therefore she wept, and did not eat."
>
> (1 Samuel 1:6,7)

Hannah's affliction related not to another person but to her own condition, [49] and it was clear that the condition related in some way to the barren state of her womb. [50] For any married woman in Israel, to be barren was a bitterness indeed, but to one who sought a child for the redemption of the nation, it was a trial almost past

---

49 That the word *tsarah* would be better rendered 'adversity' rather than 'adversary' is outlined in Appendix 3 – "What was the source of Hannah's great adversity?" on page 216.

50 The immediate context of her adversity related to the fact of her barrenness. Note the juxtaposition – "But unto Hannah he gave a worthy portion; for he loved Hannah, but the LORD had shut up her womb. And *her adversity also provoked her sore, for to make her fret*, because the LORD had shut up her womb" (1 Samuel 1:5,6).

bearing. For Hannah, her barrenness was an inadequacy that could never be satisfied. [51] But childless though she was, her condition although related to her distress, was not the primary basis for it. Her bitterness of heart was not directed against Peninnah, for she was neither obsessed with retaliation, nor consumed with self-pity. This was no brooding spirit in a woman obsessed with desire for a child, that she might vaunt herself above a rival. If that were so, then there was no explanation as to why or how she could possibly rejoice to give away her son to one who had failed miserably to raise his own offspring.

There was a deeper reason at work, a reason which was entirely consistent with who Hannah was. To receive her son and then to give him away, while singing a song of joy at doing so, was incomprehensible to the natural mind, but in perfect harmony with the spiritual mind that governed this woman of grace and faith. What then was Hannah's tribulation, that aggravated her so completely as to make her fret? There was nothing vague about Hannah's adversity, for it lay so heavy upon her that she was provoked by it to anger. But, her strength of feeling was driven by something more powerful and spiritual than a personal sense of injury or the unkindness of another. Neither of these were the true cause of Hannah's adversity, nor of the displeasure which she felt. The condition which moved her to such anger was prompted by far higher principles.

Her reason for such deep vexation of heart lay in the fact that she shared the spirit of her God, and felt His righteous indignation at the evil within His sanctuary. Her anger was the same as God's, and her provocation was brought about by the same circumstance. God was provoked to anger by the corruption of His people, [52] and the wicked setting aside of His principles by

---

[51] "There are three things that are never satisfied, yea, four things say not, It is enough: the grave; and the barren womb; the earth that is not filled with water; and the fire that saith not, It is enough" (Proverbs 30:15,16).

[52] The phrase "provoked her sore" uses a doubled form of *ka'ac* for emphasis. The word (*ka'ac*) means to be angry, to be vexed, to be indignant. In every previous occurrence, it refers to God being vexed or grieved by rebellion or sin in Israel

Hophni and Phinehas vexed His Handmaid likewise to the very core of her being.[53] She was provoked so deeply, as to make her tremble with despair.[54]

Grief can be felt in different ways. In Ramah, she felt the dull ache of being bereft. At Shiloh, she felt the sharp pain of urgent need. For it was at the sanctuary that the matter was thrown into sharp relief, and every time they came, the same bitterness afflicted Hannah. This was not a singular event, but a regular one, occasioned in some way by attendance at the sanctuary itself. Hannah's grief was not at home, where Peninnah might have had opportunity to engender strife with her words and deeds. Whatever the state of her home life in Ramah was, it was clear that her adversity, her pain, her grief was related to the matters of the sanctuary and the work of the priesthood.

Every year at Shiloh the repeated experience of an unholy priesthood and their ungodly behaviour crushed her spirit, and made it impossible for her to draw near to God. Every year at the sacrifice of the peace offering, the priests would destroy the occasion, as subsequent events would show. Every year at the fellowship meal that followed, Elkanah sought to affirm his love for Hannah with a special portion. And every year, her continued barrenness, given her higher objectives, provoked her to despair

---

(Deuteronomy 4:25; 9:18; 31:29; 32:16,21×2, Judges 2:12). The threefold use in the Song of Moses was especially significant, as this passage would be quoted by both Hannah and the Man of God. Hannah knew the feeling of God at His people's unfaithfulness. Similarly, the great majority of all other occurrences of the word, after Hannah, also relate to God's provocation to anger. It is this word which the Spirit selects to describe Hannah's depth of feeling. Hannah felt the same despair as her God at the evidence of evil among His people.

53 Hannah's troubled spirit was of the same character as Lot's who was "vexed with the filthy conversation of the wicked", and who, in dwelling among them, "vexed his righteous soul from day to day" (2 Peter 2:7,8). Both he and Hannah were righteous persons amidst great wickedness.

54 The word "to make her fret" (*ra'am*) means to thunder, and relates almost always to God who thunders upon His people. It is the very word used by Hannah in her subsequent prayer – "The adversaries of the LORD shall be broken in pieces; out of heaven shall he thunder against them" (1 Samuel 2:10). The sense is captured by GLT – "so as to make her tremble". The word is a further indication that Hannah's feelings were the mirror of her God's. It was His trembling that she felt.

in that place. It was at Shiloh that everything came into focus: the damage done by a wicked priesthood, the compromise of her own fellowship with God, and, most painful of all, the knowledge that she could not resolve the matter. Despite her fervently repeated prayers, she had not yet received an answer from God. Instead, she was distressed greatly by her inability to bear a child for the saving of the nation, that the evil of Hophni and Phinehas might be overthrown.

There had already been enough to afflict the heart in the circumstances which led to their family meal. That situation continued every year until their visits to the house of God became, for Hannah, unbearably difficult. It was the time which Hannah dreaded, for it not only reminded her that the problem was real, but also that it was inescapable. She felt imprisoned within her adversity, and its terrible constraint took its toll upon her until she mourned. She did so every year in an annual cycle of prayer and pain, from which there seemed to be no release. [55]

There must have been good reasons why Hannah did not eat, for this was a fellowship meal with her God. Whatever might have prevented her, she did not set it aside out of envy or jealousy of Peninnah. No doubt Peninnah's many children added to Hannah's sense of inadequacy, and perhaps Peninnah herself was guilty of some thoughtless words. But these were not reasons enough for Hannah to sit there while her portion remained untouched. Even as the others around the table partook of their portions with grateful enjoyment, Hannah was unable to eat a single mouthful. Instead, she wept with such bitter tears that everyone else felt awkward, and Hannah was mortified. At the very time of drawing near to God, at the very moment

---

[55] That Hannah's adversity was not focused on Peninnah but rather upon Hophni and Phinehas, is outlined in Appendix 2 – "Who were the enemies of Hannah's holy cause?" on page 212, and Appendix 3 – "What was the source of Hannah's great adversity?" on page 216. As the record of Hannah's life unfolds, other key events will all corroborate this view. The terms of her vow, the focus of her song, the purpose of the coat, and the words of the Man of God will confirm that Hannah was completely focused on the replacement of an evil priesthood.

of appointed fellowship with Him, Hannah felt estranged. This was why she could not eat. Her adversity was too great, and her resources too small to cope with the suffering it bought upon her in this place.

Elkanah's bewilderment and concern

> "Then said Elkanah her husband to her, Hannah, why weepest thou? and why eatest thou not? and why is thy heart grieved? Am not I better to thee than ten sons?" (1 Samuel 1:8)

It distressed Elkanah to see Hannah so filled with anguish, and he wished that he could smooth away the hurt. This sacrificial meal they shared together was supposed to bring spiritual refreshment to them all, and yet it was painfully obvious that it had the very opposite effect upon his wife. Worst of all was the fact that she wept at the very meal itself. Hannah was not of a spirit deliberately to destroy the happiness of others, and so her weeping on this occasion was unusual in the extreme. Moreover, he was genuinely puzzled by the depth of Hannah's sorrow in this place of all places, and at this time of all times, for all three of his questions were set at the table. "Why weepest thou?", "Why eatest thou not?", "Why is thy heart grieved?" were all prompted by the moment of the family meal.

And the focus of his questions told all. The issue of query for Elkanah was how she could possibly feel this way, at this moment of all moments. Gladly would he help to remove the cause of her pain, but he knew not what it was. He would never have asked if it was obviously a situation brought about by Peninnah and her behaviour at the table. The very nature of his questions were an indication that Hannah's grief of mind and vexation of spirit were on a higher plane than Elkanah had realised. Anxiously, he sought to assure her of his affection, believing that her adversity sprang from the feeling of inadequacy brought about by her barrenness. And his declaration of devotion, "Am not I better to thee than ten sons?" was not intended to vaunt himself above the joy of having children from his wife's perspective, but to comfort Hannah that he loved her no less than if she had many sons.[56] That was the message contained in his special portion to her, and it saddened him to know that despite his care, he could not stem the tears which she shed at this meal – tears, he was aware, that flowed from her upon every visit to this place.

His words were well intended, for Elkanah was genuinely upset to see his wife in such a state of sorrow and distress. But his comments could not help or heal her, for the cause of her grief was not related to the lack of a large family. Nor was her despair centred on bearing many children to reach equality with Peninnah. It remained for Elkanah a matter of mystery as to how different Hannah was at the tabernacle, to the companion he knew at home. In Ramah, she was the settled and loyal wife he loved and knew. At Shiloh, she was a distraught and tearful woman, who seemed beyond him. Why was it that she was so different at the sanctuary, and what was it here that caused her to be so? Whatever Elkanah might have thought, he simply did not know.

Hannah and her grief

Hannah's answer to Elkanah's anxious questions was not recorded, for there was none she could give. It was difficult for her to explain her grief, for it sprang from her very being. Her capacity to be touched by the holiness of the truth left her oppressed by the blatant wickedness of its inverse. In one whose mind yearned towards the spiritual and the sacred, the horror of seeing the vulgar and the profane thrusting its way into the sanctuary left her feeling devastated. To know what is possible, and to witness its extinguishing does more than to upset. It wounds the soul and breaks the heart. Hannah found that to seek holiness was

---

56 The phrase was a Hebraism indicating depth of love. Ruth's deep affection for Naomi, her mother-in-law, was described by Naomi's friends in the same way – "thy daughter-in-law, which loveth thee, which is better to thee than seven sons" (Ruth 4:15). Literally, Ruth was not better to Naomi than seven sons, but the phrase was expressive of the marvellous degree of love which she did feel. Elkanah uses the expression in this sense.

also to know loneliness. Why was it that others seemed not to notice or not to care? How could others accept the setting aside of divine principles when coming before the Lord of Hosts? She was bewildered and hurt by the seeming ease with which others shrugged off the common and the base as if they were of no moment, settling down to the enjoyment of their sacrificial meal as if oblivious of its significance and unaware of its defilement.

And how much worse it was to know that this spirit pervaded the sanctuary because evil priests ruled there. When the wicked are in the ascendancy and the righteous are unable to remove them, and unable to confront them, there is a deep sense of powerlessness. [57] To experience it is to know the bitter tumult it awakes within the heart. To visit at the time of the yearly sacrifice, only to witness that decline becoming more and more defiant, only served to deepen Hannah's pain.

Here was a woman of God who desired with all her heart to challenge this spirit. Yet her womanhood would not extend to the one provision by which her challenge might be made. For Hannah, her barrenness was a double blow. This woman, whose yearning to bear stood related to higher things, was unable to bear, despite repeated prayers. Her state of barrenness was but the symbol of her emptiness, for that is how she felt: empty of feeling, empty of joy, empty of hope. She saw her state as an emblem of the nation's spiritual barrenness, and her own ruptured fellowship as the symbol of the nation's estrangement from God. Her deepest wish was to bring forth a faithful priest to restore her people's fellowship with God, and her deepest grief was that she could not. Hannah's sorrow was not for loss, but for lack, and it was a grief so strong that it consumed her. This was an emptiness that brought exhaustion, and Hannah came to know that it was possible to be filled with a grief so deep, that it could not even be expressed.

There is a sorrow so overwhelming, that the sufferer knows only that all the waves and billows have passed over them. There

---

57 Proverbs 28:28; 29:2.

is a weariness so enfeebling, that the afflicted feels unable to move and unable to escape. There is a sadness so encompassing, that the mourner weeps until they can weep no more. At such a time, the world is drained of all its colour, and daily life is trapped in the dull grey of deep despair. The appetite fails, for food tastes of nothing save misery. The daughters of music are brought low, because the voice of singing is stilled. The vigour of life is lost to a listless void, where the bones ache and the feet drag. Only the dark silence remains, and in that fearful place there is no light. No light at all. Grief casts its pall upon the sufferer, and Hannah had felt its touch.

But this grief was Hannah's private desolation, to be kept within her own heart. Neither Elkanah nor Peninnah knew anything about this agony. Her desire to come into the presence of God was so earnest, and her sorrow at the evil of the sanctuary so intense, that no one had any idea where she was in her mind. It was something deeper within Hannah alone, a grief based upon a vision of the truth and what was possible, that others had not seen. Best then that she bear it alone, because it lay beyond explanation, and beyond Elkanah's full understanding. Yet even in her lowest moments, Hannah's mind was on higher things. Events would soon reveal just how high her thinking was, as she turned towards the light.

2 |

Hannah and her vow

(1 Samuel 1:9-18)

> "So Hannah rose up after they had eaten in Shiloh, and after they had drunk. Now Eli the priest sat upon a seat by a post of the temple of the LORD. And she was in bitterness of soul, and prayed unto the LORD, and wept sore." (1 Samuel 1:9,10)

DESPITE her sorrow, Hannah remained with the household while they concluded their meal. Her distress prevented her from participating, [1] but she waited until they had finished. It was not in her spirit to disturb the fellowship feast of others, despite her own pain. Nor was it her way to interrupt the worship of others by drawing attention to her own needs as if they were paramount. Such a display of self-seeking was the last thing Hannah wished to show. Her heart and mind cried out in tumult, but she stilled her soul until the meal was ended. Only then, before they left the immediate vicinity of the tabernacle, did Hannah arise to commune with God in private prayer.

She went back to the sanctuary which was close by, while the rest of the family returned to their place of lodging, since they

---

1. The record is not specific as to who it was when stating "after they had eaten", "and after they had drunk" (1 Samuel 1:9). But given the clear statement concerning Hannah that "she wept, and did not eat" (1 Samuel 1:7) the reference must apply to everyone in the family apart from Hannah. The passage will itself later corroborate this conclusion, when it records, "So the woman went her way and did eat" (1 Samuel 1:18), marking thus the change from her previous abstinence.

would not leave until the morrow. In keeping with her character, she left quietly and discreetly. "I will just offer a final prayer to God, and then return", she said, and Elkanah nodded in sympathy as she arose. She walked alone, but she walked with purpose, for she needed to be by herself, but with her God. It was not a long walk, but she felt a sense of trembling relief on entering the place of the sanctuary. She did not draw near to the place of offering, for she brought no sacrifice, other than her broken spirit and contrite heart. And, vulnerable and weak as she was, she sought no contact with others, least of all with those who distressed her so. She needed to be at the house of God, but she stood afar off in a place apart, where unnoticed, her mourning could be in private. How desperately she needed this moment in this place. The unbearable burden of her adversity had finally prostrated Hannah to the dust. There are moments in life so filled with tragedy, so imbued with agony, that the emotions of the heart are difficult to describe. Hannah however felt hers, so sharp and acrid, that they were as the bitterness of myrrh. [2] But now, safe in this moment of seclusion she gave way to the demand of mind and body which cried out for relief from her pain.

    The tears came first, engulfing her body with their sobbing urgency, as alone at last she poured out her soul in an abandonment of grief and sorrow that needed to be released before it overwhelmed her. [3] The words would come later when that first wave had passed, its fury spent. Grief can bring us to our knees. It brought Hannah to hers. But in doing so, it brought her again to prayer. Prayer is the answer to bitterness of soul, for it holds within its purview the gift of healing balm. For every man and woman of God, prayer is the pathway to peace.

---

[2] The Hebrews expressed the emotion of tragic and unpleasant circumstances as a sense of taste – the bitter. Although brought about by different circumstances, it was the common experience of Job (Job 7:11), Naomi (Ruth 1:20), Hannah (1 Samuel 1:10), Hezekiah (Isaiah 38:15) and others. The word (*marar*) is the base for the word myrrh (*mowr*).

[3] The words "wept sore" are a doubling of the Hebrew word (*bakah*). In this intense form, it is translated "wept bitterly" (RSV), and "wept copiously" (GLT).

The heart knoweth its own bitterness

She did not seek this time away from Elkanah because she wished to conceal her feelings, but rather because the experiences of both sorrow and joy can be so intensely personal that no one else ever fully knows what we think or how we feel. Even within the sacred bond of marriage, our deepest emotions are sometimes incommunicable to others. It is not because we will not share, but because the full dimensions of our feelings are unique, and are, in that sense unable to be shared. [4] But there was a lesson here which Hannah already understood. For when there is no one else, we can come before God. That which cannot be shared with others, can be shared with God, for He does know how we feel, which is of the greatest comfort. Even in the face of extreme adversity that is what the faithful do.

Our trials can either separate us from God, or draw us closer to Him. Divine providence brings us into circumstances where we must choose between trust in ourselves or trust in Him. Those times when we realise that we are quite unable to deliver ourselves are a vital step towards our learning that God can. He can save us out of the most difficult and distressing of circumstances, but He requires first that we have learned to trust in Him, and surrender to His will.

It is easy, when in the grip of sorrow and bitterness of soul, to be so focused on self as to have lost sight of our place before God. Hannah had every reason to feel a measure of personal grief, for her affliction was very personal in its bearings. But the prayer which burst forth from her was not focused on self at all.

---

4   This does not for a moment mean that husbands and wives ought not to share their real feelings. But scripture itself testifies that some things are neither felt nor known in an identical way by others even after explanation. Hence – "Whatever prayer, whatever supplication is made by any man ... each knowing the affliction of his own heart and stretching out his hands toward this house ... and render to each whose heart thou knowest, according to all his ways (for thou, thou only, knowest the hearts of all the children of men)" (1 Kings 8:38,39, RSV). "The heart knoweth its own bitterness, and, in its joy, no stranger shareth" (Proverbs 14:10, Rotherham). "For what person knows a man's thoughts, except the spirit of the man which is in him?" (1 Corinthians 2:11, RSV).

That which we pray in private, and in our deepest distress, is a window to our soul. Those words uttered before our God, which none hears but He, are an index to our genuine character, for with no witness to our complaint we unconsciously reveal our true heart, and our real spirit. Hannah's heart was in despair, but her despair related to the honour of her God, and the sanctity of His purpose with Israel, as the vow she was about to make would reveal. Whenever she prayed, whether in deep grief, or great joy, her prayers were always centred on the purpose of God whose will transcended her own.

The vowing of a special vow

> "And she vowed a vow, and said, O Lord of hosts, if thou wilt indeed look on the affliction of thine handmaid, and remember me, and not forget thine handmaid, but wilt give unto thine handmaid a man child, then I will give him unto the Lord all the days of his life, and there shall no razor come upon his head." (1 Samuel 1:11)

The making of a vow brought with it a solemn obligation for its payment. So serious was that responsibility, that God would brook no delay for the full performance of its terms, nor accept anything less than the joyful meeting of its demands. [5] Guilty was the one who vowed, but did not pay, for commitments to God could never be entered lightly. [6] To vow rashly or unwisely was censured, and therefore a vow needed to be made with calm intent and deliberate purpose, in full awareness of its final cost. Hannah, gripped by emotions so strong that they reduced her to tears, might seem to have been in no position to make such

---

5   The law taught, "That which is gone out of thy lips thou shalt keep and perform; even a freewill offering, according as thou hast vowed unto the Lord thy God, which thou hast promised with thy mouth" (Deuteronomy 23:21-23). Given that Hannah quotes extensively from the law, it is very likely she was aware of this teaching concerning vows and the importance of fulfilling them.

6   A later passage gave counsel about the special need to be cautious when making vows at the house of God itself, as God would not accept vows made, but then broken – "Better is it that thou shouldest not vow, than that thou shouldest vow and not pay" (Ecclesiastes 5:1-6).

a considered pledge. But her vow was neither rash nor hasty, for this prayer was but the culmination of many such pleadings which Hannah had offered. She knew exactly what the full measure of her vow would cost, [7] but even here, at the house of God, she was still determined to make it.

Hers was a singular [8] vow, for it involved the giving of a person. To vow someone in dedication, was only undertaken by one who yearned to give something more than the offering of praise to God. The law provided for such vows, under which the person would be given to the priests, either for service at the tabernacle or to work on Levitical lands. The right to pledge a person in such a way, only extended to members of one's own household, as these were the only individuals over which jurisdiction and authority could be held by the person making the vow. At the same time however, the law provided a means to calculate the worth of the person so pledged, and then permitted their immediate redemption by the payment of this sum. [9] The price of redemption however was high, and in setting such values, the cost acted as a deterrent against making unwise vows. For most, the vowing of a person followed this rule. It permitted the return of the one pledged, but with the monetary value for their redemption accepted as the sign of the dedication of the offerer to the Lord. By such vows, the system of the tabernacle was sustained, but without the difficulties arising from large numbers of persons being allocated to the tribe of Levi with a consequent obligation for their maintenance.

In certain exceptional cases however, the law also provided for the dedication of a person without the right of redemption, and if so devoted, then their life belonged to the Lord

---

[7] 1 Chronicles 21:24.

[8] As in the phrase, "When a man shall make a singular vow, the persons shall be for the LORD by thy estimation" (Leviticus 27:2). Here the word "singular" (*pala*) means – wonderful, extraordinary, difficult. Significantly, this was the term also used of Nazarite commitment – "When either man or woman shall separate (*pala*) themselves to vow a vow of a Nazarite" (Numbers 6:2).

[9] This was the vow of *neder* (Leviticus 27:1-8).

completely.[10] To offer a person in such a way, was to make an extraordinary vow, and was brought forth only by extraordinary circumstances. Because they were devoted by an unredeemable grant, their lives were forfeit to God.[11] Given up to Him entirely by irrevocable surrender, they became His servants, and duty bound to a lifetime of service.[12] All such devoted persons within Israel belonged to the High Priest and his family,[13] and it was this vow that Hannah intended to make in the dedication of her son. To give such a person to the priests, was in effect to give them to the Lord Himself, since the priests were His representatives.[14]

Nor was she without precedent, for in the nation's recent history, and in Hannah's living memory, a man had made such a vow, a difficult vow in dedicating a person.[15] Jephthah had promised God that he would devote a person out of his household in such a way, should the Lord grant him victory. His vow was intended from the moment it proceeded from his mouth to be an offering without redemption. To make such a vow was unusual

---

10 This was the vow of *cherem* (Leviticus 27:28,29).

11 "The basic meaning [of *cherem*] is the exclusion of an object from the use of man and its irrevocable surrender to God ... Surrendering something to God meant devoting it to the service of God or putting it under a ban for utter destruction" (*Theological Wordbook of the Old Testament*, volume 1, page 324). Context of course, would always determine which of these two applied.

12 It was important to distinguish between those devoted (*cherem*) to the Lord out of Israel, and those devoted (*cherem*) of men from the nations. In both instances their lives belonged to God without recall, but their destinies were very different. The former (Leviticus 27:28) were given as a gift to the High Priest (Numbers 18:14) and their lives forfeit to service. The latter (Leviticus 27:29) were given to destruction, and their lives forfeit in death (Joshua 6:17-21). No one in Israel could devote another Israelite to death, for that would be murder (Exodus 20:13). In the cases of both Jephthah and Hannah, their vows were to devote one from their own household to lifetime service.

13 Numbers 18:14.

14 The devoted person (*cherem*) was described as "most holy" (*qodesh qodesh*) to the Lord (Leviticus 27:28). Every other use of this expression in the book of Leviticus related to things given to the priests for their exclusive use (Leviticus 2:3,10; 6:17,25,29; 7:1,6; 10:12,17; 14:13; 21:22; 24:9). It is logical to assume that persons devoted as "most holy" also belonged to the priests.

15 See Appendix 1 – "What was the setting for Hannah's troublous times?" on page 206, under the heading, "The twin stories of dedication".

in the extreme, but Jephthah was driven by the exigencies of his situation, for he faced a battle on which the future of the nation rested.

But Hannah felt that she also was in a battle, and that the nation's destiny was at stake in its outcome. [16] The one vow became the model for the other. His, as it transpired, was the dedication of an only daughter. Hers, as she intended, would be the dedication of an only son. But whereas Jephthah intended to pledge a person in response to victory, she would offer her child as the means of victory. But that victory depended on the power of the God to whom her vow was made. Hannah was ready to vow, and knew exactly upon whom she would call to witness it.

The Lord of hosts that inhabiteth the cherubim

In listing the items to be made for the tabernacle, the law began with the ark of the testimony, mentioned first because it was the most important. And if for the Levites the ark was the focal point of the tabernacle, it was even more so for the Kohathites, whose charge included its carriage. Housed in the Most Holy, the promise of God was that there He would meet with His people, and commune with them from above the mercy seat, as He inhabited the cherubim, [17] which were over the ark. [18] Here dwelt the Shekinah glory of the Lord's presence among His people, chambered in the Most Holy as His secret abode, but represented as His shining upon them in the exhibition of His mercy and His favour. [19]

---

16 Note the close similarity of the two vows (Judges 11:30,31; 1 Samuel 1:11).

17 In references to He that "dwellest *between* the cherubim" (e.g., 2 Kings 19:15; Psalm 99:1) the word "between" is invariably in italics. A better translation is "inhabiting the cherubim" as followed by YLT, Rotherham, etc.

18 Exodus 25:21,22.

19 The following are examples of Biblical allusion to this Shekinah glory – "Out of Zion, the perfection of beauty, God hath shined" (Psalm 50:2), "Give ear, O Shepherd of Israel, thou that leadest Joseph like a flock; thou that dwellest between the cherubims, shine forth" (Psalm 80:1). The priestly blessing at the tabernacle was also a reference to this Shekinah shining – "The LORD make his face shine upon thee" (Numbers 6:25).

It was this promise that thrilled Hannah so, the prospect of fellowship with the One whose glory inhabited the cherubim. To this woman of Kohathite zeal, the ark was the centre of their spiritual life, and the place where the God of Israel dwelt. [20] It was to this God who dwelt among them, that Hannah prayed as she appealed to Him in the extremity of her grief. She besought in prayer the God she believed in, who alone could grant her victory. "O LORD of hosts", she cried, addressing Him in a manner that had never been used before. [21] It was an arresting expression, her choice of title being not only original, but a mark of how unique she was. Hannah, as always, had thought deeply about the crisis she faced and knew that the Lord of hosts could answer it.

Who then were the hosts Hannah had in mind? It was true that God was in control of the hosts of heaven, those angelic armies that could be marshalled by God for the execution His purpose. [22] But Hannah's thought was more direct, more personal as she called upon the God of her people and her tribe. She knew that her people were the hosts of the Lord, marked out as such from the moment of their deliverance from Egypt. [23] And He who inhabited the cherubim went forth at their head and on their

---

20 "Finally, beyond, lay the innermost of the three sanctuaries. There stood the Ark only, with the Mercy Seat over it, overshadowed by the Cherubim ... It was this sacred place that beckoned Israel forward and stood as the goal of its priestly calling: here was the very heart of the Sanctuary, the Presence of Yahweh Himself, that condition of perfect and permanent fellowship with Him who redeemed Israel specifically to manifest His glory in and through them" (*Law and Grace*, pages 63,64, W. F. Barling).

21 Remarkably, the title (*Yahweh Tsabaoth*) did not appear in the Pentateuch, or in the other books written before Hannah – Joshua, Judges, Job. The title was found in the narrative of 1 Samuel 1:3 concerning the family coming to Shiloh to sacrifice unto the Lord of hosts. This was significant as it indicated that the title stood related to the worship of the One who resided at the sanctuary. But Hannah was the first person recorded as having used the title, and her prayer was offered at the sanctuary to the One who had promised to meet with His people there.

22 Joshua met the captain of this host (Joshua 5:13-15), and Micaiah saw it arrayed around the throne of God (1 Kings 22:19). These hosts of angels were always intent on performing God's word, and doing His pleasure (Psalm 103:20,21).

23 The law described Israel as the hosts (*tsaba*) of God (Exodus 6:26; 12:17,41,51; Numbers 1:3; 2:32).

behalf, since the ark preceded them and the battle cry was heard – "Rise up, LORD, and let thine enemies be scattered". **24** If Israel were God's hosts in general, then the Levites were God's hosts in particular. Theirs was the spiritual warfare of the tabernacle, and their focus was also centred upon the ark of the covenant and the Lord who inhabited the cherubim. **25**

Hannah addressed her vow to the Lord of hosts that fought for Israel in their wars, and to the Lord of hosts in whose warfare the Levites fought, as she pleaded His assistance for the battle which she now embarked upon. She did not invoke God in the name of "He who will be armies" in order to win some personal victory in a feud against Peninnah. Hannah would never have demeaned her God by calling upon Him in such a special way, for such an unseemly cause. The Lord of hosts she called upon fought for Israel and the Levites because their battles were His, and she believed with all her heart that her battle was His also, that her controversy was the controversy of the Lord Himself.

If, moreover her conflict had merely been with Peninnah, she would not have asked for one child, but for an entire family that might eclipse the many children Peninnah already had. Even if the presence of Peninnah's children added to her hurt, Hannah's mind had long been fixed on much higher things. Her battle was against an evil priesthood, and for that battle she needed but one child. A female however would not be sufficient. A man child was needed for a priest to be established, and this was what she prayed for. The Lord of hosts whom Hannah called upon was the God of that people and of those priests whom He dwelt amongst. He would be manifested in them, as they marched forth in battle, and victory would be theirs because of His presence among them. How desperately did Hannah desire such victory in her own quest on His behalf. And, given that her

---

24 Numbers 10:33-36.
25 The term *tsaba* is also used of the Levites (Numbers 4:3, etc.). For a more detailed comment on the Levites as God's hosts, see Chapter 6 – "Hannah and her hope" on page 127, under the heading, "The women who assembled".

mind was never far from the ark of her God, her form of address was a remarkable declaration of her deepest belief. [26]

Look on the affliction of thine handmaid

Strong though her vow was, and strong the spirit that uttered it, there was nothing of self-importance or of self-seeking in Hannah's words. Instead, her spirit was the very reverse, as she prefaced her vow by declaring her position of deference before God. "If thou wilt indeed look on the affliction of thine handmaid, and remember me, and not forget thine handmaid, but wilt give unto thine handmaid" she cried. It was certainly an expression of service and of duty, of humility and resignation to His will. But Hannah's threefold use of the word was so intense that it revealed her deepest wish. She wanted nothing more than to be the instrument of God for salvation, and she would gladly subordinate her own will for the doing of His. This was no empty expression in Hannah's mouth, but a vow of deepest dedication to His purpose. If the Lord of hosts answered her prayer, then the one to be born would truly be "the son of the handmaid", the one in whom God's purpose would be wrought. [27]

Hannah had thought deeply about the problems of her nation, and its spiritual condition. The godly of every generation have done the same, in contemplating the challenges of ecclesial life and how they might be faced. Frequently those difficulties bring heartache to the faithful, as they did for Hannah. But the lesson of Hannah's life was not to be consumed with expressions of self-pity or personal woe, but rather to be available to what

---

[26] It is significant that from the very next time the title "LORD of hosts" was used, it would convey the richness of Hannah's faith – "the ark of the covenant of the LORD of hosts, which inhabiteth the cherubim" (1 Samuel 4:4). This episode (set during the time of Hophni and Phinehas) was while Hannah was probably still alive. The title retained that connection with the ark of the Presence (2 Samuel 6:2; Psalm 24:9,10; 80:1,3,7,19; Isaiah 6:1-3; 37:15,16; Haggai 2:7-9).

[27] This unusual phrase – "the son of thine handmaid" is found in two highly Messianic psalms which focus on the work of God in His servant (Psalm 86:16; 116:16). Hannah's words (1 Samuel 1:11), may have formed part of the scriptural background which led to this expression.

the Lord of hosts could accomplish through those who honoured Him. It was this spirit of service that dominated Hannah's thinking, and her vow was centred upon making herself the expression of the divine purpose.

How many times had God "raised up a saviour" in the days of the judges? Was not this His way with His people during those dark years? [28] And given that the darkness still prevailed, [29] why could she not help to raise up the saviour that her people needed so badly now? Hannah knew the history of her times, and was aware how often the Lord had intervened to send such a deliverer to His people. In desiring to be the Handmaid of the Highest, she offered herself to be the bearer of one through whom God might save His people again, but this time from the darkness of spiritual apostasy.

Then I will give him unto the Lord

It was very evident in the spirit of her vow, that Hannah was not motivated by selfishness but by love. She was not a woman consumed with desperation for her own need, but she did know that the nation was desperate for the saviour she had thought about. From the beginning, Hannah did not want a child for the sake of having a child. She asked for a son, only to pledge that she would return him. Her words were so clear and strong – "if … thou wilt give unto thine handmaid a man child, then I will give him unto the LORD all the days of his life". If all she had wanted was a son, why would she vow to make him a Nazarite in separation, and a devoted one in dedication to God all his life? The child would already be a Levite, and would belong to God for twenty-five years from the time he was twenty-five. [30] But Hannah promised to give him to the Lord all the days of his life. The Nazarite was made separate for just the duration

---

28 The epoch of the judges was marked by the raising up of those described as the saviours or deliverers (*yasha*) of the nation (Judges 3:9,15,31; 6:14; 10:1; 13:5).
29 1 Samuel 3:1-3.
30 Numbers 8:24,25.

of their vow, which was generally for a limited span of time, [31] but Hannah sought to extend it to the end of life itself. Her son, should she be blessed with one, would belong to God completely.

It was one thing to dedicate her son. But to give him to the Lord all the days of his life was extraordinary. It meant that Hannah's gift was so final, so binding, as to be irreversible. [32] There could be no turning back from this vow once it had proceeded out of her mouth. If it was unalterable, then she must be absolutely committed to the work her son would perform. A vow so singular, so striking, was beyond the capacity of most even to contemplate. But Hannah had not only thought about the child, she knew exactly what he must achieve for the good of his people. She vowed him for life, and events proved that she was right, for Samuel's work in Israel would indeed embrace a lifetime of service. [33] He laboured amidst the nation, but his return was always to his beloved Ramah, [34] made special by its association with his mother. Samuel's work never ceased, for he died in office and was buried in his house in Ramah. [35] None of this was known to Hannah at the time she made her vow. But her faith and her far sightedness would be vindicated by the outcome.

There could be no mistake that it was Nazarite dedication which she intended, since in offering her son to the Lord all the days of his life, she also promised that "no razor would come upon his head". Hannah's words were an indication that she knew the story of Samson and his mother, whose child was

---

[31] Numbers 6:8,13.

[32] Yet Hannah's spirit was the same as her Lord's – "for the gifts and the call of God are irrevocable" (Romans 11:29, RSV).

[33] Compare Hannah's vow – "I will give him unto the LORD all the days of his life" (1 Samuel 1:11) with the final summary of Samuel's labours – "And Samuel judged Israel all the days of his life" (1 Samuel 7:15).

[34] 1 Samuel 7:17.

[35] The record refers to Samuel's house in Ramah several times (1 Samuel 7:17; 9:25; 25:1). Given the references to Hannah's house in Ramah (1 Samuel 1:19; 2:11), it may be (as firstborn) that the house which was the centre of Samuel's work was his mother's. How wonderful if it were so!

similarly pledged to Nazarite separation from the womb. **36** But Hannah knew full well the words of the Nazarite vow itself, and used them in her own, knowing that the Lord before whom she prayed would recognise the depth of her intent. No razor was to come upon the head of the Nazarite all the days of his separation, as a mark that he was holy unto the Lord. **37** But for one vowed for life, the crown of his separation in the flowing locks of his Nazariteship would be Samuel's sign that he was permanently consecrated in holiness unto the Lord, before whom he would minister. She asked, so that she might give, and she gave without reserve. There could be no finer vow than that.

The abiding power of personal prayer

> "And it came to pass, as she continued praying before the LORD, that Eli marked her mouth. Now Hannah, she spake in her heart; only her lips moved, but her voice was not heard: therefore Eli thought she had been drunken. And Eli said unto her, How long wilt thou be drunken? Put away thy wine from thee." (1 Samuel 1:12-14)

There is something intense about the experience of personal prayer. It is an engagement at the deepest level of heart and soul and mind. Only those who have practised long in prayer, can continue long in its offering. The very demand of what prayer entails requires such a concentration of thought and word, that our powers of focus are rapidly depleted. To prepare our mind, to confess our need, to express our hope, to ask His help, to declare His right, to plead His work, to accept His will is an exercise of such proportions that the saint can be left exhausted. But to continue in prayer was rare indeed, so rare, that but a handful of the faithful were recorded as doing so. Hannah was among them, for she multiplied to pray. **38** Her prayer was not short, but

---

36 In fact, the word Hannah uses for razor (*mowrah*) is only used by herself, and in relation to Samson (Judges 13:5; 16:17).

37 Numbers 6:5,8.

38 This is the essential meaning of the word "continued" (*rabah*), as correctly noted in

neither was it filled with vain repetition. When the faithful pray, time stands still as they come before He who is timeless.

In the state of despair which Hannah felt, her prayer brought her into the presence of God, where no one else could come, and where all else no longer mattered. In prayer, her heart could be opened before Him, to find solace in expressing the inexpressible. This was what it meant to be the Handmaid of the Highest. She would place her burdens at His feet, and seek His help to fulfil His purpose. Continual prayer is the secret of those who have learned that God's timetable does not always match their own. The daily incense which burned every evening and morning was a continual offering in the sanctuary, [39] and Hannah, a faithful Levite, lived a sanctuary life in her personal standards. Her ability to offer continual prayer was the result of faithful practice, and in her was seen the mark of the true saint of God, that they ought always to pray and not to faint. [40]

This was not the first time that Hannah had offered this prayer in this place. Each year, her visit to the sanctuary sharpened the bitterness of her adversity, [41] as she faced the same ungodliness which only grew worse. It was no doubt true that the prayer of this visit was the most intense, as her bitter grief culminated in this prayer of the afflicted when overwhelmed. But, in truth, Hannah had prayed about this matter for year after year, and in doing so manifested the spirit of the Handmaid. Having begun, she would pray without ceasing, until the answer of God, whether in favour of her pleading or against it, was made plain. Continual prayer was not the evidence of her doubt, but of her unfailing belief.

---

the margin; GLT – "when she prayed long".

[39] The daily incense was called "a perpetual incense" (Exodus 30:8), the term meaning 'continual' as used also of the daily lambs (Exodus 29:38,42).

[40] Luke 18:1; Acts 1:13,14; 2:42; 6:4; Romans 12:12; Ephesians 6:18; Colossians 4:2.

[41] The wording suggests this. Note – "and when the time was that Elkanah offered" (1 Samuel 1:4) is not a comment on a single event, but on their annual practice. Likewise – "And as he did so year by year, when she went up into the house of the LORD" (1 Samuel 1:7) was her annual experience in that place.

The mistaken observation of Eli

She had stood by herself, but she was not as alone as she imagined, for the priest of God [42] sat nearby, upon his seat at the porch of the tabernacle. [43] It was true that he was an old man, but his place near the post ought not to have been there. There was no seat for man permitted in the tabernacle. The footstool of the Almighty was there, but in deference to Him, it was required of priests that they stood whilst ministering in the place of His presence. [44] Whatever reason Eli might have had, it was a departure from the divine order, and an indication that his weakness lay in accommodating the requirements of the law to suit his own preferences.

The one who was seated watched the one who stood, and he did so with a doubtful and disapproving eye, for he was close enough to see the woman's movements as she moved in unconscious harmony with her words. He noticed, because the sight of a person in prolonged prayer was unusual at the sanctuary. But what he noticed especially was that her lips moved, yet not a sound was heard. Her prayer was intense, but it was also private. Not for Hannah the ostentatious display of learned recitation, or dramatic grief out loud for all to hear. Her prayer, although offered in grief, was heard only by her God, for she spoke in her heart. [45]

Eli was quick to rebuke what he took to be the signs of inebriation. Her swaying form and mouthed words were the

---

42 Note that although Eli was a judge for forty years (1 Samuel 4:18), he is described here as "the priest". The entire focus of Hannah's story concerns the matters of priesthood.

43 When the tabernacle was finally established in Shiloh (Joshua 18:1), it seems that the nation erected a permanent canopy under which the tabernacle was pitched. The phrase – "set up" (*shakan*) means to dwell, lodge, inhabit, reside. Hence YLT – "and they cause the tent of meeting to tabernacle there". Evidently a porch was also built before the entrance to this facility. Wherever Hannah came to make petition (and she would only be permitted to the boundary where worshippers could come), she was close enough for Eli both to see and hear her.

44 Deuteronomy 10:8; 18:5-7.

45 Compare the spirit of Eliezer's prayer as the servant of God, where, although his prayer was recorded, it was only later that he revealed it had been spoken in his heart (Genesis 24:12,15,42-45).

evidence, to his eyes, of one who had tarried long at the wine. It was a sad testimony to the state of worship at the tabernacle that he should assume such a condition in one of the worshippers who attended. No doubt he had seen it before, as the intemperate behaviour of his sons was copied by the unspiritual and the unholy. "How long wilt thou be drunken? Put away thy wine from thee", he said, as he abruptly advised her to go away and sleep her wine off before returning. [46]

But Eli was wrong. Grievously wrong. There may have been reason for his assessment, but the woman who stood before him was so holy of heart that his judgment was unrighteous. He rebuked one whose spirit before God was purer than his own. If ever there was an indication that Hannah was all alone, it was here. She was at the sanctuary of her God, and yet God's priest had absolutely failed her in her time of need. There was no grace to help here. But Eli's inadequacy, and his son's iniquity were the very reasons she was here praying at all. She sought to replace their priesthood which had become corrupt through the weakness of this man, and this exchange gave proof of her cause.

She openeth her mouth with wisdom

> "And Hannah answered and said, No, my lord, I am a woman of a sorrowful spirit: I have drunk neither wine nor strong drink, but have poured out my soul before the LORD. Count not thine handmaid for a daughter of Belial: for out of the abundance of my complaint and grief have I spoken hitherto."
> (1 Samuel 1:15,16)

Hannah, startled by these words called out to her, turned towards their speaker. She saw the priest of Israel, and quickly read in his narrowed eyes and frowning face the marks of his strong disapproval. Lost in her grief, and absorbed in her conversation with God, she had been unaware that anyone might be watching her, and was shocked at Eli's intrusion on her prayer. His rebuke,

---

[46] The phrase "put away thy wine" may be taken as implying this. Cp. 1 Samuel 25:37.

abrupt and sharp, would have occasioned a less courteous reply in another woman. Unfairly interrupted and unjustly accused, there was every reason for her to feel hurt at this evident misreading of her condition. How painful, that even here at the sanctuary the solace she sought was to be denied by this interruption.

But Hannah's gravity of speech and purity of mind were not reserved for moments with her God. They were part of her whole being. Interrupted though she was from things so private, her response was in the same gracious and godly spirit which marked all her interactions. Recognising who had addressed her, she immediately showed respect for the Lord's anointed, a respect that was instant and sincere. She knew that this man's weakness had led to the evil of his sons. She knew that this man's toleration was responsible for the corruption of the priesthood. She knew that this man's compromise was the cause of the nation's ruptured fellowship with their God. Yet, such was her reverential respect for the office of High Priest, that she still called him "my lord". It is possible to acknowledge the dignity of office and the burden of authority, without endorsing the individual who holds it. Respect for those in authority is a divine principle, and Hannah's response was a shining example of how saints ought to behave, even when surprised by the unexpected.[47]

It was true that the sorrow of pain and the anguish of trial had caused her to pour out her soul before the LORD, and with such intensity that her body swayed and her lips moved. But none of this was because she was drunken as Eli had supposed. It no doubt reflected the wickedness oft seen at the sanctuary, but the old man had been sorely mistaken in his judgment on this day. The woman before him was most certainly not drunken, and her response was a gentle but firm repudiation of his charge. In her reply however, she did not use Eli's word, but spoke instead in the language of a scripture which he, of all people, should have

---

[47] The principle of honouring those in authority is enjoined upon the saints, whether of obedience to those who guide the ecclesia (1 Timothy 5:17-19; Hebrews 13:7,17,24), or of due submission to those who rule the world (Romans 13:1-7; 1 Timothy 2:1,2; 1 Peter 2:13-17).

known. Her words were not intended as a deliberate slight to him, but for all that, they were the unconscious revelation of her heart. For in denying his accusation, she answered with the words of the Nazarite vow. It was the Nazarite who was forbidden to partake of either "wine or strong drink", and these were the terms in Hannah's mouth.[48] Here was one who had not only abstained, but who had done so from the highest of spiritual motives. Instantly, she lifted the matter from the unseemly to the sacred.

But this was not an expression of a Nazarite dedication which would rest upon her son, if he was born. Such was her spirit, even in distress, that she pledged herself to a higher standard of commitment in her own life. She had already pledged her son's life, should God graciously grant him, but this vow was for herself. And there was a recent example in the history of the nation, which furnished Hannah with the basis for her own pledge of Nazarite abstention. Samson's mother, although barren, had been visited by an angel who promised her the conception of a son. Her child however, was to be dedicated unto the Lord, a dedication that would be from the womb to the day of his death. For this lifetime pledge of separation to be fulfilled however, the woman was advised that a vow of abstention must apply to her. So important was the matter that she was commanded three times to "drink no wine nor strong drink".[49]

Samson's Nazariteship began before his birth, because his mother lived as a Nazarite during the entire time of his bearing. That commitment of the mother linked her with her son's future work. Hannah was determined to do the same. And, so real was the prospect of this son she had prayed for, that she bound her own soul in a prohibition of Nazarite commitment. Her decision not to partake of wine or strong drink was a vow that she would prepare herself to the uttermost for the bearing of this child.

But Hannah needed no instruction from an angel to abstain from wine and strong drink. She made that commitment

---

[48] Numbers 6:2,3.
[49] Judges 13:4,7,14.

in the voluntary spirit which lay at the very heart of the Nazarite vow. Her decision, made without compulsion and of her own free will, was a testimony to her faith, that even in barrenness she, likewise, would prepare her body for the bearing of a special son. This pure and holy woman, whose mind was so focused on how best she might offer herself to be the Handmaid of the Lord, was the one who spoke with Eli. As he listened to her answer, so gracious and sincere, he knew immediately that he had badly misread her actions and her motives. "I have poured out my soul before the LORD", she said, and looking upon her earnest countenance, he believed her completely. And where else should such a prayer be made, but here at the place where God dwelt with His people, and promised to commune with them.

"Count not thy handmaid for a daughter of Belial", [50] said Hannah, as she pleaded for Eli to understand the depth of her sorrow. She humbled herself in seeking to revise his estimation of her, and she was even prepared to bare her grief before him so that he might understand. The one who stood before him was of sober mind and serious intent. But the depth of her grief was so real, that her body shook with the force of her feeling, "for out of the abundance of my complaint [51] and grief have I spoken thitherto". To have an abundance of grief was to be overwhelmed by it, and Hannah was overcome by hers. But her grief related to her adversity, [52] and her adversity to the sons of the man whom she stood before. Enough then, that she share the scope of her sorrow. She could not tell him its source.

---

50 It does not seem that Hannah intended it, but her words became a rebuke to Eli. She was most certainly not a "daughter of Belial", but his boys were "sons of Belial", and that by the estimation of God Himself (1 Samuel 2:12). Eli, quick to judge Hannah, had failed utterly to recognise and judge his sons correctly, whose sins were, to Hannah's, as the darkness was to the light.

51 The basic meaning of the word "complaint" (*siyach*) is to go over a matter in one's mind. It is used to describe the state of suffering and lamentation which Job felt (Job 7:11,13; 9:27; 10:1; 21:4; 23:2). Hannah may have found in Job's expression for his sorrow the word for her own.

52 The word "grief" here, is the same as "provoked sore" (1 Samuel 1:6). But that provocation in Hannah's life was centred on the spiritual wickedness of Eli's sons.

Why should Hannah have been concerned with what type of woman Eli might have thought her to be? Because the purpose which burned so brightly within her depended on the giving of a child to God at the sanctuary, and this man would be the one to whom she gave him. Her foresight was clear enough for her to know that this man must be under no misunderstanding as to who she was.

A priestly blessing of fellowship peace

> "Then Eli answered and said, Go in peace: and the God of Israel grant thee thy petition that thou hast asked of him. And she said, Let thine handmaid find grace in thy sight. So she went her way, and did eat, and her countenance was no more sad." (1 Samuel 1:17,18)

"Go in peace" Eli said, and at least he was quick to affirm his acceptance of her explanation, and to make amends for his hasty judgment. But he said more, "And the God of Israel grant thee thy petition that thou hast asked of him". Eli's wish that God would answer her prayer was more than mere commonplace. It was a prophetic assurance that her prayer was heard, as subsequent events would prove. But although Hannah had mentioned her grief to Eli, she had not disclosed the detail of her petition. He would have been shocked had he known it, for he had no idea at this moment how revolutionary Hannah would be in the nation over which he presided as High Priest. He had no awareness of the changes she would set in motion, in a succession of events that would finally reach out to overthrow his own household. But Hannah did. And yet her reply was to plead his favour, and to recognise herself as his handmaid. How could she do otherwise? She had already pledged herself as the Handmaid of the Lord. This man was the representative of God, despite his weakness, and she bowed before him in humility because of it.

That response, so filled with humility and respect, gave insight into Hannah's true spirit. "Let thine handmaid find grace in thy sight" was her reply to Eli, as she thanked him for his blessing. The woman named grace, sought for grace, and would soon become its glad recipient. [53] How was it so, that the one who came in the bitterness of her grief would depart in the gentleness of her peace? Surely, it was the outcome of her prayer and its effect upon her. Prayer, earnest and fervent, settles the heart and the mind. Although she had not yet received an answer from God, she had committed the matter to Him, and rested in that. Although outwardly her circumstances had not changed, she was now joyous and resolute, full of assurance that her prayer would be answered.

It was a different Hannah who returned to her family, a woman made tranquil and prepared in heart to eat in peace, in fellowship with God, and made whole in the partaking of her portion. "Go in peace", Eli had said, and, receiving this as the blessing of heaven, she did go back, and ate the bread of her peace offering with joy. She did not however drink. [54] It was a conscious abstention. Her vow of Nazariteship for her son extended to a Nazarite vow upon herself, that not only in his life, but even in his conception and his bearing in her womb, he would be a holy child. Even in her newly found peace and happiness, that vow would stand, must stand, as she awaited the day of the Lord's visitation in her life.

Hannah and her vow

Hannah could have vowed to dedicate her son under the law of devoted persons. Had she done so, he would have immediately come under the control of the High Priest, and been permanently dedicated for service. His life would have belonged to God, who could have used the child for whatever purpose He had in mind. But Hannah decided to dedicate her child in an additional way, that also invoked a different law. She offered her son without

---

53 Note the wonderful words of Gabriel to Mary, which alluded to the meaning of Hannah's name (Luke 1:28).
54 The record is careful to distinguish between the rest of her family who ate and drank (1 Samuel 1:9), and Hannah, who only ate (1 Samuel 1:18).

the right of redemption under the Law of the Devoted, [55] but she also pledged him for perpetual service under the Law of the Nazarite. [56] In doing so, Hannah revealed the depth and insight of her spiritual mind, for she discerned in the Nazarite vow a higher truth in which was hidden the real reason for her pledge.

The Nazarite was separated to God for the duration of their vow. Because that vow was normally for a limited time, it made possible a pledge of dedication from either man or woman that was realistic to the normal circumstances of their daily life. Such a vow permitted a level of commitment above the ordinary, for a designated period, when a person could experience a heightened awareness of coming before their God in service and praise.

But it enabled something more. The Israelite who vowed a Nazarite vow ascended to the spirit of priestly service in their lives. Whatever the extent of their vow might be, God commanded certain actions as the minimum required by Himself. The Nazarite learned thereby that even a voluntary vow carried with it obligations to heaven that He alone could determine. But the purpose of God's statutory rules carried with them an enormous gift. In keeping them, they were lifted to the standard and to the spirit not just of priesthood, but of the High Priest himself.

There were three such provisions that God enjoined upon the Nazarite. The first was an abstention from the drinking of wine. [57] That abstention related to holiness of mind, and taught the principle of mental separation. The second was an arrangement to hallow the head. [58] That arrangement related to holiness of life, and taught the principle of moral separation. The third was an avoidance of contact with death. [59] That avoidance

---

[55] As indicated by the phrase – "I will give him unto the LORD all the days of his life" (1 Samuel 1:11; cp. Leviticus 27:28,29).

[56] As indicated by the phrase – "and there shall no razor come upon his head" (1 Samuel 1:11; cp. Numbers 6:1-8).

[57] Cp. The Nazarite (Numbers 6:3,4), and the High Priest (Leviticus 10:9).

[58] Cp. The Nazarite (Numbers 6:5), and the High Priest (Leviticus 21:5,10).

[59] Cp. The Nazarite (Numbers 6:6,7), and the High Priest (Leviticus 21:10,11).

related to holiness of body, and taught the principle of physical separation. In each, the Nazarite imitated the High Priest, ascending to his standard and drawing near to God thereby. [60]

Because the Nazarite vow was voluntary, no provision was made for wilful infringement. An unintentional breach however was possible, and the law prescribed the offerings required to acknowledge failure, and renew the vow. As part of the restitution that God required, the days of separation previously observed were forfeited, and the entire term of the vow recommitted to. The Nazarite for life however, stood in a different relation to the matter. A breach of the Nazarite terms, whether intentional or inadvertent did not nullify his vow. There was no reason to forfeit the past, when there was no date for completion in the future. The Nazarite for life was a perpetual illustration of priesthood, and in this state also imitated the High Priest, since both were appointments for life. [61]

Only the thoughtful in Israel understood the true spirit of Nazarite separation. Only those with the deepest appreciation perceived that the Law of the Nazarite lifted the separated one to the holiness of priesthood, and to the spirit of the High Priest anointed among his people. But Hannah knew, and this was what Hannah wished for. She didn't seek for a man child to be dedicated merely as a Levite. She desired her Levite to be devoted as a Nazarite. This vow was not about a child for Hannah. It was about a priest for Israel. She could not offer a man from the

---

60 "The [High Priest] was the exemplar ... of all the pious ... in Israel. How then could these men and women attain to his 'holiness' and realise the ideal of self-consecration which his official role typified for them? ... The Law resolved their problem by arranging for the voluntary assumption by them of duties parallel with those of the High Priest – duties differing only slightly from his in nature, and not at all in essence" (*Law and Grace*, page 122, W. F. Barling).

61 Even a High Priest might be inadvertently defiled by contact with the dead. In that case, he would need to absent himself from the sanctuary, while observing the requirements of the law for purification (Numbers 5:2,3; 19:11-13). None of this however, negated his position as High Priest, or removed him from office. Those pledged under Nazarite vow for life would share this rule with the High Priest. A breach of their Nazarite provisions, did not negate their permanent Nazarite status, nor set aside their vow.

priestly family, but she could offer one from the priestly tribe. And her decision to offer her son under Nazarite terms was even more daring. She was asking God to take and use her son as if he was a priest, and to use him in place of the priests of that age, who although of the right family and the right tribe, were not of the right spirit.

Her vow was breathtaking in its intensity and in its grasp of her nation's need. As the Handmaid of the Highest, she begged for the privilege of providing one who might bring her people back to God. The implications of her vow were unmistakable. She was offering a man for priesthood. [62]

---

[62] The Nazarite however, because of the voluntary nature of their vow, stood related to a higher spirit of priesthood than those of the Aaronic family, who were obliged to perform their duties by virtue of their fleshly descent.

3 |

Hannah and her loan

(1 Samuel 1:19-28)

> "And they rose up in the morning early, and worshipped before the LORD, and returned, and came to their house to Ramah: and Elkanah knew Hannah his wife: and the LORD remembered her. Wherefore it came to pass, when the time was come about after Hannah had conceived, that she bare a son, and called his name Samuel, saying, Because I have asked him of the LORD." (1 Samuel 1:19,20)

ALTHOUGH the family made an early start, they still made a point of attending the sanctuary for a final act of worship before returning home. In an age of overwhelming wickedness, this household showed an outstanding spirit of dedication to the Truth, and Elkanah was a man of faith indeed to lead his family in that way. Despite their renewed attendance at the temple however, there would be no new offerings presented by the family that morning. All that they had brought from Ramah had been presented at the feast. But there was time enough to see the sacrifice of the morning lamb, to mingle their own prayer with the morning incense, and to hear the priestly blessing before they left.

And on that early sunlit morn, Hannah herself was a joyful participant. At last, she had partaken of the peace offering with her God. There at the sanctuary, immersed in holy thought, she recalled the vow she had made and remembered the words of the old priest – "Go in peace". **¹** And this day, she had heard again the benediction beloved of all Israel – "The LORD lift up his countenance upon thee, and give thee peace". **²** She felt it now, as she hugged herself in private reflection: the peace of fellowship with her God. There was a strange but powerful sense of calm, that by her prayer she had set in motion the great cause of her heart. If the Lord answered, then her calling as His Handmaid would change her destiny, and she was ready for that possibility.

So often in life, the only thing that prevents us from moving forward is our inability to believe in the possibility, and to place it before our God. Hannah would never regret her prayer of pleading, in pouring out her heart to heaven, nor her prayer of thankfulness this next morning. And somehow, in its giving, even before heaven's reply, she felt the lifting of the darkness, and the warmth of the light. It was as if, when she prayed, that the "fashion of her countenance was altered", for this would be a day of transformation in her life. She was thankful for this one last moment at the house of God, for it brought a sense of completion to a journey which had begun in despair. She would return to her own house in peace, but was unaware that several years would pass before she would stand again in this place.

When the family finally left, even the journey back to Ramah was different. This time, Hannah, in going home was stepping toward the future, not walking into the past. There was hope now. Hope and possibility. How wonderful that prayer can change us so. The same issues remain, the same problems obtrude, and yet our attitude alters in the light of the divine perspective which only prayer can bring. Prayer helps to lift our view upwards, beyond the narrow focus of our own life, to the light of God's own work. We begin to frame our requests that they might be harmonious with His purpose, **³** and in

---

1 Eli's words – "Go in peace" (1 Samuel 1:17) carried more significance for Hannah than he realised.
2 The priestly blessing (Numbers 6:24-27) was customarily offered at the morning and evening sacrifice.
3 1 John 5:14.

doing so, we learn to distinguish between the important and the mundane, the transient and the eternal, and are the better for it.

As they took the road that travelled south-west through Gilgal, and then due west across the hills of Ephraim, the sun travelled with them on their journey, warming them from behind, and finally passing beyond them in its march across the sky to traverse the far horizon of the uttermost sea. It was as if God's blessing went with them, and it lit up the face of Hannah who shone with new found tranquility. Elkanah noticed the altered expression, subtle yet distinct that had softened Hannah's countenance. [4] The sign of tears, and the anxiety of care were gently wiped away. Her smile was joyous, and her demeanour serene, and he marvelled at the change. There would be private conversation back home in Ramah between these two, for he was curious to know the reason.

A matter of mutual consent

Hannah was also preparing for their conversation, for she had much to share with him. She had made a vow, but not, as yet, with her husband's knowledge. There was no impediment to the making of such a vow on Hannah's part. The law of God authorised any man or woman to offer a peace offering, it allowed any man or woman to undertake a Nazarite pledge, it permitted any man or woman to bind their soul with a vow. Men and women are equal in their capacity to love the Truth, to worship God in the spirit of holiness, to draw near before Him in fervent prayer, to ascend into the holiest to find fellowship with Him. In that sense, there is no constraint upon a sister, that prevents her from exercising her highest spiritual faculties in the Truth.

But there are mutual responsibilities within the marriage bond, and Hannah knew that she must talk with Elkanah, to

---

4   The expression "and her countenance was no more sad" (1 Samuel 1:18) would have occasioned the attention of a caring husband, who likewise noticed his wife's moments of distress (1 Samuel 1:8).

share her vow and seek his endorsement.[5] And it was vital that she speak with him as soon as possible after returning home. She could not come together with her husband without telling everything. After all, there were huge implications. The child, should there be one, was promised to God. Yet he would be Elkanah's son as well, and he had claim to the child as much as Hannah did. How essential it was then that they be in harmony on the matter, for even the child's conception needed to occur within the sacred unity of their mutual understanding. They must be committed in their intention about what would happen if a son was born. There was no way she could share her vow with Elkanah after conception. Such a deceit would rupture their trust and destroy her vow.

The journey to Ramah gave Hannah opportunity to review her thoughts, as she tried to sort the tangled threads of her emotion and belief into a tapestry of reason and calm. How might Elkanah react to such an unusual request? What if he disallowed her vow, and made it void? What if he rejected it as being quite unthinkable? What if he refused it on the basis that he felt Hannah would regret it later? What if he repudiated it because he could not himself bear the thought of giving away their son, should one be born? How easy it would have been to magnify the difficult into the insuperable.

In her earlier state of grief, Hannah might have been distressed as she pondered the problem of how to speak with Elkanah on this matter. And yet she remained at peace. She knew with certainty, that if God could hear her, and grant her a son, then He could also work a work with Elkanah to convince him of the spirit and importance of her vow. How it might be achieved was no longer the largest issue. In the despair of our most anguished prayers, we finally discover the secret blessing of surrender to God, and learn to cast all our cares upon Him. When matters in life lie beyond our power to control, we finally

---

5   The law of vows was careful to distinguish between the day a woman uttered her vow, and the day her husband heard it (Numbers 30:6-8).

experience what it means to cast our burdens on the Lord, in the certainty that He will sustain us. He would show the way, and Hannah knew that if her purpose in seeking a man child was consistent with the divine will, then all else would follow. Being God's Handmaid began here, even before conception. It meant being ready to release her own fears. It meant being prepared to follow God's direction whenever he showed the way. It meant having confidence in God's power to work His own work.

How Hannah shared her vow

The moment of conversation did come. When Elkanah sought her out, to ask what she had been thinking of as they journeyed home, her upturned face fixed upon his, heart aflutter with the importance of it all. How much she wanted, how badly she needed him to understand. So, taking a deep breath, she told him all her heart. [6] Out poured the story of her sorrow at Shiloh, the grief she felt when the peace of fellowship was shattered by spiritual wickedness in high places, her yearning to overthrow a priesthood that robbed the nation of its spiritual heritage, her wish for a faithful priest in their place, her determination to ask the Lord to intervene by her hand, her pain that led to make her vow then and there to be His Handmaid. And most compelling of all was the truth with which she finished her words. If she was wrong, if she was at fault, if she was not to be God's means to resolve the problem, then her barrenness would remain and she would need to bear it. But if, at this moment, after this visit, given this vow, she did conceive a child, then what could it be but the answer of heaven to prayer. Surely, it was given her what

---

6 It is evident that this conversation must have taken place. Hannah could not have made her vow in defiance of her husband's role to approve it. The law was clear, that once he had heard, he then had responsibility to confirm and establish, or to disallow and make void her vow (Numbers 30:13-15). Hannah knew that the final decision still rested with her husband, and that her vow was subject to his approval. There are at least two pieces of corroborative evidence in this record which confirm that Hannah did share her vow with Elkanah (1 Samuel 1:21,23). And given that it was so, the matters suggested here would surely be amongst the things Hannah wished to discuss with him.

to speak in that hour! In her earnestness, she shone with the certainty of it all.

As Hannah spoke, the changing expressions on her husband's face displayed the passage of her story, and she saw in sequence the signs of surprise, then doubt, and finally thoughtfulness as her words came to an end. Elkanah, who had listened with growing astonishment, was greatly moved by Hannah's speech. How unaware he had been of the true nature of her burden. He was humbled by the realisation that what he had imagined were simply a woman's yearnings for a family, masked something far deeper. He had not known until now that her barrenness was, for Hannah, but the emptiness of her people. He had not felt, as sharply as she had, how fellowship with God at the sanctuary had been made impossible by a priesthood that disgraced the principle of holiness to the Lord. He had certainly not understood that she wanted a child for the nation, that she yearned for a man child to deliver Israel from such a sinful state, that she desired a son to defeat the terrible wickedness of Hophni and Phinehas. What sort of daring was this, for a woman to be ready to confront this evil at the sanctuary? Yet he had known of the ungodly behaviour for which these men were notorious. Why then had he not been disturbed enough to seek a solution? Was he not a Levite himself, called to the guardianship of holy [7] things? Why was it instead that his faithful wife had vexed her righteous soul [8] with their unlawful deeds?

There was deep respect here, tinged with not a little awe at the blazing purity of his wife's conviction. He had always known of her fervency, but this promise, this pledge, was so intense that it amazed him. And there was wonder too, that despite all her passion, she had, in the fulness of her trust, left the matter of

---

[7] The Levites as well as the priests were related to the holiness of the sanctuary and its activities (2 Chronicles 5:5; 23:6; 29:5; 30:27; 35:3).

[8] The vexation of Hannah (1 Samuel 1:6, Rotherham – "to cause her great vexation") may be compared with the vexation of Lot at the wickedness of Sodom (2 Peter 2:8). In both cases the vexation sprang from the despair of the righteous at the evil of the wicked.

her pledge in his hands. His role as husband had not been set aside. The future of her vow rested entirely with him. He could hold his peace and cause it to stand, or disallow it and make it void. The power of that choice was his, and she would yield to whatever his decision might be. But he was uneasily aware of the burden of that responsibility, for it was not a simple matter. If he agreed, how would they explain their intentions to others? If she conceived, how would they fulfil the obligations it brought? And yet her eloquent truth had inspired and convinced him. After all that she had shared with him on this day of revelation, how could he not establish her vow and allow it to stand?

For the possibility of this conception to be blessed, their union would need to be sanctified by a vow that was shared, and by prayer offered together for the Lord's blessing to rest upon them. In fact, the more he thought upon the matter, the more convinced he became that he could not just permit Hannah's vow to stand. He needed to join it. He must make her vow, his also. The initiative might have been hers, but he would add his vow to it, and so fully enter this compact with Hannah. Husband and wife would bind their souls together in this bond, their vow made final in a prayer that sealed their purpose before the Lord. It was a highly unusual circumstance. How often would a couple pray for a son to be conceived, in order that they might give him away? Elkanah was certainly aware of the effect this could have upon his household, and with the wider circle of their family and friends. It says much for his spirit that he concurred. It says as much for Hannah's that she submitted, as the blessing of their mutual understanding triumphed.

She brought forth her firstborn son

And the Lord did remember His handmaid. [9] He responded not only to her vow, but to the absolute conviction with which it had

---

9   The phrase is an echo of an earlier occasion – "And God remembered Rachel, and God hearkened to her, and opened her womb. And she conceived, and bare a son" (Genesis 30:22,23). Hannah was no doubt aware of the birth of Rachel's firstborn,

been made. He had never forgotten her, but simply awaited that moment of opportunity that was consistent with His own sovereign purpose. Learning that God always moves according to His own majestic timetable is hard for earthly time bound humans to understand. Whereas He can declare "the end from the beginning, and from ancient times the things that are not yet done", we lie caught in the reality of the present, and do not always perfectly understand the circumstances that have led to the moment, nor the events that will unfold beyond it. God however does, and all His arrangements are planned with infinite discernment. It is only when we look back that we appreciate the many events in our life which were not only for our good, but which were ordered according to "the determinate counsel and foreknowledge of God". Only later would Hannah realise the exquisite timing of the Almighty. Her child would be brought forth at the precise moment needed for the part he would eventually play, and she would marvel at the prescience of the Lord, who in His timeless wisdom knows all.

There was pure joy for Hannah when she conceived. From the outset, her determination was to offer to the Lord one who would not only be a Nazarite for life, but whose Nazarite holiness would begin at conception. She would never forget the day when she became aware of those first sensations of change, that heralded the answer of God, as her body began its work to provide a little sanctuary for the precious life that had begun within her. The "way of the spirit, and how the bones do grow in the womb of her that is with child" was a mystery which Hannah could not fathom. And as for the babe, she did not know how the Almighty would "possess his reins, nor how he was covered in his mother's womb", but she gave herself entirely to being the instrument for his bringing forth. This was what it meant to be the Handmaid of the Highest. Hannah herself was pledged in a vow of dedication that began at Shiloh, and would not end

---

conceived in response to her prayers to God, for this was the force of the phrase "and God hearkened to her". She would also have known that Rachel's son, Joseph, was similarly ordained by divine purpose for the deliverance of his people, as her son would be.

until the vow was fulfilled. Conceiving, bearing, and nursing the child would all take place within the care of a mother whose own life was kept holy for the duration, that her firstborn might be a Nazarite from the womb. [10] No wonder she had needed to share her vow with her husband. It wasn't just the child who was dedicated to God. His mother was also separated unto Him, and it would be some time before her vow could be completely fulfilled. Only a truly united couple could share this experience.

Finally, the year came full circle, and Hannah was delivered of her child on the anniversary of their yearly visit to Shiloh. [11] How blessed that the circuit of life which marked their annual pilgrimage should this time be crowned with the birth of the child for which she had petitioned a year before. The sorrow of childbearing that has been the peculiar burden of womankind from the foundation of the world, was surpassed by the joy that a man child was born into the world. As Hannah held her firstborn son close to her heart, she felt a surge of such indescribable happiness, such tumultuous joy, that her whole being was aglow with the wonder of it all. In this little babe, so perfect in his smallness, lay all her hope. His very birth was a sign that his mother could not mistake. The purpose of God was at work in this child, and she, as Handmaid of the Highest had been blessed to be part of that work. There was yet more for her to do, but for now she was content to rest in her son's safe arrival.

---

10 Her vow would follow the same constraints which the angel had strictly enjoined upon Samson's mother (Judges 13:4,5,7,13,14). But Hannah rose higher, in voluntarily imposing them upon herself.

11 The expression "when the time was come about" (1 Samuel 1:20) refers here to a circuit of time (Exodus 34:22). Although the word time (*yowm*) is the common word for day (hence margin, the revolution of days), it was also used for years (Exodus 13:10; Leviticus 25:29; Judges 21:19). It is not certain whether the reference here is to the circuit of gestation, or the circuit of their yearly pilgrimage. The writer has adopted the latter view, based upon the fact that this family measured their spiritual lives by their circuit to the yearly sacrifice, and that the term *yowm* is used to describe this cycle in the whole story of Hannah (1 Samuel 1:3,21; 2:19 ×3). If this were the case, then they were home for three months before Hannah conceived. This was more than sufficient time to discuss the matter over with Elkanah, and to reach perfect accord before conception ever took place.

And she called his name Samuel

It was Hannah who made the choice of his name. [12] It was not because Elkanah was unwilling or indifferent. He was fully involved with their vow. But just as Hannah had trusted him enough to leave to him the approval of her pledge, so he loved his wife well enough to leave to her the naming of their son. She justified his confidence, for the name she selected, Samuel, was chosen with wisdom and special care. It did not commemorate his mother's asking him of the Lord, though of course she had, but that the Lord had responded to her request. It was not so much the offering of prayer, but the answering of prayer that Hannah was so thankful for. Samuel was conceived and born because of answered prayer, and his special name celebrated that truth. [13]

But this was not the chief reason for the name she chose, for this, after all, was Hannah. She always thought beyond the measure of her own life, and even beyond her own joy. A far deeper purpose ran behind the name. It was true that her prayer had secured the response of heaven, but Samuel was not a name to celebrate her role, but the child's. She desired him to be Heard of God, for he was marked out for a priestly part, to be the spiritual intercessor the nation sorely needed. The essence of that work lay in a man whose prayers would be heard by God. And her faith in naming him thus was vindicated, as the work of Samuel amidst his people was revealed. This "son of her womb", this "son of her vow", would become famous for his prayers of petition on behalf of the nation and for the fact that God heard him. [14] Never had a child been better named in anticipation of his destiny. Never had a mother been more deeply aware of that destiny than Hannah. The

---

[12] It was not altogether unusual for a woman to name a child (Genesis 29:32-35; 30:6; 38:4; 1 Chronicles 4:9; 7:16), but the role of Hannah in this story is so pronounced that her involvement in choosing the name is to be noticed.

[13] Samuel does not mean 'asked of God', but 'heard of God', from *shama* – to hear, to understand, to obey. The force of the passage lies in the idea that Hannah had asked, and God had heard.

[14] Hannah's choice of the name Samuel was prophetic of his office. Her son would indeed be "Heard of God", as time and time again he offered intercession for his people after the manner of Moses of old (1 Samuel 7:9; 12:18; Psalm 99:6; Jeremiah 15:1).

divine guidance would rest upon this woman and her son from the beginning, as the babe lay nestled in his mother's arms. Already the foreshadowing of another mother and child could be seen in this house at Ramah. The fulness of that foreshadowing was yet to be unfolded, but when it was revealed, the picture and the pattern would be so exact that only the Spirit of God could have drawn it.

> "And the man Elkanah, and all his house, went up to offer unto the LORD the yearly sacrifice, and his vow. But Hannah went not up; for she said unto her husband, I will not go up until the child be weaned, and then I will bring him, that he may appear before the LORD, and there abide for ever. And Elkanah her husband said unto her, Do what seemeth thee good; tarry until thou have weaned him; only the LORD establish his word. So the woman abode, and gave her son suck until she weaned him." (1 Samuel 1:21-23)

The time for their annual pilgrimage to the sanctuary had come again. Elkanah had begun the arrangements for the journey they knew now so well. But there was something more purposeful this time in his preparations. A special peace offering was to be taken to the sanctuary, and so another animal was added. It signified the completion of his vow, and he was anxious to make the offering at this time of Samuel's birth, since the vow [15] related to the child. As the father, he also was involved in the decision to lend Samuel without redemption to the Lord's service, and he was ready to pledge his commitment to that course. He would do so without reserve, for this would be his personal offering of thanksgiving. Hannah was certainly with her husband in spirit, and dearly wished to be with him at this special moment. Yet despite the significance of the occasion, Hannah decided not to

---

15 Why now are we informed (for the first time) of the existence of a vow which Elkanah had made, and of his intention to symbolise its completion? Why does his vow deliberately occur in the narrative only after the making of Hannah's vow? Why does it follow hard on the heels of the announcement of Samuel's birth? The implication of the narrative is strongly suggestive of the view that Elkanah had added his vow to Hannah's, and that both vows related to the conception, birth and dedication of their firstborn son.

join him. She did not make demand, for there was no need. She knew already that Elkanah would understand her thinking.

The woman abode, and gave her son suck

Hannah had always shared her husband's earnestness in following the yearly cycle of their family visits to Shiloh. It was no doubt her dedication as much as his that took them to that place every year, so her determination not to attend on this occasion was a departure from her normal and desired routine. It was, as always, driven by careful thinking on her part. The child Samuel was but new born, and too little to make the journey just now. And, much as she might have wished to attend, there was a wider issue that reached beyond this next pilgrimage. Her decision not to visit the sanctuary until Samuel was weaned might have been construed as a means to delay the fulfilment of her vow. Certainly, by settling the moment of his weaning as the date, she extended the time she might have with Samuel. Yet her resolve not to bring him up until he had been weaned was not an endeavour to avoid her obligation, but a striking confirmation of her determination to fulfil it.

She knew, as only a mother could, that until the child was independent of her, he could never be the Lord's in the absolute sense. But, the Lord's he would be, and Hannah was certain in her mind who her son belonged to, and what her son's purpose in life was to be. Of all those who "appeared before the LORD", the priests pre-eminently were those who were chosen to "come near", and it was this work of priesthood that Hannah had in mind for her child. It had never been otherwise from the moment she sought the divine assistance as His Handmaid. And her decision was final and irrevocable that the child, once presented, would continue to appear before the Lord, remaining in that role for ever. This was no temporary commitment, but the offering of a lifetime. The child was destined for the sanctuary and everything she did now was to prepare him for that moment, for his earliest visit to that place would mark the beginning of his new life. But, she could not bring him up until she could end his dependence upon her, and she could walk away and leave him there. The break must be complete and final at that moment, for there would be no turning back. She knew, even then, how desperately hard that moment would be. And as much for the child as for herself, Hannah did not want to accustom Samuel to going and returning from Shiloh, only to experience the burden of a visit, all too soon, when he would be left behind there for good. His first journey to that place must be his final one. She nodded to herself, as she decided that this indeed was the wisest course. She would not visit Shiloh until she could complete her vow.

But everything she did now, in their house in Ramah, was designed to prepare her son for that moment, and her work of preparation was not yet fulfilled. As a married woman, she was not free to make a lifelong vow. Her obligations as a wife would limit her ability to be dedicated in the way that an unmarried woman might. But for this crucial period, she might extend her vow, so that everything from his conception to his weaning was related to the spirit of separation and holiness. Elkanah did understand. He knew that Hannah was seeking the most prudent way for her vow to be fulfilled, and readily agreed with her decision to remain behind. He was, as always, confident that his wife's motives were pure, and her thinking clear as to how best to accomplish this. Although he would travel to offer his offering of thanksgiving on this visit to Shiloh, he was prepared for Hannah to do what she thought appropriate. And although he could not enter fully into the depths of her feelings, he did realise that the completion of her vow would be far more difficult than the fulfilment of his vow which he was about accomplish at the sanctuary. Gracious in allowing Hannah to find the right way, he wisely framed his permission with the wish that God might thereby establish that which had gone forth out of her mouth.[16] Elkanah saw the entire

---

16 The KJV renders this, "only the LORD establish his word". The sense would be that the Lord might bless the child towards the purpose for which he had been brought forth. However, the LXX renders the phrase – "May the LORD establish that which is gone forth out of thy mouth". There is something to commend this translation,

matter as divinely orchestrated by God who was at work in their lives, and he encouraged his wife to complete her part.

When therefore Elkanah gathered his household together, they set out for Shiloh without Hannah and Samuel in the company. There was the customary bustle, as children and baggage, offerings and provisions were counted, and then the journey began. Suddenly, the family was gone, and Hannah was alone with her firstborn son. She drew a deep breath as the silence settled softly around her. Time at last to think and to pray. And most of all, time to plan. She would use these days of solitude to begin the nursing of her child through to his weaning. She knew that even then he would still be small, but these first few years would give her the opportunity she needed to imbue him with a love of God that would never leave him.

Even from the earliest age, a child can be touched by scriptural ideals and values, [17] and these can be imbedded so deeply at the outset, that they affect an infant for their entire future. [18] From the beginning, Hannah intended to nurse her child in such a way that her son's direction would be set for life. [19]

---

since there was no recorded specific word of God for Hannah (or God Himself) to establish. But Elkanah's wish was that God would give Hannah the strength to fulfil that which had gone forth out of her mouth, and thereby enable her to complete her vow. This rendering highlights the fact that the word "establish" is an allusion to the role of a husband in confirming a vow (Numbers 30:13,14), and the phrase "gone forth out of thy mouth" is an allusion to making a vow (Numbers 30:2; Deuteronomy 23:23). Elkanah asked for God's help, that Hannah might complete the promise of her own word uttered in vow (1 Samuel 1:11).

17 The apostolic comment, "from a child thou hast known the holy scriptures" (2 Timothy 3:15) is remarkable for its use of the term *brephos* – meaning a newborn child or even an unborn one!

18 The admonition to "train up a child in the way he should go" (Proverbs 22:6) means literally to train up a boy at the mouth (*peh*) of his way. Although the word 'mouth' no doubt is used to mean the opening or beginning of his life, it is reminiscent of the earliest moment a child suckles its mother (1 Peter 2:2).

19 Hannah no doubt knew also of the example of Jochebed, who performed her crucial work in nursing her own child (presumably until he was weaned) before giving him to Pharaoh's daughter (Exodus 2:7-10). Aware (as Hannah was) that hers was a special child (Acts 7:20; Hebrews 11:23), she didn't just suckle him, she nursed him into the ways of God. Ever after, although he might be called 'the son of Pharaoh's daughter', he was, in truth, Jochebed's son. And was not this special

Time alone would tell the depth and quality of her nurture, but it would later be seen that "the child was father to the man". [20] The power for good that lies in the early formative years should never be underestimated. A mother deeply influences her child in the first years of their life, for they are open to the receiving of godly impressions, which, gently but firmly pressed upon the tables of their heart, make a mark which rarely alters. Every mother sustains a special relationship with the little one who depends upon her for every need, and a wise woman knows that in this mysterious and magical time they do far more than feed their babe. They nourish its very spirit, as tiny hands clutch tight, and little eyes and ears begin to look and listen to the world that their mother opens to their gaze. Their first sense of security comes from her voice, and their first experience of love from her touch.

In the case of Hannah, the influence upon her son was profound. Fed on a rich diet of his mother's milk, and his mother's mind, he absorbed it all. That charge of motherhood was, for Hannah, made more urgent by the fact that her time with her son was to be so limited, that every moment must be made to count. These early years would form Samuel's entire outlook, and shape his whole perspective. She needed to capture those moments, and fill his mind with all that was holy and sacred concerning the Lord of Hosts who inhabited the cherubim. And capture them she did. Instruction by repetition is a divinely wise principle, [21] and Hannah was no doubt committed to it from the moment her son arose each day, until the moment he lay down to sleep each night. She taught him so diligently that his first words, his first rhymes, his first tunes, were all stored deep within him, locked from infancy into a spiritual code. His earliest memories centred on the sound of her voice, offering prayers and singing songs.

---

child, Moses, also set to be the deliverer of his people, as Hannah desired Samuel to be?

20 A line taken from the poem – "My Heart Leaps Up" by William Wordsworth.
21 Deuteronomy 6:7. The word 'teach' (*shinnantam*) appears to be derived from *shanan* – to repeat, to iterate, to do a thing again and again, hence to whet or sharpen which is done by repeated friction.

He had heard them both from the womb, and knew the sounds by heart. By the time he went to Shiloh, the ideas of prayer and praise were already woven into the fabric of his life. **22** This was his mother's birthright, a special portion bequeathed to her firstborn son. He received the imprint of his mother's own spirit, and it would remain upon him for a lifetime. **23**

A child weaned of his mother

And it was not just a question of instruction in spiritual principles. It was vital that she prepare his mind for the time of his dedication in such a way that Samuel felt its pull. It was a matter of choice. She could either fill his mind with the sadness of their coming separation, how hard it would all be, and how much she would miss him. Or she could fill his heart with the thought that to be given to the Lord was so high a privilege, so precious a calling, that it was an honour to have such an opportunity. She would determine the spirit of the child when he came to Shiloh to commence his new life. She could either make the occasion one of sorrow and loss, or one of wonder and joy. She could either give him a burden of duty that distressed him, or a sense of destiny that enthralled him.

And in painting for him the picture of his calling to priestly things, it was crucial to his spirit that he did not see her pain, or feel her sorrow, that he did not sense the price that she would pay. Instead, he only ever saw her warm courage, her positive spirit, and her bright smile, that filled him with comfort and certainty that his future must be blessed indeed. Another woman might have indulged in sufficient self-pity to have clouded his certainty. But that was something Hannah would never do. And because she would do what was right before God, and what was

---

22 Matthew 21:16.

23 The prayers of Samuel were marked by a peculiar and urgent cry (1 Samuel 7:9; 15:11). It is most likely that he first heard that cry in his mother's prayers, which were given with such passion that the priest imagined (in her fervency) that she must be inebriated (1 Samuel 1:12,13). Samuel learned his manner of prayer from his mother!

best for the Truth, He chose her to be His instrument. This was what it meant to be the Handmaid of the Highest. For Hannah, God-centred at her very core, there was only one way. The child belonged to God, and would be returned to Him. Nothing would divert her from that work.

> "And when she had weaned him, she took him up with her, with three bullocks, and one ephah of flour, and a bottle of wine, and brought him unto the house of the LORD in Shiloh: and the child was young. And they slew a bullock, and brought the child to Eli." (1 Samuel 1:24,25)

Three years is not long. Filled as they were with her love, nurture and care, the seasons sped past, and so did the years. In all too short a time, the moment for the weaning of her child came. It was a significant milestone in his life, for it marked the first stage of his physical independence, as he relinquished his claim upon his mother's nourishment. But it was also the first stage of his moral development, since this first step towards individual responsibility lay in yielding to a higher authority. He had learned to submit to the will of his mother, in the moment of his weaning.[24] Now the next step was to occur. At the house of God, he would learn to submit to the will of his Father.

It was a special day when Samuel reached this moment, and his weaning feast[25] was held. For with his weaning, the next stage of his spiritual education could commence. Not only would he progress in his physical diet from milk to meat, but in his spiritual growth to the discernment of good and evil.[26] For Hannah, the day was bitter-sweet. The joy of seeing this first step in her son's journey to manhood was balanced by the sorrow of the loss of her sucking child, and a painful awareness of his

---

[24] Psalm 131:2.
[25] Evidently, from earliest times, weaning was already considered a special moment for celebration because of its significance (Genesis 21:8). It wisely imbued the child with a positive sense about this development in their life, as they were encouraged to continue in their growth. It turned the occasion of weaning into a memory of family happiness and support.
[26] Isaiah 28:9; Hebrews 5:12-14.

coming departure. The next stages of his growth would not be hers to see and share, apart from a meeting once each year, which would be painful in its brevity.

Yet, true to her vow, Hannah began to prepare for their yearly visit to the sanctuary. After all, his weaning had been accomplished with this in mind. It was always her plan to bring him to Shiloh at this moment, but there was a marked resolution to her actions which showed how strong her sense of purpose was. She had weaned him, she would bring him, she would present him. [27] She was ready. Any vow was accompanied by its appropriate sacrifices, chief among which was a corresponding burnt offering. [28] Hannah had chosen one to complete her vow, and to signify Samuel's dedication. Her choice was marked by that depth of thought which was so characteristic of her. From Ramah, they had taken with them a bullock of three years old. [29] The animal represented the child, and it was the perfect symbol, since her son was also three years old at the time of his dedication. [30] But this child was to be dedicated for life. And this bullock, offered as a whole burnt offering, totally consumed to ascend as a sweet-smelling savour, was to be the child's exact counterpart.

---

27 The phrase – "And when she had weaned him, she took him up with her" (1 Samuel 1:24) is eloquent in presenting this moment as her initiative.

28 Psalm 66:13-15.

29 The LXX has – "a bullock of three years old". There are reasons to consider this rendering as correct, rather than the KJV – "with three bullocks". The phrase echoed the similar term – "an heifer of three years old", which was a commonly used expression (Genesis 15:9; Isaiah 15:5; Jeremiah 48:34). In this case however, Hannah would offer a male from the herd (a bullock), since the animal was to represent Samuel. The Samuel text in the Dead Sea Scrolls corroborates the LXX version (rather than the Masoretic Text as followed by the KJV).

30 The only Biblical reference to the likely time of child weaning occurs during the reign of Hezekiah (2 Chronicles 31:16), who in making provision for the Levites and priests, included children from three years old and upwards; which is a presumptive proof that prior to this age they were wholly dependent on their mother for their nourishment. A passage during the Inter-Testamental period is also relevant, since it is an historical statement concerning child weaning as uttered by a Jewish mother. "O my son, have pity upon me that bare thee nine months in my womb, and gave thee suck three years, and nourished thee, and brought thee up" (2 Maccabees 7:27).

The journey to Shiloh was far more sombre in mood on this occasion. Hannah was not weeping with sorrow, but there was an air of solemnity about the little group, as they travelled north to the place of the sanctuary. How could it be otherwise when step by step she marched towards the place of destiny and dedication. It was impossible for her not to contemplate the enormity of what was about to occur, and much of her journey was passed in quiet reflection. Elkanah marched in full sympathy, but not comprehending the full weight of the burden this would bring upon Hannah's heart. Even Peninnah was subdued, for all the family knew what was to occur, and none dare breathe a word that might disturb the mind of the child. Samuel, stealing a glance at his mother was reassured by her warm smile, but he also sensed that this day was special.

The dedication of Hannah's firstborn son

Arriving at the sanctuary, the family made their way to the door of the tabernacle of the congregation, for this was the place where those who had offerings were to gather. [31] How well had Hannah chosen. She presented a bullock, the most valuable of all burnt offerings, because this was not the dedication of any child. This was the child of promise, and the child of purpose, and her offering called attention to that fact. A bullock was the burnt offering which would be made by an anointed priest, [32] and in choosing one, Hannah associated the dedication of her son with the priestly role.

But now the moment of reality had arrived, and as Hannah placed her hand [33] upon the head of the bullock, her eyes filled

---

31 Leviticus 1:3.
32 The size of the offering indicated the status and importance of the person offering. For this reason, the sin offering for a priest was the highest value animal, which was a bullock (Leviticus 4:3). The schedule of burnt offerings, although voluntary, provided a similar graduation of sacrifices from a bullock to a pigeon. A priest, again guided by that principle, would have offered a bullock as their burnt offering (Leviticus 1:3), since it represented the pinnacle of what an individual could offer.
33 The prescription of the law expressly required the offerer to slay their own sacrifice (Leviticus 1:4,5). Given Hannah's complete involvement in this vow of dedication, it is reasonable to infer that she was directly involved in identifying with the

with tears. The simple act of touching the creature, still alive in its warmth, was intended as an act of identification, and Hannah understood only too fully the outworking of the symbol. The time had come for her son to be committed to the Lord's service. It would be all consuming in its effect, because his whole life would be given to ministering before the Lord in a spirit of dedication, just as completely as this bullock would now be given as a whole burnt offering unto God. There was a pause, and then the thing was done, as Hannah, in concert with Elkanah slew the bullock, [34] and then brought the child to Eli. Even the sequence of the moment gave witness to the symbol. [35]

These were not separate deeds, but exact counterparts of each other. To slay the bullock, and to dedicate the child were complementary actions, and in recognition of that significance, Hannah moved swiftly from the one to the other.

> "And she said, Oh my lord, as thy soul liveth, my lord, I am the woman that stood by thee here, praying unto the LORD. For this child I prayed; and the LORD hath given me my petition which I asked of him: therefore also I have lent him to the LORD; as long as he liveth he shall be lent to the LORD. And he worshipped the LORD there." (1 Samuel 1:26-28)

Moving from the altar which was near the door, she brought Samuel to the very spot before Eli's seat, where she had come previously. It was a special moment to stand again in that very place, made holy now by the remembrance of her prayer. She took a deep breath as she approached, for she would need to live that prayer again now in all its earnestness, and remember all that she had promised her God on that tear-filled day. As Hannah came close, with her son beside her, the old man looked up, and the

---

sacrifice, no doubt cooperating with Elkanah in the action. That inference is supported by the force of the phrase – "And they slew" (1 Samuel 1:24).

34 The phrase in the Hebrew is actually – "they slew the bullock [*eth happar*]" (1 Samuel 1:25), indicating that there was only one bullock, as previously suggested.

35 The two expressions "slew the bullock" – "brought the child" exactly matched each other in spirit and meaning.

flicker of recognition broadened into a dawning sense of wonder as the woman began to speak. "Oh my lord" she said, and Eli at once recognised the greeting and the voice. Her respect for the anointed of God still caused her to address him with the dignity his office deserved, and before she spoke again, he knew what she would say, or at least he thought he did. For the little boy standing so close by her, nudging into the skirts of her robe, with the imprint of his mother so fresh upon his countenance, was obviously the child for which she had prayed. The words came. "I am the woman that stood by thee here, praying unto the LORD". How could he ever forget! He had seen nothing like it before she came, and had certainly seen nothing like it in the four years since. For all the throngs of the faithful whom he had met in their pilgrimages to the sanctuary, the day of their meeting still stood out vivid in his mind.

"For this child I prayed; and the LORD hath given me the petition which I asked of him." There was something very gracious about Hannah's words to Eli. For these were his words, which Hannah now quoted so joyfully back to him. [36] "This is what you said. And this is what our God has done." She invited him to recall the wonder of that mutual moment, and remember it he did. It was kind of her to include him in the matter, for with her comment Eli felt the blessing of his own involvement. He recalled the day so clearly, but he had not until now remembered what he had said to comfort the woman, in fulfilling his priestly part. But it was something more than kindness that prompted Hannah to remind him that they had been joined in this matter before heaven, there was also wisdom in her words. She needed to prepare him for the climax of her speech, for whatever part he had played thus far, his involvement was about to increase dramatically.

Hannah and her loan

"Therefore also" she said, looking earnestly and directly at the old man, "I have lent him to the LORD." It took a moment for Eli to

---

[36] "Go in peace: and the God of Israel grant thy petition that thou hast asked him" (1 Samuel 1:17).

realise what she must mean. He had known of her desire for this child, but he had no idea that she intended to offer him to God, and he was astonished at her words, and amazed at their implication. Struggling to confirm their import, he looked again at Hannah whose gentle resolution in the nodding of her head told him all. In answer to the question in his face, she confirmed the impossible, "as long as he liveth he shall be lent to the LORD". Here then was the completion of her vow, and in her words Hannah rose above herself. She had never asked for herself, but that she might devote the child to the Lord's service. Her petition had always been about the fulfilment of God's purpose, and this loan was the proof of it. He was loaned to the Lord, but it was a loan for life in the spirit of joyful surrender, for Hannah's "as long as he liveth" was her conscious and deliberate recollection of her own vow. [37]

The one thing she could not tell the old man was her deepest reason for the loan of the child. She did not believe in the likelihood of the repentance of Hophni and Phinehas, for her prayer from the outset was a plea for God to reverse their evil. Her son, born in response, was therefore set on a course, which, if prospered by God, would result in the eventual overthrow of Eli's own household. But it was not for her to make such comment. Let God Himself work His own work with the child. Her part was met in the completion of her loan. But how enormous was its cost, when this day for its payment finally came.

A firstborn son represented the future of his family, for in him was vested the right of inheritance, the right of priesthood, and the right of rulership. [38] A firstborn son was the beginning of his father's strength, and the opening of his mother's hope. A sense of commitment to things divine already encircled the child, as upon him was laid from the earliest of times the mantle of responsibility within the household. [39] Who could doubt

---

[37] Her earlier prayer had stated – "if thou wilt give unto thine handmaid a man child, then I will give him unto the LORD all the days of his life" (1 Samuel 1:11).
[38] Genesis 49:3.
[39] Exodus 13:12,13.

then, that the greatest grief imaginable was the bitterness of the loss of a firstborn son. **⁴⁰** When the time came for Hannah to complete her loan, a measure of this grief came upon her soul, like a piercing sword, and there was bitterness indeed. True she was not losing her child completely, but the wrench of the parting was so sharp, the reality of the loss so deep, that she knew a pain that few could ever know.

It is one thing to make a vow. It is another to perform it. Hannah had not been hasty to vow, for hers had been long in the making, but the fulness of its cost could never have been known until now. She had prepared for this moment for the last three years, completely aware of its time. But when the day had come, when she stood there at Shiloh with Samuel by her side, his tiny hand clutching hers, so forlorn in his littleness, who could stay the feelings of motherhood which came coursing through her body, like the advancing of the tide? All the warmth of her maternal love to protect, all the depth of her desire to nurture, all the yearning of her instinct to keep and to hold were so powerful, that only the strongest resolution enabled her to continue. **⁴¹** How could she leave her only son here in Shiloh, at the very centre of wickedness in the land? How could she leave such a small child with Eli whose own lack of fatherly discipline had brought about this crisis in the nation? How would the needs of such a little one be understood, and properly met? How could she permit him to stay in this place, when all her heart cried out that the risks and the dangers were too great?

But this child had not been brought to Shiloh to be with his mother. He had been brought to Shiloh to be with his Father. And Hannah was not loaning Samuel to Eli. She was loaning him to God. Her very act in leaving him there was not evidence that

---

40 Jeremiah 6:26; Amos 8:10; Zechariah 12:10.
41 The courage and love of Hannah in this action was not unlike those Jewish mothers who gave up their children for the Kindertransport in World War Two, in a desperate attempt to provide a safe future for their offspring, some no doubt as young as Samuel. But whereas they gave up their children to save them, Hannah gave up her child to save the nation.

she was irresponsible or negligent or foolhardy, although others no doubt thought it so. Her act was driven by her absolute belief that if the logic of his gracious birth made necessary the logic of his joyful return, then his joyful return made possible the logic of his providential care. She gave to God the firstfruits of her womb, knowing that she gave to Him what was already His own, received by her as a blessing of trust. But only until this time. Nothing other than her passionate belief in this truth could make sense of this dramatic moment. Her conviction that Samuel belonged to God gave her the emotional strength to surrender. She brought him from their house in Ramah, to the house of the Lord in Shiloh, and there, in his Father's house, the little child would grow in wisdom and favour with God who would overshadow his every moment. And all would be well when she left, for in that place Samuel [42] would come to know and worship God, just as she had believed. So there [43] now he was, and in Shiloh Samuel would grow into the Lord's minister exactly as the Lord intended, and exactly as Hannah desired.

---

42 Who might be referred to in the phrase – "and he worshipped the LORD there". Most Biblical commentators suggest that it cannot be Samuel, since he was too little, and that therefore the phrase either refers to Eli on receiving the child, or to Elkanah on joining with Hannah in giving the child. But the context favours the idea that the 'he' of this phrase is Samuel himself, since all the other pronouns in the verse refer to him. He obviously did not worship God in full at that moment, but the phrase is indicating that in this place the little boy began to develop that special relationship with God that would mark him out as a faithful priest. This passage begins a series of such descriptions concerning the child (1 Samuel 2:11,18,26).

43 Even the word "there" is an echo of Hannah's earlier promise – "that he may appear before the LORD and there abide for ever" (1 Samuel 1:22).

4 |

Hannah and her song

(1 Samuel 2:1-10)

IT was in that moment of offering her son, as she lent him to the Lord, that the greatness of Hannah was seen. Only her deepest commitment to the purpose of God saw her through the moment. Only her strongest conviction that His sovereign will was at work permitted her to complete her vow. That which had gone out of her lips she would keep and perform.[1] She knew this principle well. It had been the secret of her inspiration for all that she had done, and she would not fail it now, for it was in the difficulty of the vow that its preciousness lay. No burnt offering can be offered without cost,[2] but there would be few who would ever match the magnitude of Hannah's loan. She would pay her vow, with all the voluntary joy that a freewill offering required.

It was on her part an act of extraordinary faith, for despite the logic which told her that God would protect the child, the emotional price of this day in her life was enormous. She had every reason to feel a desperate sadness, a weeping of tears, as committed but sorrowful, she felt the final, real cost of her vow. And yet, remarkably, her spirit was the very opposite. She gave the little Levite with a joy so fierce, it was breathtaking in its intensity. How could she possibly be joyful on that day? But then

---

1   Deuteronomy 23:23.
2   1 Chronicles 21:24.

this was Hannah – the Handmaid of the Highest, the one who saw ahead to higher things, as her song was about to declare.

There may have been others at Shiloh on that day, watching with curiosity as the woman brought the little child forward to stand with her before Eli. They may not have heard the passage of conversation between these two, but they did hear Hannah's voice rising in joy immediately after. For gripped as she was by the transcendent importance of the moment, Hannah suddenly burst forth into prayer. In a paean of praise, she sang her song of thankfulness at the very moment of giving her child away. [3] Yet so earnest was her focus, there was not a trace of lamentation or loss. Instead, there came an outpouring so steeped in Biblical thinking, [4] so devoid of personal vindication, [5] so full of spiritual exaltation, [6] that it was as if she had stepped into the Holy Place itself.

At the point of her prayer, she crossed the threshold of the sanctuary, and entered into fellowship with her God. Her song recognised the Lord and not herself as the primary force behind all these events. It was a revelation of Hannah's mind, for in spirit she lived in the presence of the Lord of hosts, being there to do His bidding, and ready to fulfil His will. Here surely was the work of God, and this was the song of His Handmaid.

---

3   Mary offered her prayer of thanks at the prospect of receiving her child (Luke 1:46). Hannah offered her song of praise at the point of giving her child away. It was an astonishing spirit of sacrifice that few could comprehend, and even fewer could emulate.

4   In Hannah's age, there were few inspired writings that could inform her thinking, apart from the Book of the Law, and the Book of Job, which had both been completed before her time. Her song captured many thoughts from these two sources. It indicated that she was vitally aware of the 'holy scriptures', using their thoughts and words to frame her own expressions to the Father.

5   All personal reference to Hannah is limited to the opening verse, and even then, her rejoicing was seen to lie in the advancing of the divine objectives, and not in the vindication of self. Beyond the opening expressions, her prayer would reflect entirely on God's power and purpose.

6   There are five references to Hannah, all of which are found in 1 Samuel 2:1. But there are twenty references to the LORD in this short prayer. Hannah was utterly God centred, and her prayer proved it.

That song, as with other Spirit inspired utterances, saw ahead to speak of future things, but her words were embedded in the power of this present moment. Her prayer reflected what this occasion meant to her, and in that meaning the significance of the future would also be discovered.

Rejoicing in a higher cause

> "And Hannah prayed, and said, My heart rejoiceth in the LORD, mine horn is exalted in the LORD: my mouth is enlarged over mine enemies; because I rejoice in thy salvation. There is none holy as the LORD: for there is none beside thee: neither is there any rock like our God." (1 Samuel 2:1,2)

"My heart rejoiceth in the LORD" she began, and in these first words, so telling in their focus, she revealed herself. Even in her own rejoicing, Hannah was not concerned with personal recognition, or private vindication. There was no trace of self at all in her prayer, for her thoughts were far above her own situation. In glorying, she gloried in the Lord. As His Handmaid, she found reason for happiness in the higher cause of the One whom she served. Her own joy was discovered in the outworking of His will. But on this day, this day of days, already filled with tumultuous feelings and heightened thoughts, she felt inspired with the sense that God had brought her to this moment, and that if He had, then her controversy, her contest was now set in motion on His behalf.

It was as if her place and purpose were now made clear. But her true worth and value were only to be seen in Him, for her horn was exalted "in the LORD". [7] This was the key to Hannah's life. Those who seek to serve a cause higher than themselves find more fulfilment than those who have sought for self-recognition.

---

7   The term "horn" is the symbol of a person's power or influence. Hannah appears to be the first person to use the expression, but it will be taken up in many other places (Psalm 75:10; 92:10; 112:9; Luke 1:69). How important to note that Hannah did not say that her horn was exalted, but that her horn was exalted in the Lord. The phrase declared her God-centred outlook. Truly she was His Handmaid!

It is a God ordained paradox, that those who lose themselves in the greatness of the Truth find happiness beyond compare. For those who do not, the search for happiness is one of the chief sources of their unhappiness. This is a truth which all God's saints come to discover over time, for it lies at the heart of the calling to manifest God. It is not affected by whether our life is lived in the married state or as an unmarried individual. All God's people find their true focus in the inspiring power of His glorious plan, and the amazing wonder of His mercy in condescending to involve us in it. Here is the only sense of worth that need concern us. Our God has called us, and if we are of worth in His eyes, then nothing else matters.

It was in that new found certainty that her mouth was "enlarged over her enemies", [8] for she felt not only God-sanctioned, but God-directed to declare these words of censure against those who were not just her enemies, but God's as well. [9] She was made eloquent to declare the Lord's disapproval of them. Speaking on His behalf and in His name, she uttered words, not of personal recrimination but of divine disapproval. [10] It is common to the weakness of our nature to take the hostility of others personally. It is uncommon to react only to those things which are an affront to our God. Hannah, whose spirit was exceptional, rose above the personal and saw instead the perspective of heaven. Those enemies that Hannah had in mind could not be Peninnah, for the plural term made that impossible. Perhaps she had endured the pain of comments from Peninnah,

---

8 The word "enlarged" (*rachab*) refers to breadth or expanse, and is used colloquially to mean – 'to give room', 'to set free', 'to give relief'. In its essence, it refers here to the faculty of speech being made of greater effect (*Theological Wordbook of the Old Testament*, volume 2, pages 840,841).

9 For although the song begins with the phrase – "mine enemies", it will end with the expression – "the adversaries of the LORD". The two were the same, for as the Handmaid of the Highest, Hannah was opposed to those who were against her Lord.

10 Her reproof against those of arrogant words (verses 3,4), and her rebuke against those of aggressive deeds (verses 9,10) were uttered by Hannah on behalf of God, as later events would show.

some unjust, some unkind, and possibly some even cruel. But Hannah's mind, in this climax of song, was lifted far above and beyond whatever difficulties Peninnah might have caused in her life. Her heart, her strength, her mouth, were all committed to God. Her rejoicing was in the Lord and in His salvation, which she saw as being made possible in the giving of this child to Him.

The salvation of God was not to be seen in some individual triumph over Peninnah. And blessed though she was at the birth of Samuel, his arrival did not give her ascendancy over a woman who boasted at least four or more children already. Hannah was not concerned with such rivalry in her song. She was intent upon a far greater cause, and both the birth and the presentation of her child were bound up in its fulfilment. No, these enemies, whom she had striven against from the first, were Hophni and Phinehas, steeped in wickedness, and opposed to God. She referred to them throughout her song, and before it ended, she had, with prophetic insight, seen their impending death by divine intervention against them. Here was a contest indeed, and out of it the salvation of the Lord would be seen, not only for Hannah, but for the nation itself. And in her controversy against the priests, the mystery of why a song of thanksgiving should also sound like a stirring battle cry was made plain in the process. [11]

She was already certain of the outcome, for she had now seen its beginning and believed in its end. Whence then this confident rejoicing on Hannah's part? It did not rest upon her own ability, for the times of her barrenness had taught her not to trust in self. Her certainty sprang from a conviction that God was at work in her life, declared in a threefold chorus that upheld His unrivalled supremacy. "None holy as the LORD", "none beside thee", "no rock like our God". [12] The words were not Hannah's own, for she had sourced each expression from the book of the

---

[11] See Appendix 4 – "What was the import of Hannah's special song?" on page 221.
[12] The three lines all begin with the same word *en* in the Hebrew. This is a tricolon, with emphatic, short stress lines which all attribute supremacy to God.

law. Her use of them showed not only her wonderful recollection of scripture, but a remarkable understanding of their setting. [13] In these marvellous opening lines of song that flowed unabated from her mouth, Hannah's belief in the greatness of the One she served was seen to be absolute.

Reproving the spirit of arrogant words

> "Talk no more so exceeding proudly: let not arrogance come out of your mouth: for the LORD is a God of knowledge, and by him actions are weighed." (1 Samuel 2:3)

It was precisely because of the all surpassing supremacy of God that it was so wrong for any to speak with pride or arrogance. But Hannah's enemies had, and she reproved them with all the authority vested in her by the Spirit, which gave utterance. This was not a reproach against the Philistines. Nor was it a reprimand to Peninnah. There was only one arrogant speech recorded in the story of Hannah's life, and it would emanate from the Sons of Eli in their strident demands upon the worshippers at the sanctuary, [14] Phinehas himself being the epitome of such hard speeches which ungodly sinners had spoken. [15] Their bold words revealed their hubris, made worse by the fact that of all people, the mouth of God's priest was supposed to be the repository of peace and truth. [16]

There was every reason for Hannah to speak such words of rebuke to those who disgraced their office in such a way. Upon

---

13 The words "none holy as the LORD" were an allusion to the nation's song of victory when facing impossible obstacles (Exodus 15:11), "there is none beside thee" was an allusion to the lawgiver's exhortation to obedience in the face of corruption (Deuteronomy 4:35,39), "no rock like our God" was an allusion to the song of Moses concerning the abiding stability of God in contrast to the fickle perversity of His people (Deuteronomy 32:4,5,15,28-31). All three circumstances were relevant to Hannah's own situation. She not only used scripture, but did so in context!

14 See notes on this episode (1 Samuel 2:15,16).

15 See notes on the first appearance of Phinehas (1 Samuel 1:3).

16 Cp. "The law of truth was in his mouth, and iniquity was not found in his lips … For the priest's lips should keep knowledge, and they should seek the law at his mouth" (Malachi 2:6,7).

them would come inevitably the judgment of God, who was always aware of the words and actions of His people. Hannah understood that God was the ultimate arbiter of human destiny, the final authority who would weigh each life in the balances. She knew that in the end, God who knows altogether the "word in our tongue", and who knows the "secrets of the heart", will hold everything to account. There was immeasurable comfort for Hannah in this thought. The wicked would be judged, and none of their words would be forgotten. It was so important to remember that the Lord was omniscient in His knowledge. Sometimes the circumstances of life cause us to imagine that perhaps He does not see, or does not hear, but He always does. He knows all things occurring in our lives, and being cognisant of them responds according to His sovereign will. Hannah, in understanding this, and despite the provocation of sore trial, could rest in the knowledge that God weighs the spirits and ponders the hearts.[17] Those like Hophni and Phinehas, who used their words to coerce others into submission, would be dealt with according to God's infallible knowledge. She saw it now, through the eye of faith and the insight of the Spirit.

> "The bows of the mighty men are broken, and they that stumbled are girded with strength. They that were full have hired themselves out for bread; and they that were hungry ceased: so that the barren hath born seven; and she that hath many children is waxed feeble." (1 Samuel 2:4,5)

Whatever sharp words Peninnah might have uttered, she was not the subject of Hannah's thought when she envisaged the breaking of "the bows of the mighty men".[18] Nor did Hannah

---

[17] Proverbs 16:2; 21:2.

[18] The term "mighty men" (*gibborim*) is both masculine and plural, and cannot be a reference to Peninnah. But it does have an immediate and obvious application to Hophni and Phinehas who were the *gibborim* of their age. Within the epoch of the judges, Gideon was a *gibbor* (Judges 6:12), Jephthah was a *gibbor* (Judges 11:1), and Boaz was a *gibbor* (Ruth 2:1). Its use indicates those who were prominent in status or influence at the time. In Hannah's day, Hophni and Phinehas had already assumed that position, as the record carefully noted at the start of this story (1 Samuel 1:3).

have the Philistines in mind. **[19]** She was focused on the men of the day who held the power, and who made the decisions within Israel. And who were these mighty men of the moment, but Hophni and Phinehas, who, ensconced in the place of greatest spiritual authority, held the nation in their sway as they exercised the priestly office. Eli might still have been present, but all the nation knew who was really in control. These were they to whom Hannah referred, as she saw ahead to the removal of their influence, and to the breaking of their arrogant words by which they kept the people in subjection.

Words are powerful weapons of control, and these two used their bows to "shoot privily at the upright", and to "shoot in secret at the perfect" as their arrows of scorn were directed against the righteous. **[20]** Hannah had witnessed their power to destroy godly life, and she felt cause for deep rejoicing at the thought that this evil influence might be removed. How much she wanted to see these bows broken, and those arrows snapped. Yet this was not a prayer of personal revenge on Hannah's part, but a fervent wish that the nation might be delivered from a spirit that all too long had burdened and oppressed them, so that "men abhorred the offering of the LORD".

But hope now lay at hand, in the form of the little child lent to the Lord. Through her work on this day, Hannah felt at last that though fainting, she might again be girded with strength. She knew what it felt like to know the feebleness of inability to change the wrong. In the face of the man of aggressive deeds and the man of arrogant words, who was she, but one woman against

---

[19] Hannah's subsequent words in 1 Samuel 2:5, will be seen to refer not to the Philistines, but to the ultimate fate of the priests – Hophni and Phinehas, as the record will later show.

[20] In the context of the proud talk and arrogant words of verse 3, the bow (*qesheth*) here is not a symbol of military force, but of boastful speech. The symbol of the bow as the mouth, and its arrows as bitter words is certainly used elsewhere (Psalm 11:2; 64:3,4; Jeremiah 9:3). Of special significance is a passage (Psalm 37:14,15) where the same term (*qesheth*) is not only used figuratively, but where the phrase "their bows shall be broken", is clearly an allusion to Hannah's own expression here.

the control of such corrupt men. To know their spiritual evil, and to realise their ascendant power, was to know the helplessness of the saints when overwhelmed. Yet that is the moment when the faithful pray for strength beyond their ability, but not beyond their God's. Hannah felt a surge of strength now, as her heart outpoured its thoughts, strength for the battle which she had now embarked upon. There was no doubt in her mind that it was a contest. For these unholy and ungodly men had abused their office to satisfy their own fleshly desires. The fulness which the priesthood enjoyed was notorious. In their greed, they had seized the sacrificial portions to feed their desire for dainty meats, in brazen disregard for the spiritual havoc they wrought among the offerers. [21]

Their fulness of bread was but the token of a life of riches, as the service of the sanctuary was sequestered for their private pleasure. But all this was to change. Hannah knew that she could not remove this evil, but she was certain that God could, and that even now, that work had begun in the son she had returned to Him. The house of Eli was to suffer a reversal so complete as to change their abundance into want, and their fulness into deficiency. She knew it now, and her triumphant words – "they that were full have hired themselves out for bread", declared her certainty by describing the future in the present. Her words would be confirmed by heaven, for the reversal which she saw was exactly God's intention. [22] The Handmaid knew her Master's mind.

Nor would their demise be the end of the matter, but rather, that in their removal, the spiritual life of her people could be started afresh. How deeply did Hannah yearn to be fed with spiritual sustenance, and where else should that have been found

---

21 1 Samuel 2:17,24.
22 There could not have been a stronger endorsement of Hannah's statement than the use of that same expression by God's own spokesman (1 Samuel 2:36). And this deliberate echoing of Hannah's words is evidence that the focus of her prayer was indeed on the removal of Hophni and Phinehas, that true worship in the nation might be restored.

but at the sanctuary. **²³** And yet, how many times had Hannah visited that place, only to depart feeling empty and unsustained. Not everyone feels that yearning. Hannah did. Yet even now, that first sense of an assuaging of her hunger had come. In time, the place of the peace offering would again be the place of the fellowship meal, and then she would be filled. But for now, she rested in the joy of knowing that it would come. When it did, she would eat and be satisfied, and in that day, all those who were hungry would cease to be so. **²⁴**

As her mind ranged over the enormity of what this day promised, she could see the nation's destiny found within her own family. Peninnah had borne children with such ease, as indeed the nation did in producing the natural seed. But the begettal of true spiritual offspring was a work which lay beyond the natural power of procreation. **²⁵** Hannah knew the reality of divine intervention in her life, and saw in Samuel the type of one to come who would be the deliverer of his people. She understood that she could not personally bring forth the Messiah, but her child was a foreshadowing of the one in whom the nation would find redemption. **²⁶** Hannah of course had not borne seven children at this moment, nor would she ever do so. But her statement – "The barren hath borne seven" was her way of describing the sense of completeness which the birth of Samuel

---

23 Deuteronomy 12:18.

24 Mary fully understood the meaning of Hannah's words, for in her prayer she quoted them exactly in context. "He hath filled the hungry with good things: and the rich he hath sent empty away" (Luke 1:52). In the gospel of Luke, with its special focus on the priesthood of Christ, the term 'rich' is a key idea, and has marked application to the priestly class who controlled the wealth of the temple. There was a Hophni and Phinehas family in the time of Christ!

25 The circumstances of Hannah and Peninnah were typical of the spiritual and natural seeds, seen also in Sarah and Hagar, and in the allegory of their lives, so carefully wrought by the apostle as he depicted the two sons, the two women, and the two mountains (Galatians 4:22-27).

26 That Hannah saw a national, rather than a personal aspect to her words is also seen in the comment of the prophet, where, in allusion to Hannah's words, the matter is also given a national application (Jeremiah 15:7-9). This was not about Hannah and Peninnah, but about how the nation's experience was mirrored through them.

brought into her life.[27] There was purpose now, and a sense of fulfilment which was very real. Even the agony of giving Samuel up could not diminish it, for his giving was part of that purpose. As always, Hannah's mind was on higher things.

Reversing the vicissitudes of life

> "The LORD killeth, and maketh alive: he bringeth down to the grave, and bringeth up. The LORD maketh poor, and maketh rich: he bringeth low and lifteth up." (1 Samuel 2:6,7)

God controls all the circumstances of life, and there is not a person who can escape His omniscient presence. But His ability to make dead or alive stands related to the question of our final destiny. God could take life as He would in the case of Hophni and Phinehas. Hannah believed that God could remove them, and that He would do so by the divine intervention of judicial death.[28] But He could also give life as he did in the miraculous conception of Samuel. Hannah knew that power, in the bringing forth of her firstborn son from the deadness of her womb. In both cases, there was a divine involvement, as God used the power He holds over life and death in the furtherance of His purpose.

And yet further, she saw with prophetic insight that reached beyond her own state to the issues of final destiny. Where one would be brought to the grave to remain, another would experience the power of resurrection. God's purpose relates to eternal things, and its outworking will involve the miracle of a bringing up from the grave of certain who have gone there. In a remarkable demonstration of her spiritual mind, Hannah spoke of the hope of that resurrection with a clarity rarely known in her age.[29] She believed in One who held the power to exert sovereign

---

27 A similar expression was used concerning Ruth's relationship with Naomi (Ruth 4:15).

28 Her words were again a quotation from Moses (Deuteronomy 32:39), reflecting upon the all-pervasive power of God. To 'kill' here was not simply death by natural means, but God's power deliberately to take away life.

29 Hannah knew the book of Job, and may well have been aware of his testimony – "For I know that my redeemer liveth, and that he shall stand at the latter day upon

control over those processes normally regarded as fixed and immutable.

But, in addition to the matters of final destiny, are the matters of present reality. Whilst these are more proximate in their bearings, they are nevertheless ordered by God towards our ultimate end. To be made poor or made rich, to be brought low or to be lifted up, are alike within the power of God who permits such things for our development.

Hannah, on this day was acutely aware of what the Father could do in her life, for the power of providence interwoven into daily experience was something she knew and believed in. She had learned to recognise the hand of God in both the good and evil in her life. Since God is the author of both, [30] we must accept that either may come, and seek rather to understand what the Father would have us to learn from the experience. [31] The presence of trials in our life does not mean that He has rejected us, but rather that He is at work in our lives. Our wisdom is to respond, that He might shape us as He pleases.

But there is an order. First the darkness and then His marvellous light. First the suffering and then the glory that should follow. First the sorrow and then the joy that no man taketh away. The Lord maketh poor, and maketh rich, He bringeth low, and lifteth up, and in that way, we thereby experience the fulness, having first known the emptiness. The trials brought upon us by God are designed to strengthen and direct us in His way. It is easy in lives of purposeful activity to forget that all things are regulated by the divine hand. Hannah had known the

---

the earth: and though after my skin worms destroy this body, yet in my flesh shall I see God; whom I shall see for myself, and mine eyes shall behold, and not another; though my reins be consumed within me" (Job 19:25-27).

30 Isaiah 45:7.
31 Hannah's words are again reminiscent of Job's (Job 1:21, 2:10), whose thoughts she may well be echoing. Despite his suffering, he was lifted out of it by God, and made better in the process. And his final restoration came when he prayed for his three friends (Job 42:10). Hannah likewise, was lifted out of her grief, after she had prayed for the needs of her people.

poverty of barrenness and the lowness of reproach, but God had graciously altered her circumstances. God can and will reverse the vicissitudes of life, but even then, it is His purpose that is being advanced, and not our own.

Recognising the balance of divine control

> He raiseth up the poor out of the dust, and lifteth up the beggar from the dunghill, to set them among princes, and to make them inherit the throne of glory: for the pillars of the earth are the LORD's, and he hath set the world upon them." (1 Samuel 2:8)

The poor in the dust and the beggar on the dunghill were the social outcasts of society. Their position was such a lowly one that they were constantly aware of it, like the dust which covered them, for they were unable to improve their lot or make demand of others. Vulnerable and anxious, deprived and ignored, their lives were lived in a state of perpetual need. To sit in dust or ashes was an act of mourning which symbolised just how low the suffering one had been brought.[32]

> Hannah was not literally among the poor or the beggars, for her station in life was secure. But of all people, they epitomised that feeling of degradation and despair that Hannah knew only too well. Hers was the result of the social stigma that the reproach of barrenness brought upon her, and with that flash of insight so marked in Hannah's mind, she saw the poverty of the poor as a parable of her own barren womb. She had known the misery of being oppressed in heart, but now she knew the marvellous freedom of release. In blessing her with a son, God had alleviated her need, and lifted her out of the dust of her wretched state. And to be lifted out of the dust was but the first step to being washed clean, and clothed afresh, and set on high. The exaltation of spirit she felt because of God's hand upon her was so real and so uplifting, that she could not help but praise Him.

---

[32] Notice again how reminiscent Hannah's words are of ideas expressed in the book of Job, as her mind found expression in the language of scripture (Job 1:20; 2:8,12,13; 16:15; 30:19; 42:6).

But she saw in her own experience an earnest of the coming exaltation of her people. Israel, oppressed as they were by the ungodly who had left them so spiritually bereft, would be raised to better things. This dramatic change in her own life made her sure of it. Nothing could speak of that reversal more eloquently than for the poor in the dust to arise and sit with princes, and for the needy on the dunghill to ascend to inherit the throne of glory. There was blessing indeed about to come. She felt it in her bones, this tingling certainty that God was at work in these very things to restore the nation to the honour of fellowship with Him. [33]

She knew the character of the God she served. It has always been a divine paradox, that He that inhabiteth eternity, and who dwells in the high and holy place, is also He who dwells with those who are of a contrite and humble spirit. [34] He who dwelleth on high, is He who humbles Himself to respond to those in need. The very mark of His greatness is to be found in His willingness to stoop down and consider those who are His special care, the poor and needy. [35]

"He can raise the poor to stand, with the princes of the land": He does not do so merely for their advancement, but for His. He who holds all things in His sway is intent upon the

---

[33] Hannah's phrase "the throne of glory" is quite possibly an allusion to the temple (Jeremiah 14:21; 17:12). Just as Hannah saw in her bearing of a child the raising of the nation, so with no less focus did she see the same lesson in her son. Little Samuel, plucked from obscurity and sent to the temple, where the spiritual decisions of the nation would be made, was a parable of the same thing. His elevation to the place of God's throne of glory stirred her heart with its possibilities of restoration to fellowship with God. After all, Hannah's mind was never far from the ark of God's presence and the sanctuary where it resided.

[34] Isaiah 57:15.

[35] The very words of Hannah's song are quoted in the book of Psalms (Psalm 113:7,8). Here, the raising of the poor is undertaken by the God who dwelleth on high, yet who humbleth Himself to behold the needs of His saints (Psalm 113:5,6). The final proof of His power to elevate is seen in His intervention in the life of the barren woman, to make her a joyful mother (Psalm 113:9). The psalmist knew of Hannah's situation, and not only quoted her words, but her own special circumstance before God, and His response to her need. The psalm moreover, is addressed to the priests, that they might understand this lesson of divine care (Psalm 113:1,2).

ordering of His own sovereign purpose. But those who might be poor in resource, yet rich in faith towards Him, suddenly find the might of God arrayed behind them, and the world is turned upside down. This was how Hannah felt as she sang her song, fully aware, fully conscious of things now made possible, she might never have dared to contemplate. That God governed all the world was never in doubt in Hannah's mind. But to see His hand at work in her life and in the life of her son, was to see it made real.

She knew as few others did, how completely the world rested upon the foundations which God had fastened from the beginning. [36] And she knew also how everything depended upon the stability of the pillars which God had set the earth upon. [37] But how like Hannah to picture her world as a temple for God, where the pillars of the building were the stay and support of the whole edifice. [38] For her, the pillars were but the entrance to the world over which God presided. [39]

And since that delicate balance of all the circumstances of life rested in the hands of the Father, the whole world was subject to a divine control which could disturb that balance at any moment of time. [40] Suddenly those who felt secure could be shaken out of their place, and those who felt unstable could remain.

All God's saints are brought through this experience. The ability of God to turn the world upside down leaves His people

---

36 Job 38:4-6. The word 'foundations' used here (*eden* – sockets) relates to the supports for the pillars of the tabernacle (Numbers 4:31,32) which the Levites were responsible for.

37 Job 9:6.

38 The temple of the Philistines furnishes an example of the type of pillars Hannah no doubt had in mind – "the two middle pillars upon which the house stood" (Judges 16:29).

39 The term Hannah uses (*matsuwq* – molten support, from *tsuwq* – to pour out or melt) conveys the idea of the molten cast pillars of the temple, which Solomon later fashioned (1 Kings 7:15,16), and placed in the entrance porch of the temple (1 Kings 7:21).

40 Hence Rotherham – "For, to Yahweh, belong the pillars of the earth, and he setteth thereon the habitable world".

thankful that when the earth shakes, it is God that "keeps steady its pillars". **41** Only when we have felt the powerlessness of times when our own world is shaken to its core, do we know the wonder of how God can keep us upright in the place of falling. But He can, and He will, when His own purpose is at work.

Rebuking the spirit of aggressive deeds

> "He will keep the feet of his saints, and the wicked shall be silent in darkness; for by strength shall no man prevail. The adversaries of the LORD shall be broken to pieces; out of heaven shall he thunder upon them: the LORD shall judge the ends of the earth; and he shall give strength unto his king, and exalt the horn of his anointed."   (1 Samuel 2:9,10)

In fact, it is in those very moments when the balance of life can be upset so easily, and so dramatically, that the faithful ought never to fear, because "He will keep the feet of his saints". Hannah knew this in her own life. Looking back, she saw the steps that had led her to this day, and knew with certainty that the Lord of hosts had seen her journey, and chosen her path. But this song of thanks which now she breathed, was not for herself, so much as for her son. From the moment of his conception, nay, from the moment of her prayer, she had believed that the child was destined for the Lord's work. And if he was, then it was into the Lord's charge that she now left him, certain that He would guide his footsteps. The thought brought both calm and consolation to Hannah, as she readied herself to leave her little boy in Shiloh.

The Lord would recognise a priestly spirit in him, **42** and would watch over him for good. How else would the lad manage

---

41 "When the earth totters, and all its inhabitants, it is I who keep steady its pillars" (Psalm 75:3, RSV). And this, in a psalm which resonates with allusions to Hannah's prayer (Psalm 75:5,7,10)!

42 The word "saints" (*chaciyd* – pious, holy, godly) is used in parallel to the word priests (2 Chronicles 6:41; Psalm 132:9,16). But in the Hebrew text, the word is in the singular – "the pious one". This one, so lovingly disposed toward God, as to be called 'his holy one' – was Samuel! His mother knew the child's heart, for she had taught him since he was a babe.

in this place, unless in his weakness and smallness, the hand of the Almighty overshadowed him. When all in life seems hopeless, when all our strength seems powerless, this assurance of an invisible, invincible spirit of guardian care brings comfort to grieving hearts. The saints of God are precious to Him, and whether it be the journey of our own life, or the pathway of a child who we resign into His care, "the foundation of God standeth sure, having this seal, The Lord knoweth them that are his". **43**

But God also knoweth them that are not His, and their destiny was not to be found in the light. The proud and the lofty whom God would cast down were not the national foes of Israel, but the ungodly within the nation. And the poor and wretched whom He would exalt were the holy and the righteous in the land. The wicked who would be silent in darkness were not the Philistines, for Hannah's thoughts were not focused on the fear of foreign domination. The wicked were those whose spirit was so opposed to divine principles that God Himself was their enemy. Their influence was to be removed by the termination of death itself, for the silence of darkness was but the stillness of death.

Why was this calamitous overthrow to come upon them? It was because of a spirit which vaunted itself against God. If Phinehas was the representative of those who were arrogant in their words (the man of the brazen mouth), **44** Hophni was the symbol of those who were aggressive in their deeds (the man of the clenched fist). But even a mighty man could not prevail against the divine purpose. Even one given to aggressive deeds could not succeed in exerting the force of his power when it came to opposing God. No matter what trials come upon us, the will of

---

43 The apostle's statement (2 Timothy 2:19), is a quotation from the episode of Korah's rebellion against Moses and Aaron. Moses declared that "the Lord will shew who are his, and who is the holy one" (Numbers 16:15). The priesthood of Aaron was confirmed, and the wickedness of Korah declared. It was this same controversy Hannah had set in motion with the challenge of Samuel against Hophni and Phinehas. The Lord would soon declare who was His holy one in Shiloh, and this is the theme of Hannah's song.

44 Compare the earlier terms in Hannah's song which refer to the spirit of Phinehas (1 Samuel 2:3).

the Father will always prevail, and none can stand against it. Not even a Hophni. "By strength shall no man prevail."

In truth, the judicial decree of God had already been determined in this matter. These men were the enemies of God, and it was His intention to oppose them. It was a dreadful thing, for their spirit had already sealed their destiny. The wrath of God against His adversaries was terrible indeed, for God would not hesitate to shatter those who stood in opposition to Him. Hophni and Phinehas were completely unaware that their doom was declared, but Hannah, through the Spirit, knew it of a certainty. [45] God Himself would utter His strong disapproval upon them from on high. The thunder of heaven, terrifying in its power, was as the voice of God Himself. [46] And when that word of judgment fell, there would be no right of reply, for the decision would be final. None would be exempt, and the judgment of God after falling on the sons of Eli would extend across the entire nation. [47] The inevitability of this day was deeply comforting to Hannah, as it is to all who await the answer of God against an evil age. The day of judgment was not hers to announce, nor hers to execute. But when it came, and once it began, it would move forward with ever increasing force until it became unstoppable.

Revealing the hope of a better age

As her inspired utterance drew near to its close, her thoughts came full circle. As the Handmaid of the Highest, she sought

---

[45] Her words were strong indeed. Rotherham – "As for Yahweh they shall be shattered who contend with him"; GLT – "They who strive with Yahweh will be smashed". Hannah did not utter these words based upon her own personal feelings. They were the decree of heaven expressed through her, and God Himself endorsed her words (1 Samuel 2:25).

[46] The metaphor of the thunder as the voice of God, was to be found in scriptures which Hannah had access to (Exodus 9:28; Job 37:4,5; 40:9).

[47] This is of course what happened. Not only were Hophni and Phinehas slain, but Eli died, the ark of God was taken into captivity, Shiloh was destroyed, and the nation plunged into trouble. In this series of events when the Lord judged to the "ends of the earth" (Israel), was foreshadowed the great judgment to come when Messiah shall judge all the world, that the adversaries of the Lord might be shattered.

only to advance the divine purpose. Her song from start to finish was never about Hannah's objectives, but the Father's. And so, those whom she first described as "mine enemies", were at the end none other than the "adversaries of the LORD". She saw how important it was to be working with God, rather than against Him, for those found to be contending with God will be overthrown. Alone in her weakness, and bereft of the instruments of control which these two wielded, she served in humility, but would be victorious through submission.

It is one thing to pluck up and to pull down that which is evil, but quite another to build and to plant that which is good. Seeking to overthrow the wrong is negative. Striving to establish the right is positive. The latter is much more difficult to achieve than the former, for to destroy can be the work of a moment, but to create is the labour of a lifetime. The great epochs of spiritual vitality in the history of God's people all came about because of the labour of those who sought something better. Hannah was such an one. She desired not so much to remove as to replace, not so much to put an end as to make a start. For her, the dedication of Samuel promised the start of a new and better age for the faithful in Israel. And, such was her grasp of divine principle and divine promise, she knew exactly what that age would involve.

Guided by the Spirit, she saw the overthrow of those who were evil, but as her mind soared beyond her own day, her words gave utterance to the Spirit's promise of the final victory of Messiah in the age to come. God's king would be given strength. God's anointed would be exalted. But his elevation was related to and consequent upon the overthrow of the adversaries of the Lord. His rise was the counter to their fall, and in coming to replace them, his work was to fulfil that which they would not do. The height of Hannah's prophetic anticipation did not lie in the advent of a king, but in the appearing of one who would also hold priestly powers. This anointed one of whom Hannah spoke, could not just be a king, for his work was to bring about a better priesthood, to replace forever the sacerdotal order so disgraced by Hophni and Phinehas. She anticipated one to come in whom kingship and priesthood would be united, and with an anointing to the dignity of both offices. [48] This was Hannah's understanding, marvellous in its insight, and that it was so would be made plain by her subsequent actions. [49]

Realising the promise of another priesthood

The terrible rupture of the fellowship meal which Eli's sons so cruelly caused was the reason for Hannah's grief. That the precious associations of this meal could be so abruptly set aside was the basis for her righteous indignation. But in her deepest meditation upon scripture, Hannah found the basis for her hope. For in an earlier age, and in the tabernacle of Shem, where the true worship of God had been found, a man had stood to minister before the Lord. His spirit did not destroy the beauty of holiness, but rather upheld it. And the work of Melchizedek as king and priest had inspired the patriarch Abraham to make his own pledge of faithfulness to the Most High God. [50]

The prospect of such a man who brought forth a meal of bread and wine and graciously invited those present to share it with him, [51] was like a blazing light to Hannah's mind. How

---

48 It has been rightly observed that Hannah was the first person to use the word Messiah (*mashiyach*) as a title (1 Samuel 2:10). But Hannah was not the first person to use the word itself, for it appeared in the book of the law, which Hannah was familiar with. Its use there however exclusively referred to the anointing of the priesthood (Leviticus 4:3,5,16; 6:22), the holy anointing oil being the mode of appointing the High Priest to office. What Hannah spoke of in prophecy was the coming of the one with the rights of Melchizedek, to be both king and priest upon his throne (Zechariah 6:12,13).

49 See Appendix 5 – "What was the lesson of Hannah's little coat?" on page 225.

50 The vow of Abraham uttered to the Most High God (Genesis 14:22) immediately after his conversation with Melchizedek who had already used that title (Genesis 14:19,20), showed the impact that this king-priest had on the patriarch. In paying tithes to him (Genesis 14:20) he declared the greatness of Melchizedek above his own station in God's sight (Hebrews 7:7,8).

51 The very verse which identified Melchizedek as holding both the offices of king and priest, also mentioned the fellowship meal he provided to share with Abraham (Genesis 14:18).

different was this one, who had ruled in Salem, and brought forth blessing on those who came to the tent of meeting. And how sacred was this fellowship feast, prepared and offered by a priest whose aim was to exalt all who ate together. In this episode, Hannah found the example and the spirit which she desired to see renewed in Israel. Surely another man like he, was what the nation needed.

And was not that possibility enshrined in another promise made in patriarchal times? When Jacob blessed his sons, he uttered a promise which the faithful in Israel knew. His words to Judah promised that one called Shiloh would come, a mysterious man in whom would be vested a similar authority to Melchizedek. [52] But only a Hannah would discern the deeper meaning of the promise, for hidden in his description was one who would hold the sceptre of the king, but also wear the blood sprinkled garments of the priest. The gathering of the people would be unto him, not only through his rulership exercised with power, but because of his redemption wrought in sacrifice. [53] There was probably none else like her in the nation at this moment, as she looked ahead to things unseen by others. Her heart was in the Holiest of all where the ark of God's presence promised both atonement and fellowship. Hannah knew that the fulness of both would only be realised when a King of Righteousness was exalted, but in him she also saw the Priest of the Most High God.

And far off though that moment might have been, she saw all this in the birth of her son. Of course, he was a man of Levi,

---

[52] That the Shiloh promise related to a person not a place was made evident by the passage itself (Genesis 49:10-12). The terms clearly indicate an individual – "unto him shall the gathering of the people be", "binding his colt", "he washed his garments", "his teeth white with milk". Both the personal pronouns and the personal actions concern a special man.

[53] This twofold aspect of kingship and priesthood in the Shiloh promise was recognised in other scriptures. Ezekiel referred to an overturning "until he come whose right it is", in unmistakable allusion to the Shiloh promise. Until that one should come, both the mitre of the priest and the crown of the king would be held in reserve for him (Ezekiel 21:26,27). Zechariah spoke of one who would appear on Shiloh's ass, to ride as king and claim dominion, but who would also bring salvation as priest through the blood of the covenant he would mediate (Zechariah 9:9-11).

and therefore unable to fulfil the terms of the Shiloh promise which awaited a man of Judah. But, she recognised in her child a model for the work of Messiah himself. It was an ideal to be striven for by every godly mother: to have such a desire for the development of their children, that they might grow to reveal the very spirit of Christ within them. Hannah was filled with joy at the triumph of the Lord's honour, and the triumph of the Lord's purpose focused in her son as the instrument for its achievement. And when the last line of her song left her lips, her own vow of Nazarite dedication was accomplished, completed in the giving of her child. How gloriously would her words end, just as her song had begun. For her first cry – "My horn is exalted in the LORD", would at the last become – "the LORD ... will exalt the horn of his anointed". Her status and her purpose would be subsumed into the exaltation of God's anointed. She would be made whole, she would be made strong in him.

Hannah and her song

In wonder, her song saw ahead to the ultimate fulfilment of God's purpose, reaching its climax in the expectation of one to come, who would be both king and priest after a different order than that of Hophni and Phinehas through the line of Aaron. From the outset, she had envisaged another priestly line that would supersede the existing order at Shiloh, and in her song, she saw that older order being swept away. Whatever trials Peninnah had caused, whatever threat the Philistines had brought, these were not the adversaries of the Lord that Hannah had controversy with. Her contention was against the evil priesthood of Hophni and Phinehas, and their destruction of the nation's fellowship with their God. As she prayed, she was right there at the sanctuary where they officiated, and her awareness of them was acute. Her prayer, in their presence, was about God's triumph over them, and the most powerful and poignant reason for Hannah's joy expressed in song, was that for her, the giving of Samuel to the Lord was not the conclusion of the matter, but the very beginning. This was exactly what she had yearned for, and exactly what she had prayed about. Let now, the voice of recompense to His enemies be heard! Let now, the vengeance of His temple be seen! The controversy of Hannah was the controversy of the Lord Himself. Her song was the celebration of its start, and her words resounded with all the spirit of possibility that this beginning opened.

How dramatic was this moment, when she brought her child, offered him to God, and sang her hymn of praise. Those who heard must have wondered at the words, so stern and strong, so exalted in spirit and tone, as to make the hearers feel they had entered the Holiest on that day. Hannah was already there in her mind, drawn toward the light of the presence of God, where no darkness can be. Despite the anguish of this moment she had never felt so alive as this day. There was a sense of fulfilment so strong, that it verged on ecstasy. [54] In that moment, as time stood still, and the onlookers were hushed, she prayed with closed eyes and uplifted countenance, made radiant in the certainty of her conviction. The Lord had spoken through His Handmaid, whose mind, as always, was fixed on higher things.

There were moments in the divine record, when a man or woman of God ascended into the heights of worship with such fervency and zeal, that they were transported beyond the mundane. It is not an experience shared by the many. It is possible to read from scripture, to stand and sing a hymn, to give our amen to prayer, to partake even of the emblems, yet all the while be far from God. To draw near to Him, is an act of deliberate intent that demands our earnest focus, but when we do, we experience an aspect of the Truth that fills our being with joy and wonder in equal parts. The great ones of scripture knew such moments. They lived lives that brought them close to God, to a place where intellect and emotion were bound together in reverent awe.

---

54 Who, reading Hannah's song, could fail to discern her exalted state of mind, and her heightened sense of purpose, so evident in her words, as guided by the Spirit she gave utterance to things that reached far beyond herself. Her song, focused on God throughout, is one of the most moving passages in scripture. This truly was the song of His Handmaid.

Hannah was certainly among them, for her words this day, ascending on high, marked her out as the Handmaid of the Highest. Those others who stood framed within the tableau, were but silent witnesses. Elkanah, her astonished husband, who knew now the fulness of his wife's faith, and the depth of her understanding. Eli, the old priest who heard her word of prophecy, but had not yet seen the role the child would play in the overthrow of the Lord's adversaries. Hophni and Phinehas, the mighty men of the age, who if they heard at all, were scornful and dismissive of so strange a prayer, and knew not that their own bows were about to be broken. Peninnah who stood with her children, thankful that it was not her son being given, and struggling to comprehend what Hannah had done.

And Samuel himself, who although so tender in years, knew with some inner stirring that this day was a very important one in both his life and his mother's. Watching her every movement, hearing her every word, the child drank in the scene and imprinted it forever upon his heart. Only when he was grown to maturity would he understand the full import of this day. But his mother's prayer would become the basis for his own, as his impassioned pleadings for his people echoed this cry of his mother, whose heart was so committed to the nation she loved.

5 |

Hannah and her child

(1 Samuel 2:11-19)

"And Elkanah went to Ramah to his house. And the child did minister unto the LORD before Eli the priest." (1 Samuel 2:11)

HANNAH'S song ended, and she knelt to embrace her child, holding him close, feeling his warmth, hugging him tight. 'The LORD be with you, my son' she whispered, and as she arose, a woman from the tabernacle stepped forward quietly, and took Samuel by the hand.[1] 'Come, little one. Let me show you your new home', she said, as she led Samuel away to his new house in one of the buildings about the sanctuary. The die was cast. The battle was joined. The outcome was now in the hands of the Almighty Himself. Hannah turned and walked away from the tabernacle. She did not look back. It would have been too hard.[2]

Their journey home was not an easy one. Hannah's elation in praise was followed by an unbearable sadness, as each homeward step marked the absence of the little boy who had walked alongside her on the journey there. It was to be expected, but she felt it all the same. The ache of the loss inside her was more painful than she ever could have imagined, a pain impossible to describe. She would come to realise that her pain would never go

---

1 See Chapter 6 – "Hannah and her hope" on page 127, under the heading, "The mysterious guardian of the child" for thoughts as to who this woman might have been.
2 Cp. Genesis 19:26; Luke 9:62.

away, for it was part of her. The cost of giving her son was not just to be felt in the moment of his giving, but for ever after in the permanence of his loss. She felt unutterably weary, as the toll of four years of prayer and preparation were suddenly completed. From her first beseeching to this last surrender, these years had been focused on one thing only: the birth, nurture and return of the son for whom she had prayed. Now she uttered in private the prayer she would offer so many times over this next year, that the Lord would watch over her son, and "keep the feet of his holy one" in Shiloh. But the little boy was already being watched over by the One into whose care she had consigned him. When Hannah left Shiloh, so did Elkanah, and Samuel was now also to be separated from his father, and his father's house. From this moment, he would live in another house, and serve another Father according to a higher principle than flesh and blood. [3] Within the shelter of that sacred care, his life and work was sacrosanct, as he learned to "be about his Father's business". [4]

It was too soon for Samuel to know the meaning of the temple service he was now joined to. But even in his innocence as a little child, Samuel was intent upon ministering to the Lord. [5] To the degree that his age permitted, Samuel began to learn the priestly role, and the priestly law. He would, early on, begin his instruction in the Torah, which he would learn to read, then to

---

[3] This is the idea suggested by the narrative. For although it is evident that Elkanah and Hannah returned home together as on other occasions (1 Samuel 1:19; 2:20), the record focuses attention on Elkanah alone. The implication is that Samuel was not just weaned of his mother, but would now be separated from his father. The meaning is seen in the balance between the two sentences which convey this idea. Rotherham – "Then went Elkanah to Ramah, unto his own house – but, the boy remained ministering unto Yahweh" (1 Samuel 2:11).

[4] The expression is rendered by YLT – "in the things of my Father it behoveth me to be" (Luke 2:49). How significant it is that these are the first recorded words of Christ, and how remarkably well they echo this moment in the life of Hannah's son.

[5] The word "to minister" (*sharath* – to minister or serve) does occur in some political and domestic contexts. But its most frequent use is for the service at the sanctuary (Exodus 28:35,43) with its priestly overtones, and it is so used here (1 Samuel 2:11).

recite, and finally to teach. Of course, everything that he did was done under the watchful eye of Eli, who set and approved the tasks he could perform, but even now the spirit of the child was that he ministered unto the Lord.

Only now was it seen how well Hannah had prepared her son for life at the sanctuary. The three precious years she had spent with him were enough. Samuel had not just been given to the Lord in person, but in spirit. She had not just brought him to the sanctuary, she had given him a sanctuary mind. She had not just left him to serve, she had imbued him with the spirit of sanctuary service. This child belonged at the house of God, and it was his mother who gifted him with that sense of belonging. Hannah's example would become the benchmark of every aspiring mother in Israel, whose wish was to train up their child in the way they should go, so that when they were old, they would not depart from it. Samuel never did depart from the way of his mother, for she instilled in him a love of the God of Israel. From his first moment in Shiloh, Samuel grasped his calling to the priestly office. He was a little priest in the making, and just as well that he was.

The sons of Belial that knew not the Lord

"Now the sons of Eli were sons of Belial; they knew not the Lord." (1 Samuel 2:12)

There was every reason for Hannah to believe that her contest had begun with the giving of her son, for the situation at the sanctuary was dire indeed. Such was the evil of the priests at Shiloh that God had determined on a course that would bring judgment upon them, the very judgment Hannah had seen by the Spirit in her song. The sons of Eli, called to a life of holiness in priestly service, never attained unto the honour of that state. Hophni and Phinehas were undoubtedly the mighty men of the age, but in spirit they were not the sons of Eli. Their father's name commemorated the great principle of ascension to things divine, that going up to the sanctuary permitted, and was imbedded in the law of the burnt offering which signified the dedication of the worshipper. **⁶** But these men were not 'sons of ascension'. Instead they were the very reverse, for in both speech and action they were but the 'sons of worthlessness'. They had never ascended into the heavenly places of spiritual thought and worship where Hannah walked. They had never set their affection on things above, for their thinking was but carnal and base.

At the most fundamental level of their lives, they knew not the Lord, **⁷** and it was because they knew Him not that they engaged in words and deeds of such blatant defiance. To know the Lord is a journey that moves from intellectual assent to experiential surrender. What the counsels of the word have inscribed upon the tables of the mind, the hand of providence can then inscribe upon the tables of the heart, but only in that order. Divine principle cannot be written into human experience in the absence of its mental assimilation. But when both are joined in harmony, a person is seen who thinks and acts like God, and thereby knows Him. Hannah was such a person, for her pledge to be the Handmaid of the Highest was to absorb first the mind of her Master, and then seek to do His bidding. Her prayer and her song revealed that she knew Him whom she served, and her speech and actions were the very antithesis of those displayed by Hophni and Phinehas.

The law of the peace offering

To know the Lord was to seek fellowship with Him, and Hannah desired that more than anything else in her life. She knew that she could never enter His temple, but was ever thankful that she could "bring an offering and come into his courts". Her desire to "worship the LORD in the beauty of holiness" would continue to draw her unto the place which He had chosen to put His name there, where offering and sacrifice should be made. And there was one offering above all others that excited and exalted and

---

6   Eli means 'ascension' and is from (*alah* – to ascend), which is in turn the root word for (*olah* – the ascending sacrifice) or burnt offering.

7   Their spirit certainly reflected the character of the times of the judges (1 Samuel 2:10).

enthralled her with the prospect of the fellowship it promised. For Hannah, the climax of drawing near to her God lay in the law of the peace offering. [8] She could recall earlier visits to the sanctuary, and held precious memories of a time when the offerings were offered in the manner prescribed by the law. Those visits had been the highlight of her year, and the basis of her attachment to the sanctuary that prompted their yearly pilgrimage.

She remembered what it felt like to arrive before the priest of God with an animal carefully chosen as the best they had. She knew how it felt to place her hand upon the warmth of its head before it was sacrificed, and how, as they slew their offering, the priest stood ready to capture the blood and sprinkle it upon the altar round about. But he stood ready to do something else. For no sooner was the offering slain than it was cut asunder, to remove the inward fat and the two kidneys. [9] The priest would guide them as to how and where the knife should cut, so that this special part, the portion that the Lord Himself sought might be made ready. [10] Once removed, they had brought it to the altar themselves, and only then did the priest take the fat directly from their hands, [11] to offer it by fire before the Lord upon His table. She could vividly recall those moments at His altar, because it was the nearest she would ever come to the place of His presence. And she remembered the pleasure and approval she felt as she had watched the priest take the fat of their offering and place it upon the daily lamb which was already burning there. [12]

---

8   Given that Hannah's story revolved around the peace offering (1 Samuel 1:4-7; 2:13-17), and her desire to replace the priesthood of Hophni and Phinehas because of their corruption of that offering, it would seem reasonable to infer that she had a thorough understanding of its significance, as the following paragraphs suggest.
9   Leviticus 3:3,4,9,10,14,15.
10 The word "fat" (*cheleb*) means the best, choicest, finest (Numbers 18:12; Psalm 147:14).
11 This seems to be the inference of the law, which strongly emphasised that it was the offerer himself who offered the fat, bringing it with his own hands, even though the priest then took and burnt it upon the altar on their behalf (Leviticus 3:14-16; 7:29-31).
12 Leviticus 6:12.

Seeing God's portion, [13] offered first unto Him, brought her the greatest satisfaction, for she understood its meaning. The finest was to be God's. Even voluntary offerings of thanksgiving must needs acknowledge the supremacy of God as the first condition of acceptable worship. This fat of the inwards, so esteemed by the Almighty, belonged on His table and nowhere else. Hannah loved that moment of highest privilege as they approached the altar to offer the "food of the offering", for she treasured its teaching. The Lord desired the richest part of her life as His. Her innermost thoughts and her deepest emotions, the best of her labours and the fulness of her loyalty belonged to Him. She would not have had it otherwise. Even her marriage vow was made stronger by the spirit of her dedication to God, for "a woman that feareth the LORD, she shall be praised". [14]

After the fat had been offered, those other parts of the sacrifice were separated which would be given to the priests. The first of these was the wave breast, a large and tender piece of meat, which belonged to the priestly family as a whole. [15] Without these, Hannah knew, there could be no approach to God at all. It mattered not what her desire was to draw near in worship, the presence of the priest who acted on her behalf was the divinely appointed protocol which both permitted approach yet upheld God's holiness. He could only be approached through the mediatorial office of the priest, and she would not forget it. Both priests and Levites themselves had been made a wave offering in their consecration to the Lord for their priestly service. [16] The wave breast, given to the priestly household, reminded Hannah that God, no less than these, sought the full consecration of her own heart before Him.

---

13 So insistent was God upon the receiving of this as His chosen portion, He forbad all Israel from ever consuming the fat of the sacrifices (Leviticus 7:23-25). His prohibition was stringent and absolute. No one was ever to take of the fat of the sacrifices for their own use under any circumstances – "all the fat is the LORD's" (Leviticus 3:16,17).

14 Proverbs 31:28-31.

15 Leviticus 7:30,31,34.

16 Noted of the priests (Leviticus 8:22-28), and the Levites (Numbers 8:10-13).

One more portion was to be given to another before they could enjoy their fellowship meal. For what the priests represented in general was seen in the work of the priest who offered for them on the day they came to the tabernacle door. She knew how the hind leg of the animal was carefully severed from the whole, and given solemnly to the priest who officiated at the sacrifice. How robust and vigorous was that right leg, how full of power and force it was. Surely all the strength of the animal was here in this portion of meat which the priest would eat as his appointed share. But before he did so, it was offered up as a heave offering to God. He would eat this portion, but he would do so as God's representative. Hannah remembered watching him, and feeling the wonder of the fact that in eating, he would symbolise that God had indeed accepted their offering. How necessary then, if she was to eat with Him, that all her strength might be devoted unto the Lord with whom she had to do.

With every peace offering, the offerer was more involved than with any other sacrifice, an involvement that lasted from its beginning to its end. Now, in Hannah's eyes, came the most wonderful involvement of all. With all the portions that belonged to others now distributed as the law required, it was time to share this meal with her God. She always felt the same when this moment came, for she knew an indescribable feeling of wonder and privilege that made this meal like no other. It was more than a meal, for even its eating was an act of worship. There was a portion here "to seven and also to eight", for even after the parts which went to God and His priests, the rest of the animal promised a feast which her entire family would be more than satisfied by. There was meat for all, and with it a generous basket of unleavened cakes, unleavened wafers, and cakes of fine flour mingled with oil and fried.[17] But, in addition to these, there were freshly baked loaves of leavened bread as well.[18] Hannah remembered how a basket of all these cakes was offered to the

---

17 Leviticus 7:11,12.
18 Leviticus 7:13.

priest, [19] so that they might truly share in the sacrificial meal together.

It was strange that these leavened loaves should be permitted, when unleavened bread was the standard of all meal offerings. [20] But Hannah knew why it was that they were offered, accepted their lesson, and bowed before it in reverent humility. They taught her that this meal, shared in fellowship with God, was not to be eaten on the basis of her own righteousness, but on the basis of God's grace. The unleavened cakes promised her that one day, fellowship with God would be made possible to the full, but only when sin was at last removed. The leavened loaves reminded her that in this mortal age, sin would be ever present in our lives, [21] and that fellowship with God was only permitted through His mercy and subject to His conditions. In appreciating the lesson of the loaves, Hannah knew that the meal of the peace offering was a privilege so high, that it was an honour to participate. It was not necessary for Hannah to be reminded that only those clean could eat of the peace offering. [22] She would never have permitted herself to eat with her God whilst unclean, but her standard of personal holiness exceeded the ceremonial of the law, and reached to that purity of heart and mind that made true fellowship with the Father possible.

Of all the peace offerings, the most important was that of thanksgiving, also known as the sacrifice of praise. [23] So holy

---

19 As part of the peace offering, the law stipulated, RSV – "And of such he shall offer one cake from each offering, as an offering to the LORD, it shall belong to the priest" (Leviticus 7:14).

20 The law of the meal offering rigorously excluded the use of leaven (Leviticus 2:11). The only other occasion where leavened bread was permitted was in the two wave loaves offered at the Feast of Pentecost (Leviticus 23:17). It should be noted that these also were associated with a peace offering (Leviticus 23:19,20).

21 The leavened loaves however, were only for the consumption of priest and offerer, and could not be placed upon God's table. The normal meal offering which accompanied even the peace offering (and which would be burned upon His altar) had to be of unleavened bread only (Leviticus 2:11).

22 Leviticus 7:20,21.

23 Unlike the vow and voluntary peace offerings, the "thanksgiving" (*towdah*) offering had to be eaten the same day, indicating its higher importance (Leviticus 7:15;

was this sacrifice, that the fellowship meal which followed had to be eaten on that very day. Hannah had known the joy of that meal, for to her, a life made up of praise in every part, and a spirit of thanksgiving in worship, was the essence of who she was. The joy she felt in bringing praise, and the fellowship she knew in offering it, was the transcendent point of her spiritual life.

But these were all memories of a past and better age when worship at the sanctuary brought such fulfilment and peace. For a long time now however, the wickedness of the sons of Eli had not just brought the sanctuary into disrepute, but had filled the hearts of the faithful with distress and indignation. The meal of the peace offering, which should have been eaten with rejoicing, [24] instead brought only sorrow. In fact, it was only the strength of their conviction concerning the Lord's command to appear before Him, that kept Elkanah and Hannah in attendance. [25] Her fears that the worship of Israel might be corrupted beyond recovery, were entirely justified. But the arrival of Samuel in that place marked the beginning of a challenge to their order. It was time the issue was joined, and already Hannah was deeply involved in advancing that cause. It was none too soon, for the iniquity of the priests had come to the full.

The sin of aggressive deeds

"And the priest's custom with the people was, that, when any man offered sacrifice, the priest's servant came, while the flesh was in seething, with a fleshhook of three teeth in his hand; and he struck it into the pan, or kettle, or caldron, or pot; all that the fleshhook brought up the priest took for

---

22:29,30). To offer a sacrifice of praise (*towdah*), was to recognise and exalt God, a spirit which the Lord delighted in (Psalm 50:23).

24 Deuteronomy 12:6,7,12; 27:7.

25 The general wickedness that prevailed at the sanctuary must have discouraged many a faithful Israelite from coming to Shiloh at all. The persistence of Elkanah and Hannah in adhering to the requirements of the law (Deuteronomy 16:16,17) was a remarkable example.

himself. So they did in Shiloh unto all the Israelites that came hither." (1 Samuel 2:13,14)

The law was very precise regarding the portions of the peace offering. It regulated the portion for the Lord, the portion for the High Priest, the portion for the officiating priest, and the portion for the offerer. Each received their part, in descending order of importance. The order set down within the law was part of the teaching of God to uphold His supremacy. But these men had decided to establish their own law of sacrifice, in a rule that violated all that the peace offering symbolised. They did not greet the arrival of faithful worshippers with the sense of honour that was theirs, to lift their brethren to the high calling and wonder of worship which this offering permitted. Instead, they saw it as an opportunity for personal gratification, at the expense of those who came.

They sought to intimidate, and the moment they chose was shocking. The offerer had first sacrificed a sin offering, to declare before God a full realisation of their sinful state and their desperate need for atonement in their lives. That principle of confession was followed by a burnt offering, in that vow of renewed dedication that should always accompany the state of cleansing from sin. With those vital offerings completed, the offerer was ready to turn with joy to the fellowship meal which their peace offering promised. The animal had been sacrificed. [26] The fellowship feast was being prepared at the very time. The meat was cooking, and all the other arrangements for the meal were being finalised. They were just about to sit down and eat with God. There could be no higher occasion of fellowship than this. Yet, this was the moment that the priest's servant came to make demand in a belligerent spirit that would brook no argument. There was no decency or decorum in their actions; only their open avarice, displayed in a sequence of aggressive deeds which left the offerer with no choice but to give up a significant part of their own fellowship portion.

---

[26] That the term for sacrifice here (*zebach*) relates to the peace offering is clear, since it refers to the offerer's portion, which only occurred with the peace offering (1 Samuel 2:13,14).

The three-pronged fork or fleshhook, was one of the instruments of the sanctuary, [27] and counted as one of the holy things relating to the tabernacle. [28] They belonged to the service of the Lord, but Hophni and Phinehas took God's instruments from His altar for their own ends. Strong enough to pull up the biggest pieces of flesh out of the pot in which the offerer's portion was cooking, they were well suited for the exercise of greed the priests had in mind. They had already received the best parts of the animal, but these men wanted more. Both the wave breast and the heave shoulder were theirs by descent and office, so they had already received the chiefest portions. But it was not enough. They wanted the best part of what was not theirs. And, so grasping was their spirit, that to fulfil their desire they were prepared to resort to ruthless and cruel intimidation. [29] They did not ask, they simply took. They arrived, and without word or warning, they plunged their fleshhook into the meat of the offerer's portions, and took it for themselves. The spirit of giving and sharing that the offerer had joyfully submitted to, was not shared by the very priest supposed to officiate on their behalf. Theirs rather was the spirit of keeping and taking. No one was exempt. Everyone suffered the same indignity and loss, for this was their common practice with all who came to the sanctuary. It had become their settled routine of ungodly behaviour, as their spirit reached out to destroy every aspect of the worship of God in His holy place.

They challenged the portions of the offering, and by interfering with the seething of the flesh within the cauldron they

---

27 The term (*mazleg*) relates to the fleshhooks of the altar of burnt offering (Exodus 27:3; 38:3), used to move the parts of the sacrifices on the altar. Hence, GLT – "the priest's servant came when the flesh was boiling, with the three-toothed hook in his hand" (the definite article indicating that the fleshhook was a tabernacle instrument).

28 As were all the instruments of the altar (Numbers 4:4,13-15).

29 Here was the spirit of the man of the clenched fist (Hophni) who exemplified the sin of their aggressive deeds. The phrases describing their treatment of the offerer's portions at the time of sacrifice, illustrated their entire behaviour and demeanour – "the priest's servant came ... with a fleshhook", "he struck it into the pan ... all that the fleshhook brought up the priest took for himself." "So they did ... unto all the Israelites" (1 Samuel 2:13,14). The focus was upon their actions.

destroyed the people's fellowship meal, and came between them and their God. All that was wonderful about the moment was lost in this despicable act of common theft, blatantly demanded and brazenly enforced. It was enough to make the heart despair. But what did these men care? All that mattered was their own enrichment, without regard for consequence to others. Hannah had witnessed this spirit. She had seen the portions of the peace offerings exploited by the priests, and knew the spiritual anguish it caused.

The evil of arrogant words

> "Also before they burnt the fat, the priest's servant came, and said to the man that sacrificed, Give flesh to roast for the priest; for he will not have sodden flesh of thee but raw. And if any man said unto him, Let them not fail to burn the fat presently, and then take as much as thy soul desireth; then he would answer him, Nay; but thou shalt give it me now: and if not, I will take it by force." (1 Samuel 2:15,16)

But worse was to follow. Not content with robbing the offerer of their portion they came even earlier, and in effect robbed God of His. The law was insistent that not only did all the fat belong to the Lord, but that it must as a priority be offered upon His altar before any other portion be dealt with. That which belonged to Him had to be given first. There was no offering acceptable to God which denied His supremacy, or set it aside. That principle, which lay at the heart of the fellowship meal which followed, was impressed upon the offerer as they participated in the sacrifice itself. The bringing of the Lord's own portion was the first thing the offerer attended to. In their respect for the Lord of hosts who inhabited the cherubim, they were anxious to carry this choicest part to His altar, and to witness for themselves the evidence of the fat placed upon the table. But in Shiloh, the priests used this very moment to press their claim.

They sought to interfere, and the timing of their speech was dreadful. The animal had just been slain, and the fat removed.

The portions for the priests had also been prepared, and now the one who sacrificed was ready to gather up the fat and the kidneys in their own hands, to walk to God's altar. For every Israelite, that walk brought them into the place where priests alone could minister. High was this privilege which permitted them to draw near and present the Lord's portion at His table. And yet, it was at this moment, when all was focused upon the Lord, that the priest's servant demanded a further share of the offerer's portion, before it had even been placed in the cauldron for seething.

They had the advantage of control. They simply refused to offer the fat unto the Lord until they had been given the extra portion of raw meat they sought. And, if the truth be known, these unthankful and unholy men were sufficiently corrupt, that some of the fat of the sacrifice itself may well have been purloined to add to the flavour of their roasts.

Part of the spirit of the peace offering was that the offerer became the host, and God and His priests, his honoured guests. It was the privilege of he who sacrificed to wait upon his guests in service at this sacred meal. The wave breast and the heave shoulder were ready to be given, as soon as the Lord had received His part, and the offerer himself looked forward to partaking of a good piece of flesh and a loaf of bread. But all that was sacred and wonderful at that moment was shattered by this demand for more.

It was to the credit of those who offered, that, faced with such obnoxious and arrogant words, they were prepared to give way, and if necessary to be defrauded in the process. Here was the peaceable spirit of those who were willing to surrender much of their own portion, provided the Lord was honoured with His rightful due. Yet their request, consistent with the very spirit of the offering, was met with a vulgar brute demand. Hophni and Phinehas wanted what they wanted now, and were indifferent as to whether they interrupted the burning of the fat as a matter of holy priority. **30** And so determined was their desire that they did not hesitate to employ caustic and abusive threats. **31**

They challenged the order of the offerings, and by interrupting the burning of the fat upon the altar, they destroyed the Lord's fellowship meal, and came between Him and His people. The offerer had come to witness the giving of the best to God, and to watch as the fat was placed upon the altar to be burnt before the Lord. And for the priests to present an ultimatum at that moment for more was scandalous. Bluntly demanded and brutally enforced, it offended every sense of exalting God above all else, in the spirit of thanksgiving and the sacrifice of praise which the peace offering represented. How was it possible to honour God in the heart, when His primacy was ignored and thrust aside by His own representatives? What point was there in bringing an offering and coming into His courts, when its spirit was spurned and its holiness profaned? Why would the faithful come at all? This was iniquity of the worst kind, and its damage to the spiritual life of the nation was incalculable.

When men abhorred the offering of the Lord

> "Wherefore the sin of the young men was very great before the LORD: for men abhorred the offering of the LORD."
>
> (1 Samuel 2:17)

It wasn't just the evil of their aggressive deeds and arrogant words. Their sin lay in a contempt for divine principles which first permitted, then encouraged and finally legitimised a similar

---

30 In this passage – "Let them not fail to burn the fat presently, and then take as much as thy soul desireth ... Nay; but thou shalt give it me now" (1 Samuel 2:16), the word "now" is used over against the word "presently". The implication was that burning the fat unto the Lord didn't come first; giving the priest the portion he sought was to come first.

31 Here was the spirit of the man of the brazen mouth (Phinehas), who exemplified the evil of their arrogant words. The terms describing their treatment of God's portion at the time of sacrifice, revealed their whole spirit and attitude – "the priest's servant came and said ... Give flesh to roast for the priest", "if any man said him, Let them not fail to burn the fat", "then he would answer him, Nay ... I will take it by force" (1 Samuel 2:15,16). The focus was upon their speech.

spirit of ungodliness among the people. When the priest wanders from the narrow way, it is no wonder that the people stray. [32] Those charged with the sacred responsibility to lift the nation in prayer and praise were the very ones who destroyed the spirit of the truth amidst the people of God.

Everything they did was so destructive of the real objective of godly worship. When the consecration of all one's labours brought before the Lord in holiness was rudely seized for personal gain, what was the use of striving to worship in spirit and truth? It thoroughly disheartened the faithful, who for the most part were the only ones in the land to come to the sanctuary with their offerings at all. Worst of all, the climax of the peace offering centred on worshipping a God who desired to share a fellowship meal with His people, and at that sacred, precious, special moment, these spiritual scoundrels came and destroyed it all. To worship the Lord in the beauty of holiness was not possible in the face of such licentious behaviour.

That challenge of spiritual decline which Hannah faced so resolutely in her age, has always been present in the household of faith. Changes are made to the decorum and the dignity of the worship of God in ecclesias. Many of the changes are small, but they are always incremental and in one direction. They come about because of agitation for change, and yet a sound scriptural basis for them is frequently doubtful and most often absent. The mood of the ecclesia alters. The atmosphere declines. The sense of reverence that once touched every heart is lost by degrees which are themselves so gradual, that it seems unreasonable to object. But over time the characteristics of vigorous spiritual life that once revolved around a reverent respect for the Lord, a deep desire to uphold the counsels of His word, and an appreciation of the greatness of His purpose, is replaced with a style more suited to the wishes of the worshippers. Speech, dress, music, prayer, posture, order, are all made the subject of adjustment to make things more human, more relaxed, more comfortable, in

---

32 Hosea 4:9.

a manner which unsurprisingly reflects the surrounding world. Some know that the changes are spiritually damaging to the higher purpose of the Truth. But it is easier to say nothing, less challenging to give consent through silence. This is how spiritual decline occurs. Beware the triumph of gradualism. It begins with the few who seek to change the way of worship. It ends with the many who in practice if not in purpose, abhor the offering of the Lord. In the process, worship continues on earth, but may no longer be accepted in heaven.

The record of Hophni and Phinehas gives warning as to how spiritual life can be destroyed when ecclesial shepherds fail to guard the heritage of the Truth. It occurs when those who guide ecclesias do not know where the ancient landmark has been placed, or why it has been placed there. Almost every custom in ecclesial life has come about because of a scripturally reasoned principle which stands behind the practice. When those in authority do not know where those boundary stones of the Truth lie, then they will not guard the Truth's heritage, and fail to pass it on safely to the next generation. In this age, as in every previous epoch of time, there are those who seek to move the boundary stones on everything. Ignorance of where the ancient landmarks of doctrine and practice within our community lie, is not a defence that ecclesial elders can claim. To be an elder is to accept the responsibility of guarding the Truth. They of all must know where the boundaries of the Truth lie. Where that charge of guardianship is upheld, the Truth will flourish and continue. Where it is abandoned, the Truth will eventually be lost. In both cases, ecclesial elders will be held accountable, as Hophni and Phinehas would be in their day, for safeguarding the sacred charge of the Truth.

Hannah's controversy with the sons of Eli

Was it any wonder then that Hannah could not properly partake of the fellowship meal, when they brought their peace offerings to Shiloh? There were obviously many who accepted that such ungodly behaviour was just the way things were at the sanctuary.

But evil at the house of the Lord affected Hannah far more intensely. To one whose spirit rejoiced at the thought of holy things, the blunt vulgarity of these greedy hypocrites smote her at the heart. Peninnah was not the source of her deepest grief, but these men were. She had witnessed for herself their deliberate refusal to burn the fat unto the Lord, and she was left sick at heart at the dishonour done to Him. She had seen first-hand the robbing of their family portion, so that their fellowship meal was ruined, and she knew the feeling of spiritual emptiness and destitution that it left behind. **33** The real source of Hannah's adversity was not Peninnah or the Philistines, but these two men as the representatives of their own corrupt priesthood.

Was it any wonder that she was angry with such terrible dealings? She hated their spirit, and she hated it on God's behalf. **34** She shared His righteous indignation at the defiling of His ways and the corrupting of His truths. To have known this just once would have been intensely distressing. But Hannah had seen this wickedness and felt this pain for year after year, until the burden of its wrong lay so heavy upon her heart, that only black despair remained. The yearly visit to the sanctuary became the cause of Hannah's grief, and this evidence of their treachery was the reason why. This was why she wept and could not eat.

Was it any wonder that she prayed with all her heart for a son, and vowed to give him to God? These years of agony had also been years of pleading and petition as her thoughts grew more and more focused on what she could do to resist and confront the wickedness of these men. The intensity of her love for the Truth, and her strong desire to turn the heart of Israel back to their God, had led to this thought which captured her mind. It was so daring that it left even Hannah breathless, but she could see no other way. Hophni and Phinehas could only be defeated by being replaced.

---

33 The statement that Hophni and Phinehas robbed those portions from all who brought them to Shiloh (1 Samuel 2:14), is clear evidence that Hannah had personally experienced this behaviour. This was the catalyst for her grief, and this was the focus of the record.

34 Psalm 139:21,22.

But a better priest would not come from their line, of that she was certain. A new man offering new hope was the only way. But where was such a man to be found? Suddenly she knew. He would only be found if someone provided him. But the man she had in mind needed to be focused from the very beginning. Only a child dedicated from infancy could achieve the outcome she sought. It was too late to train him up in the way he should go after he arrived at the sanctuary. His education must begin from the day of his birth. In fact, she wanted his journey to holiness to begin in her womb, such was the standard she would set for his life.

What Hannah contemplated was a battle against spiritual wickedness in high places, where the weapon of warfare would be her beloved son. In the clarity of her understanding she knew, she believed, that only by giving her firstborn could this battle be waged and a victory won. **[35]** Only by offering her son could her people be delivered from the thraldom of sin which bound them. But all this resided in her mind before it became real. Her son did not exist when she first envisaged his priestly calling, but faith clothed the future with substance, and this woman of faith saw things that were not yet, as though they already were, and asked for God's help to turn vision into reality. There was no one else in Israel who thought thus. There was no one else who implored God with such a bold and dramatic plan in mind. There was no one else prepared to pay the price of a firstborn child, who having known the joy of receiving him, would willingly suffer the pain of giving him away in the agony of accomplishment.

Hannah so loved her people that she gave her only begotten son, that the nation through him might be saved. In her, the spirit of God was seen, a living embodiment of the purpose of the Lord of hosts. This was what it meant to be the Handmaid of the Highest, and this was why God so delighted to answer the prayers of His Handmaid. He would bless her with that son which she had

---

[35] That Hannah saw the work of her son in terms of a warfare to be fought is confirmed by the tones of the battle hymn found within her song of thanksgiving (1 Samuel 2:1-10). See Appendix 4 – "What was the import of Hannah's special song?" on page 221, under the heading, "The riddle of the battle theme".

petitioned of Him, and in the story of Hannah and her firstborn, the purpose of God with His only begotten Son would be set forth. The greatest battle of all, the battle against sin, would be fought and won when God sent forth His Son, made of a woman, that the world through him might be saved. Hannah's work with Samuel would point the way to the work of God, who "spared not his own Son, but delivered him up for us all", [36] and in his giving, freely gave us all things. And now, with the presentation of Samuel that he might appear before the Lord, the next chapter of Hannah's controversy was about to be seen. Leaving him at Shiloh was but the first step in Hannah's plan to confront the sons of Eli. Although returned to Ramah, she was already at work to advance the conflict further, if God might but prosper her plan.

But Samuel ministered before the Lord

> "But Samuel ministered before the LORD, being a child, girded with a linen ephod. Moreover his mother made him a little coat, and brought it to him from year to year, when she came up with her husband to offer the yearly sacrifice."
>
> (1 Samuel 2:18,19)

In truth, that warfare had already commenced, for whereas Hophni and Phinehas sinned before the Lord, Samuel ministered before Him. [37] They did what they did against the face and in defiance of God, but Samuel did what he did before the face, and in honour of God. Of a certainty, the battle was joined already, right at the place of the sanctuary, but Hophni and Phinehas did not even know that it had begun. The conflict however was soon to emerge, for Samuel's spirit and his work was in complete contrast to these two. In his demeanour and in his example, he was everything that they were not. It was such an unusual thing for a child to be so at home in the place of the sanctuary as

---

36 Romans 8:32.

37 The opening "but" which with the verse begins, indicates that a deliberate contrast is intended between the little lad and these grown men. Rotherham – "But, as for Samuel, he was ministering" (1 Samuel 2:17,18).

Samuel was, but within a short space of time, it seemed as if he had always belonged there.

Where then did this spirit of ministering come from? Why, from the woman whose child he was. This "asked one" left in Shiloh was uniquely Hannah's child through and through. The spirit of this woman, so deeply imbued with a love of things divine, glowed in the heart and shone in the face of this child who gladdened the spirit of all who saw him. [38] He was nought but a boy, but then he wasn't any boy. He was Hannah's child, and therein lay the secret of his role, for he absorbed his mother's spirit. His own life of Nazarite dedication would embrace Hannah's vow and make it his own. Girded with a linen ephod, [39] and already busy with his tasks, he began to reveal the seriousness of purpose that would characterise his future work in the nation. Service at the sanctuary developed in Samuel a knowledge of the law of God, and an awareness of how little the nation knew that law. He determined to teach them. From the beginning, he was marked out for priesthood, but based upon a higher order than that of Aaron.

Hannah's gift to inspire her son

While Samuel was busy with his new life at Shiloh, his mother was intent upon the nearness of their next meeting. She knew, from the day she had lent him unto the Lord, that their contact would be limited. The pilgrimage of the family in coming to Shiloh for the yearly sacrifice would be her only opportunity to connect with her son, to refocus his direction, and set the scene for the next year of his life. All her love and care would be poured into these yearly visits. But thinking upon him and about him back at Ramah, she pondered the question of how best she could make their meeting special. What could she do to increase her influence upon him for good? What could she bring that would leave her son with a

---

[38] There was almost a sense of wonder about the phrase – "being a child", for the record would repeat it several times (1 Samuel 2:11,18; 3:1).

[39] The ephod was a distinctly priestly garment (1 Samuel 2:28; 22:18; 23:9), which was associated with the role of divine communication.

greater sense of purpose when she returned home? She thought about it with her customary care and spiritual discernment. It needed to be something that would bind them together, but that would also inspire her son to the greatness of his calling.

Suddenly she knew the answer. She had thought of a gift that she could give him, that would need to be renewed every year, but a gift so unique, that her son would never forget it. She would make him an article of clothing, a special garment which showed him all her mother's love. But there would be more than love involved in its making, for this garment, a little coat, was sewn with threads of purpose. Long before her journey, the little coat was ready. Carefully cut and skilfully sewn, it lay folded in a special bag she would carry with her to the sanctuary. When that first year in Ramah was passed, and she came to Shiloh, she brought with her the little coat. Hannah had deep reasons for doing so, and they were much deeper than most people might have imagined.

When the feasts of Israel were ended, and harvest was complete, the season of autumn was heralded by the falling of the former rains. The trees, obedient to the signal of cooling days began to shed their leaves, as the starkness of winter began. In the months that followed, the land would receive a blanketing of snow as the crisp of cold increased. There were many weeks of such cold before the comfort of spring would return in its cycle, and even Shiloh would feel the bite of those chilly days. How natural that a mother's love should seek to provide a garment to warm her child during her absence from him, that he might not be "afraid of the snow". [40]

The hidden lesson of the little coat

But this little coat was not made to keep her child warm. If it had been, she would have left it with him at Shiloh. But she didn't leave it there, she took it home to Ramah with her. Each year she brought it up, and each year she took it home. There was not so

---

40 Proverbs 31:21.

much a succession of little coats, as a succession of occasions a little coat was brought up for Samuel to wear. [41] As he grew she adjusted its size, until eventually it was replaced with a larger and longer garment. But he only ever saw the little coat once a year, and always at the same time, for she brought it with her at the yearly sacrifice. Why did Hannah do that? Why did she not give him the coat to keep? Why did she not leave it with him there? And if she did take it home, what was the point of bringing it with her in the first place? There was a puzzle here, a mystery about the little coat which only Hannah knew. But what she intended would be made plain on her first visit to see her son.

How long it seemed to her before the time for their yearly sacrifice came again. It was exactly one year since she had left him at Shiloh, but the wait for its anniversary seemed interminable. Yet now, at last they were there again, and the moment had come. A message had been sent to fetch the child, and as she waited at the door of the tabernacle, she trembled in anticipation. What would he look like? How would he behave? What was he feeling? She need not have been concerned. "Ima, Ima", shouted Samuel in excitement, as he sped to his mother. "Shalom, ha-ben sheli" she cried, as she knelt to receive him, and as she held him tight, she noticed that his head was already now above her shoulder. Her little boy had grown in stature. He was just as high as she had imagined him to be. She knew both laughter and tears, but these were tears of happiness which welled up within her as deep as the spring of her motherhood itself. How blessed she was. How thankful she felt for this moment. And, as was always the case in Hannah's life, there was a deep sense of purpose to this meeting, that even her boy realised, as she looked upon him so intently. Ever after, Samuel would remember that gaze of his mother. It

---

41 In the Hebrew, the phrase – "from year to year" does not govern the action of making the coat, but the action of bringing the coat. Hence YLT – "and a small upper coat doth his mother make to him, and she hath brought it up to him from time to time, in her coming up with her husband to sacrifice the sacrifice of the time" (1 Samuel 2:19). The clear meaning of the passage is to indicate that Hannah brought up the little coat each year, which also meant that she took it home with her.

was at once warm and earnest, loving and kind, but her eyes were the eyes of one whose mind looked ahead to higher things.

"I have brought you a present" she said, and from the bag which lay beside her, she drew forth a garment, and held it out for him to see. "This is a special robe which reminds me that you are a priest now. I hope it will help to remind you too. This will be your special gift to wear while we are together, you and I, at the sanctuary. It is like the robe that Eli wears, but I have made it just for you." **42** She was glad that she had rightly estimated his height. Slipping the robe over his head and shoulders, she adjusted it upon his form until it fitted perfectly. Standing back, she looked at him intently, and then nodded with satisfaction. "It fits you well" she said, turning him around to see him from all angles. "And now, you must tell me what you have been doing at the sanctuary."

Hannah and her child

Hannah's action in clothing him with that robe was extraordinary. This was her peaceful yet powerful repudiation of Hophni and Phinehas, and their vile priesthood. Hannah could not openly oppose these men. She had no force at her disposal to order their removal, or to place them on trial. But she could place the little coat over the shoulders of her son, and in that simple act of quiet determination, she disassociated herself completely from their work and would have no part of it. The moment was so unobtrusive, and so natural between mother and child, that the sons of Eli would not have even noticed. Yet Hannah declared in that singular deed that she recognised Samuel as her sole legitimate priestly representative. He might be only little, but he was her priest in principle.

This was why she only brought up the little coat once in a year. The high priest did not always wear the robe of the ephod and the ephod, but only while he fulfilled his priestly office. Hannah sought to clothe Samuel for a similar purpose, but she was not proclaiming him to be the priestly representative for

---

42 See Appendix 5 – "What was the lesson of Hannah's little coat?" on page 225.

the nation. That would be a matter for God Himself to decide and for God Himself to confirm. But he could be her priest in prospect. And she claimed that right only in the context of her own appearance at the sanctuary once a year. At that moment, at that time, she declared her rejection of Hophni and Phinehas, even while submitting to their ungodly behaviour. But her resistance, silent yet strong, showed her absolute conviction that in this child lay the hope of a new and better priesthood.

The story of 'the mother and the child' that would echo into the New Testament and into one gospel especially, had its beginning here in the story of Hannah and Samuel. Her influence upon him was profound, and through this child, requested of God and returned unto Him, she brought spiritual deliverance to her people.

The little coat was his calling to office, and his mother would reinforce its meaning with more understanding each year, as she visited her son. And in clothing him so, she inspired him, for that one single action was so full of meaning, so rich with import, that it set the boy's heart alight for the rest of his life. Who but Hannah could have known how powerfully the story of the robe would operate upon her child? All that she intended was blessed by God, for what she did in faith truly set the direction of Samuel's entire life. He accepted the burden of responsibility which that robe put upon his shoulders, and in spirit he never put it off. The little coat became the mark and the badge of his special calling for the rest of his long and faithful life. [43] When Samuel was grown to manhood, his flowing mantle and flowing locks declared his priesthood, but not according to the order of Aaron. His priesthood came from a higher source. [44]

---

[43] The word for the little coat (*me-iyl*) is also the word used for the mantle which Samuel wore throughout his life, and for which he became famous (1 Samuel 15:27; 28:13,14).

[44] His priesthood was of Nazarite origin and therefore stood outside the Aaronic order. Its voluntary nature rendered it superior to the Aaronic priesthood in certain vital respects, relating to the character of the person so dedicated, and in all this Samuel would foreshadow the Lord.

6 |

Hannah and her hope

(1 Samuel 2:20-26)

AS her time with Samuel came to its close, Hannah felt again the same sense of impending loss that she had known on her previous journey home from Shiloh.[1] Her visit to the sanctuary had been filled with such purpose, that only now did the reality of departure bring its turmoil. It was to be another bitter-sweet moment. The sunlight of her joy at seeing Samuel would be darkened by the cloud of her sorrow at leaving him. She was even more convinced of the rightness of her actions, and not a little comforted that her boy was well, and even thriving in his new home. But now, she had to brace herself for the journey that would take her away from his side. Her thankfulness at his present state of safety, jostled with the emptiness of the long road to Ramah, and the even longer year which stretched out ahead of her before she would see her son again.

But before she and Elkanah left, there was to be a startling development that would transform her life, and lead her again into the light. Following their normal practice,[2] they rose early on the day of their departure to spend a last moment at the sanctuary. The morning service began by offering the daily lamb with its meal and drink offering.[3] The offering of the daily, was in turn the

---

1   Isaiah 49:15.
2   1 Samuel 1:19.
3   Exodus 29:39,40.

signal to burn the morning incense before the veil that was by the ark of the covenant. **⁴** It was customary for worshippers to await the priestly blessing, which followed the offering of the incense. To those who remained came the comforting words – "The LORD bless thee, and keep thee: the LORD make his face shine upon thee, and be gracious unto thee: the LORD lift up his countenance upon thee, and give thee peace". **⁵** Hannah knew those words, and treasured them as the climax of the meal which followed her peace offering. They embodied that exalted state of fellowship with her God that she sought so earnestly in her sanctuary visits.

The wonder of Eli's priestly blessing

> "And Eli blessed Elkanah and his wife, and said, The LORD give thee seed of this woman for the loan which is lent to the LORD. And they went unto their own home." (1 Samuel 2:20)

But this time, for Hannah, the priestly blessing would take an additional and altogether more wonderful form. As their visit came to an end, Eli, watching their preparations for departure moved forward to intercept them. **⁶** The words he was about to speak were not for the hearing of others, but for Elkanah and herself alone, and it was Eli who was anxious to initiate this meeting. Ineffective though he had been in disciplining his own sons, he clearly had an affinity for Samuel, and a genuine admiration for the spiritual integrity of his parents. Hannah especially commanded the respect of the old priest, and her appearance at the sanctuary a year after leaving Samuel there, prompted a warm response on his part. Her son had already profoundly touched him, as had her own example, and in this 'child of God' and his faithful mother, Eli saw all that he had lost in his own family. Eli had never forgotten his dramatic meetings

---

4   Exodus 30:6,7.
5   Numbers 6:22-27.
6   The juxtaposition of the phrases, "And Eli blessed Elkanah and his wife", followed by, "And they went unto their own home" (1 Samuel 2:20) suggests that this blessing was given at the point of their departure.

with this woman, nor the power of her amazing faith. The presence of Samuel at the sanctuary every day brought her story vividly back to his mind.

The magnitude of her gift so deeply affected him that he felt compelled to speak. As he looked upon the woman and her husband, Eli pronounced a blessing upon them. He spoke in his capacity as High Priest, and his words were more than the expression of a pious wish. They were given under divine inspiration, and with the prophetic insight of the Lord's spokesman, as the record would later confirm. [7] His priestly blessing would involve them both, but it was clear that the basis of the blessing related to Hannah's vow, and especially to her gift. [8] It was a moment that Hannah would remember ever after with deepest gratitude, that moment when Eli drew near to them both.

He began by addressing Elkanah, but almost immediately fixed his eyes on Hannah, [9] as he explained the reason for the divine blessing. The offspring to be promised were in return "for the loan which is lent to the LORD", and as Eli said this, a look of understanding passed between he and Hannah which could not be mistaken. [10] It was his promise to her in person that he recognised her offering, and acknowledged the child as God's. He would do what he could to watch over him on her behalf. Hannah then, was the cause of this spontaneous outpouring by Eli, as he foretold that the Lord Himself would bring a fulness of

---

[7] The High Priest was the channel of divine communication in Israel, and Eli's words were followed by the comment that the Lord did indeed visit Hannah in fulfilment of this message. This promise was of God (cp. John 11:51).

[8] Note the link between Hannah's words, "I am the woman that stood by thee here, praying unto the LORD" (1 Samuel 1:26), and Eli's, "the LORD give thee seed of this woman for the loan which is lent to the LORD" (1 Samuel 2:20).

[9] The natural reading of the passage would suggest that Eli directed his attention to Elkanah, but then looked directly at Hannah with the pronouncement of the words "give thee seed of this woman". It would have been quite incongruous to utter them whilst ignoring her.

[10] The scripture is decisive in this matter. The words of Hannah were – "the LORD hath given me my petition which I have asked of him: therefore also I have lent him to the LORD; as long as he liveth he shall be lent to the LORD" (1 Samuel 1:27,28). The loan was Hannah's, and the words of Eli were God's response to her loan.

recompense into their lives in return for her supreme gift – the gift of her firstborn son. Here was priestly intercession indeed.

Under the guidance of the Spirit, the terms of Eli's blessing evoked memories of an earlier occasion where a special woman was empowered to bear a special son in the purpose of God. [11] Ruth had been the subject of a similar blessing by the Lord. Her story was probably known to Hannah, its outcome a source of comfort to her now as she absorbed the wonder of Eli's words. She had every reason to believe him. After all, his previous intercession on her behalf had been heard. [12] Why should this blessing on his part not also be effective? How excited Hannah must have felt to hear this solemn proclamation. Here was the promise of repayment for her offering. She had not sought it, for her offering was unconditional, but it must have been a thing of wonder all the same.

Yet this blessing of children, following the giving of Samuel illustrated a principle. God has promised to reward the spirit of those who show care for others, and those who give to the poor are the subjects of His personal requital. [13] By what means and in what measure He might repay lies within His sovereign prerogative, but that He will do so, is a matter of testimony. In Hannah's case, she had given to alleviate the nation's spiritual poverty, and Eli's blessing was the proof that the Lord would recompense her work.

Nor was this a single act of blessing on Eli's part, heard only on this visit, when Hannah first brought her little coat. He was so moved by the giving of the child, that he repeated his blessing in successive years. [14] Each year Elkanah and Hannah made their pilgrimage, and each year Eli pronounced his priestly blessing upon them before they went home. Hannah's life was marked by a yearly

---

11 The account is certainly similar – "of the seed which the LORD shall give thee of this young woman. So Boaz took Ruth, and she was his wife: and when he went in unto her, the LORD gave her conception, and she bare a son" (Ruth 4:12,13).
12 1 Samuel 1:17-19.
13 Psalm 112:9; Proverbs 19:17; 22:9; 28:27.
14 That this was not a single act on Eli's part is evidenced by the text. Rotherham – "And Eli used to bless Elkanah and his wife and say"; RSV – "Eli would bless Elkanah and his wife … then they would return to their home".

celebration of Samuel's priestly work, and a yearly promise of further fruitfulness. How aglow with happiness she must have been on her journey home to Ramah, not only this time, but in subsequent years as well. The Lord had made His face to shine upon His Handmaid.

A family of three sons and two daughters

> "And the LORD visited Hannah, so that she conceived, and bare three sons and two daughters. And the child Samuel grew before the LORD." (1 Samuel 2:21)

Upon Hannah then came the blessing of divine visitation and favour, similar not only to Ruth, but reminiscent of Sarah of old. Like Sarah, Hannah suffered from an impediment to conception, which prevented her from bearing children. [15] And like Sarah, the reversal of that predicament came by means of the visitation of God in her life. [16] The result was a child of special significance and destiny, Samuel being in his generation another Isaac. But this promise that came upon her now concerned the bringing forth of further offspring, in a blessing that was centred on Hannah herself. [17] This time the promise of seed was the promise of an entire family, made possible in the firstborn son who had been given. They would be brought into being because of he who had gone before them. In a sense, they owed their existence to him, in a way which would be true also of Christ's brethren. [18] And these five, like Samuel, would all count Hannah as their mother.

The birth and nurture and weaning of Samuel had aroused all of Hannah's maternal traits. His giving left her as a woman

---

15 Their respective accounts show the similarity. Sarah (Genesis 11:30; 16:2; Romans 4:19), and Hannah (1 Samuel 1:2,5,6). Both women needed the divine hand upon them.

16 The account here that "the LORD visited Hannah, so that she conceived and bare" is a direct echo of Sarah's experience – "And the LORD visited Sarah as he had said … For Sarah conceived and bare" (Genesis 21:1,2). These are the only two women in scripture who are said to have been visited by God to enable their conception.

17 Notice the way in which the phrase, "And Eli blessed Elkanah" is given its sequel in the succeeding phrase, "And the LORD visited Hannah" (1 Samuel 2:20,21).

18 Hebrews 2:11,12.

yearning for motherhood, but unable to express it. And as the mother that she had already proved herself to be, it was in the justice and love of God that He visited His Handmaid in fulfilment of the words of prophecy given by His priest. The measure of the Lord's recompense was gracious indeed, for unto Hannah He gave five children in return for her one. In these five children, who would be rightfully hers to raise at home, Hannah received a full measure of the Father's grace upon her. In the goodness of God, Hannah's life, from the time Samuel was left at the sanctuary, was filled with the pleasure of child rearing for many years. The aching void that had been in her heart was filled by a loving God who thereby honoured His Handmaid.

But none of these, despite their excellent upbringing, would play any part in the purpose of God, such as would be recorded in the book of books. Their lives may have been of the highest standard of godliness, given their godly parents, but only Samuel would receive a mention. The Bible was not a record of family history, or of personal achievement, but was instead the chronicle of divine purpose. Both Hannah and Samuel would only find their place in holy writ because of the part they each played in the greater plan of God.

The arrival of five more children spanned a period of several years. [19] It was a busy time in Hannah's life. Her burgeoning household of precious children brought such fulfilment and happiness, that Hannah felt her cup was running over. And no matter how small her children were, even the babe in arms was brought on the sacred visit each year to the sanctuary. It was a mark of their faithfulness, that their visits did not cease. Their spirit of dedication had always brought them to the place where God met with His people. But now, the importance of seeing Samuel again, and observing his growth gave added impetus to their journeys. On several of these visits, Hannah had a new brother or sister to

---

19 It may be estimated that this was at least ten years. Mothers nursed their offspring for longer in ancient times, and the cycle of bearing children was likewise extended. Keturah bore six sons, and (based on the assumption that they came between Ishmael and Isaac) did so over a period of thirteen years (Genesis 25:2; 16:16; 17:1).

introduce to Samuel, and he became aware of his family connections, which were strengthened with each passing year. Eli also saw these little ones, and rejoiced to know that the Almighty had blessed this woman and her husband with the fruit of the womb.

When Hannah brought these children with her to Shiloh, they learned that although Samuel was their brother, he lived at the sanctuary, and had his place and daily tasks at the tabernacle. It was strange for them to meet him there, but they needed to understand that their older brother was called to a special calling, and that even now, he was involved in the work of his Father. He was of their household, and yet he was different. Their experience would be shared in another age by another family from Nazareth, who also had to learn of their older brother's higher calling in God's sight. [20] Despite the lively bustle of these times, and the busy activity of her household, Hannah never forgot to bring the little coat to Shiloh each year for the continued instruction of her firstborn. The gracious provision of other children did not deviate her from her purpose in Samuel. This child was still the embodiment of her highest spiritual objectives, and already to her observant eye, he was a child no longer, but a lad with the first signs of manhood upon him. Each year, she noticed every change, and was content that her early instruction had laid deep foundations for his entire life. [21]

But his instruction now lay with another, for while Hannah lived in Ramah, and rejoiced to raise her other sons and daughters, Samuel remained in God's special care. The transfer was complete. He was a son in his Father's house now, made possible by the sacrifice of his mother who had surrendered him to the future she believed in. In that house, he abode under the shadow of the Almighty, and in that secret place, he grew before the Lord. This was His son now, and He would mark the stages of his development. Every year he increased in wisdom and in

---

20 John 7:2-5.

21 Early childhood development studies have noted the critical importance of the first three years in a child's life, as setting the basis for their entire future. It was these three years of fervent nurture that Hannah gave as a lifetime gift to her son. Their power to direct should not be underestimated.

stature, and God was fully involved in the raising of the child. [22] He did not just grow before the Lord, but grew with Him. [23] How wonderfully was Hannah's confidence in giving her son to God vindicated. All that was necessary for the child's care and growth was provided by Him who neither slumbers nor sleeps. He would be the boy's keeper, and He would preserve him from all evil, both in his going out and his coming in. [24]

The woman that assembled at the door

> "Now Eli was very old, and heard all that his sons did unto all Israel; and how they lay with the women that assembled at the door of the tabernacle of the congregation." (1 Samuel 2:22)

The males of all three families of the Levites, Kohath, Gershon and Merari were appointed to the charge of the sanctuary. But the work assigned to these men demanded such commitment and loyalty to God, such effort and endeavour, that their calling became a commission to the warfare of the tabernacle service. [25] Whatever their specific duties might have been, they were seen to be engaged in the warfare of God's truth. Mustered and assembled, organised and conscripted for service, these Levites in their collective multitude constituted the hosts of God. [26] The military figure of the fighting hosts and their serried ranks of

---

22 God used an agency of course, in the form of Eli and others, who taught Samuel. But the record indicates that God nevertheless was the real superintendent of the child's growth, consistent with the higher purpose He had marked out for Samuel.

23 The word "before" here (*im* not *paniym*) is better translated this way. Hence Rotherham – "Thus did the boy Samuel grow up with Yahweh".

24 Psalm 121:4-8.

25 Their appointment is recorded with the term *tsaba*, which is rendered as both host, and (margin) warfare (Numbers 4:3,23,30). Similarly, the law prescribing their length of active service uses the same term *tsaba* (Numbers 8:24-26).

26 The following note is instructive – "*tsaba* has to do with fighting [but] it has also a wider use in the sense of rendering service. Interestingly four uses have to do with the work of the Levites in the tent of meeting. No doubt service for Yahweh is seen as involving total dedication and careful regimentation, and since God is Yahweh of hosts, enthroned between the cherubim housed inside the tent of meeting, work associated with the tent may be considered spiritual war" – (*Theological Wordbook of the Old Testament*, page 750).

soldiers, was echoed in the order and control of these ministers of the sanctuary. There was something very disciplined about their labours, for the service of the tabernacle required a great deal of organisation and routine for its proper continuance. That spirit of warfare would find its counterpart in the structure and activity of the ecclesias of God in later times. [27]

But there were females associated with this battle as well, for from the beginning there were willing-hearted women who gave gifts for the tabernacle. [28] Some went further, for even before the Levites were set to their tasks, there was a company of devoted women who loved the Truth with such fervour that they assembled at the door of the tabernacle of the congregation. These gave their looking-glasses unto Moses for the fashioning of the laver, renouncing the outward adorning to uphold the principle of inward washing.

If the Levites were God's hosts, then these faithful women were God's troops, [29] for they also had come to war the warfare, and to devote themselves to the sanctuary. Their work may have included some role as porters at the entranceway, with their companies as troops replacing one another that a group might always be on watch in that place. [30] As time progressed however and the routine of tabernacle worship was established, the men

---

[27] It is more than possible that this theme of spiritual warfare (*tsaba*) forms an Old Testament basis for the apostolic expression – "This charge I commit unto thee, son Timothy ... that thou by them mightest war a good warfare" (1 Timothy 1:18).

[28] Exodus 35:22-29.

[29] The reference to these devoted women occurs before the distribution of Levitical tasks noted in the early chapters of Numbers (Exodus 38:8). The expression – "the *women* assembling, which assembled at the door of the tabernacle of the congregation", is given in the margin as "assembled by troops". This is correct, as the word here is another participle of *tsaba*.

[30] The phrase "assembled at the door" (Exodus 38:8) suggests this. GLT – "the serving women, those assembling who served at the door". That their service might originally have involved an aspect of door keeping is consistent with the role of women in other passages who were used in this capacity. The LXX refers to a female porter in the house of Ishbosheth (2 Samuel 4:6, cp. also Josephus: *Ant*. book 7, chapter 2, paragraph 1). A damsel kept the door at the palace of the High Priest (John 18:16,17), and Rhoda acted as the porter in the house where the ecclesia met (Acts 12:13).

were confirmed as the porters in their office, [31] whilst other tasks would naturally fall to the lot of these women who dedicated themselves in such a way. These holy women spent their lives in devotion to spiritual things. Sanctuary worship involved holy instruments, holy utensils, holy garments, and holy provisions, and there were daily tasks required for the use and maintenance of all these. Whether in making, or cleansing, or preparing; whether in fasting, or praying, or singing, they served at the sanctuary, and contributed to the spiritual life of the nation which was centred in that place.

To these honourable women were added yet others who augmented their numbers for the work of ministration. During the battle against Midian, Moses placed a levy upon the womenfolk who were captured, which provided female ministers for the service of the tabernacle, all of whom were virgins. [32] It is likely that most of these remained unmarried, and attached to the tabernacle as part of the retinue of sanctuary servants. They appear to have been present at Shiloh in an earlier time of the judges, [33] and even now in Hannah's time, such godly attendants evidently still resided in the tabernacle compound. [34] A handmaid, who probably waited on the priests, was employed as a message bearer in David's time. [35] The building of the house of God under Solomon did not alter this practice, as the temple arrangements were of such greater magnitude, that the need for ministrants was only increased. The work and the role of such virgins continued through many generations, for centuries later at the overthrow of Jerusalem by the Babylonians, the sacking

---

[31] 1 Chronicles 9:19-27.

[32] The women spared were all virgins (Numbers 31:35), of whom thirty-two were placed under the authority of Eleazar as High Priest elect (Numbers 31:40,41), and three hundred and twenty were given to the Levites for assistance in the service of the tabernacle (Numbers 31:47).

[33] Judges 21:19-21.

[34] The phrase used – "the women that assembled at the door of the tabernacle" (1 Samuel 2:22) clearly suggests a continuity of practice from the time of Moses (Exodus 38:8).

[35] 2 Samuel 17:17.

of the temple was mourned as a national calamity which affected both the priests and the virgins of the sanctuary.[36]

There was a special degree of dedication in such virgins. Exempt from the commitments of family life, they focused on the privilege of ministering, devoted in their work to attend upon the Lord without distraction. The example of these faithful ministers survived even to the time of Christ,[37] and within the ecclesias there would be women who served in similar devotion, and with apostolic approval. Their highest joy was to care for the things that belong to the Lord,[38] and "freedom in service I would find" was the song of their life.

The "women who assembled at the door" then, was a phrase expressive of the highest spirit of dedication. Here were women, "holy in both body and spirit", who gave themselves in service so completely, that their lives were an offering of praise. In all they did, they did it as unto the Lord, and for the sake of His honour.

It was these women that Hophni and Phinehas committed immorality with. It seemed incomprehensible. Perhaps they were far removed from the godly spirit of those who gave their mirrors to Moses in rejecting the vanity of outward appearance. If so, then they were but a reflection of how far the Truth had fallen in the time of Eli's sons. But, given the special character of these godly and faithful ministers, it is far more likely that these women, dependent as they were on priestly approval for their food, and clothing, and lodging, had been bluntly told

---

[36] "All her gates are desolate: her priests sigh, her virgins are afflicted, and she is in bitterness" (Lamentations 1:4). The mention of priests and virgins together is unique to this passage, and indicates that even five hundred years after Hannah's time there was still a contingent of faithful women associated with the matters of sanctuary worship.

[37] The example of Anna being witness, of whom it states – "she … departed not from the temple, but served God with fastings and prayers night and day" (Luke 2:37).

[38] The apostolic advice on virgins centred on how they might care for the things of the Lord, that they might be "holy both in body and spirit" (1 Corinthians 7:32-35). Paul's counsel on their ability to attend to the matters of the Truth without the distraction of other cares, may well have been drawn from the example of these holy women who served in Old Testament times in both tabernacle and temple.

that more was expected of them if they wanted to remain. For such, with no other place of abode or livelihood, their situation was made precarious by their very devotion to the tabernacle system. Vulnerable, and unable to defend their cause, they may have been compelled to acquiesce against their will. If this were true, then it marked the depth of depravity which these evil men had descended to. There could be nothing more despicable than that those who upheld the holiness of the sanctuary should themselves be the subject of such an offence by the priests of that sanctuary. Hannah, married, and safely living in Ramah with her own family obligations was not present at the tabernacle to witness such depravity, but in spirit she belonged there. She had heard of this terrible behaviour against the women who assembled, and felt their same sense of violation.

Eli's last witness against his sons

> "And he said unto them, Why do ye do such things? For I hear of your evil dealings by all this people. Nay, my sons; for it is no good report that I hear: ye make the LORD's people to transgress." (1 Samuel 2:23,24)

At some point, Eli's age prevented him from supervising all the tabernacle activities personally. Since there was no term of office for high priests, only death or illness prevented his continued service. [39] There must have been a gradual stepping back from more strenuous activities however, occasioned by Eli's increasing infirmity and frailty. In the end, the tinkling of the golden bells which signified that the high priest ministered in the sanctuary was heard no more. [40] The sounds of his service were silenced, stilled by the fact that he could no longer stand, but took instead his place as an observer only, whilst sitting on his seat. [41]

---

39 Numbers 35:25,28; Joshua 20:6.
40 The robe of the ephod had golden bells attached to the hem, that sounded as the High Priest walked (Exodus 28:33-35).
41 The cessation of Eli's activity is implied in the references to his seat (1 Samuel 1:9; 4:13). Eli was no longer 'standing to minister'.

But even before that time had come, his sons had established a corrupt form of worship which he had neglected to challenge, and failed to check. Now his advanced years made it impossible for him to reverse it. He was no longer in charge. The sons of Belial were in control. From where he sat, he did hear of all their evil dealings, for the people came to make their complaint before him. He could not pretend to be ignorant of those things which were common knowledge, nor could he deny those sins which so many in Israel had informed him of. He knew beyond doubt that their spirit was very wrong. But there had been too many occasions where Eli had not 'frowned upon them' in rebuke. [42] Both as High Priest and as their father, he had the authority to curb their evil, and if necessary to remove them from office. But this he would not do, and in the end, that failure to correct and to discipline enabled their poor behaviour to be imbedded in their characters. There was nothing to the credit of Eli in this matter. His unwillingness to direct his sons in the way of truth was a sin against God, a sin against his people, a sin against his sons, and a sin against himself.

Now at the last however, after years of wilful neglect, something caused the old priest to speak with his sons in rebuke. Perhaps the presence of the child at Shiloh and the visits of his mother contributed to Eli's final protest. Prompted by her holiness and Samuel's godliness, his conscience was stirred to perceive the full iniquity of his sons, and stirred sufficiently to utter a last despairing witness against them. It was of course too late. The horrifying story of the virgins defiled proved that his sons had reached the point of no return. Nothing would now deviate them from their chosen course of action. Their father was powerless to stop what he himself had first condoned, and even this final remonstrance was far too mild to bring about change. He had brought neither his power nor his authority to bear on their discipline and guidance, and it would be to his ruin and theirs. The charge of too little, too late, lay upon Eli, and God would hold him to account for that failure.

---

42 1 Samuel 3:13 (see margin).

When matters of wrong doctrine or wrong conduct are made manifest in ecclesial life, the answer never lies in ignoring them. Wrong, left unchallenged, spreads and widens – it never diminishes. It is a strange perversity within human nature, that justifies leaving such ills unchallenged. Many a heartache in the ecclesia of the living God has occurred because changes to the detriment of the Truth have been introduced, and left undealt with. The mistaken idea that such problems will resolve themselves leads to compromise under the guise of compassion. Seeking to guard the heritage of the Truth is not an invitation to be aggressive or confrontational. All our dealings must be conducted in the spirit of Christ, and in a manner as becometh saints. But the Truth is of such precious value that when a matter arises which strikes at the foundation of our faith, to turn a blind eye or a deaf ear, is to be complicit by that silence which becomes consent. This was Eli's sin, made darker by its contrast with the light of Hannah's quiet but determined striving against the same evil, which he would not oppose.

Ye make the Lord's people to transgress

The tragedy of Eli's lack of leadership lay not just in the fact that his own sons became wayward, but in the spread of spiritual decline they caused within the nation. His poor example in wilfully disregarding the wrong of his sons had brought this evil consequence upon all Israel that came to worship. "I hear of your evil dealings by all this people" he said, and condemned himself by this admission. Their wickedness was so notorious that it was evidenced by widespread and general complaint. The life led by the priests so publicly in the sanctuary with their scornful abuse of holy ordinances, [43] and their unblushing immorality, [44] had corrupted the inner religious life of the whole nation, so as to make them transgress.

That transgression was seen in a people where some cried out [45] in either pain or protest at priests who violated God's

---

[43] 1 Samuel 2:12-17.
[44] 1 Samuel 2:22,23.
[45] See margin for "to transgress" where the alternative is "to cry out" (1 Samuel 2:24).

law and profaned His holy things. Foremost among these was Hannah, who cried out indeed, but directed her cry to God, and sought to be part of His answer. Others no longer wished to honour God or to worship Him, for they abhorred the offering of the Lord. [46] The wickedness and excess of the priests had led them to such despair that they no longer came to the sanctuary at all. When the effect of God's priests was to cause others to cease their worship, [47] then this was a sin of the worst kind. Still others delighted to follow the corrupt teaching of the priests, and join a form of worship so far removed from God's holy law that it was a travesty of His teaching. Yet even in rebuke, Eli was sadly ineffective. "Nay, my sons; it is no good report that I hear: ye make the LORD's people to transgress" he said, but his words lacked power, and in the absence of any consequences would bring about no change.

Here was the source of Hannah's grief, and the reason for her actions. She believed that the impact of these men in destroying the spiritual worship of the nation was inexcusable in those who knew better. Of all those in Israel, the priests held a special responsibility to guide the people aright. Moses had delivered the law into "the hands of the priests the sons of Levi, which bare the ark". [48] To them fell the task of reading the law before all Israel, that they might hear, and learn, and fear, and do. Upon them came the work of reading distinctly in the law of God, to give the sense and cause the hearers to understand the reading. Hannah herself had most probably heard the book of the law, as it was read in the solemnity of the year of release in the feast of tabernacles. [49] She, personally felt the sacredness of that

---

[46] 1 Samuel 2:17.

[47] The phrase – "ye make the LORD's people to transgress" (*abar* – to pass beyond) is translated by LXX – "ye make Yahweh's people cease to worship him".

[48] The connection between the teaching of the law and the care of the ark revealed how special was the charge which lay upon the priestly tribe (Deuteronomy 31:9). If the ark was the symbol of the divine presence among His people, then the law was the sign of the divine will and mind in their midst. The priest's role to teach God's will, and faithfully handle His law was their highest duty.

[49] Deuteronomy 31:10-12.

charge as a member of the priestly tribe, [50] but Eli did not guard the responsibilities of the priesthood with sufficient zeal to hold his sons accountable.

The principal task of the priests in Israel was to set forth the law of God in truth, and their sternest condemnation came because of their failure to do so. [51] For Hophni and Phinehas not only to sin in their own lives, but cause others to go astray, was a double sin, and a rejection of all that their priesthood implied. Many generations later, a prophet of God would describe the evil of the priests in his own day with these scathing words – "For the priest's lips should keep knowledge, and they should seek the law at his mouth: for he is the messenger of the LORD of hosts. But ye are departed out of the way; ye have caused many to stumble at the law; ye have corrupted the covenant of Levi, saith the LORD of hosts". [52] Alas, the spirit of Hophni and Phinehas would live on beyond their own age, and corrupt generations yet to come. The condemnation that was about to be uttered against the sons of Eli would come down upon the heads of these priests who followed them, and the same God to whom Hannah addressed her vow, would judge them. Their destiny would be decided by the Lord of hosts, and they would not escape.

Notwithstanding they hearkened not

> "If one man sin against another, the judge shall judge him: but if a man sin against the LORD, who shall intreat for him? Notwithstanding they hearkened not unto the voice of their father, because the LORD would slay them."   (1 Samuel 2:25)

---

50 As witnessed by her vow, her loan, her speech, her song, her visits, her coat. In all the major episodes of Hannah's life there would be continual references to the teaching of the Law of Moses. It was evident that Hannah passionately believed in the law of her God, and acted in accordance with its requirements.

51 Hence this recurring refrain throughout the prophets – "the priests ... that handle the law knew me not" (Jeremiah 2:8), "her priests have violated my law" (Ezekiel 22:26), "thou shalt be no priest to me: seeing thou hast forgotten the law of thy God" (Hosea 4:6,9), "her priests ... have done violence to the law" (Zephaniah 3:4).

52 Malachi 2:7,8.

The sins of Hophni and Phinehas had left them alienated from the Lord. They did not understand that reality, and even less did they grasp the consequences of their estrangement. For priests of the Lord to be at variance with He whom they served, was to place themselves in an invidious position. Eli knew it, and sought to warn them just how perilous their state was. His warning was a proverb which struck at the heart of their dilemma.

When one man sinned against another, God interposed to pass sentence and settle the dispute. [53] Controversy between individuals was made subject to the sentence of the law, that the righteous might be justified and the wicked condemned. [54] But in the case of a man's sin in defiance against the Lord, who could interpose between the Almighty and the one who sinned against Him? When their opponent in controversy was the Lord Himself, who indeed could intercede for them. [55] No man could stand between the parties as mediator or advocate, God's sovereign majesty could not permit it. At best, a sinner might have sought the intercession of the Lord's priest. But in the case of Hophni and Phinehas, who had personally sinned against the Lord, who could they go to for intercession? They already were the priests. In the matter of their sin, there was no one who could interpose, none who could intreat God on their behalf. Their sins had left them defenceless before the judgment of God, and there was none to deliver. Eli pleaded with his sons to realise the enormous predicament they had placed themselves in.

---

[53] In the text of the phrase "the judge shall judge him" the noun is *Elohim*. Most translations render it as God, which is consistent with the context. It is true that He judged the case by means of his earthly representatives, who bore the name of *Elohim* (Exodus 22:8,9,28; Psalm 82:1-8), but through their agency, God Himself became the arbitrator.

[54] Disagreements between brother and brother were to be brought before the priests who clearly acted on God's behalf to judge in such matters (Deuteronomy 17:8-13; 19:17-19; 25:1).

[55] To "judge" and to "intreat" here are both the word *palal*. The force of the proverb lies in the use of the same word, but in different voices. The first "shall judge him" is in the *Piel* and means to arbitrate. The second "shall intreat for him" is in the *Hithpael* and means to mediate. In the first, to intervene, in the second to intercede.

But if they were unable to intercede for their own sins, then they were unable to intreat for others also. Their special role as intercessors for Israel was made null and void by their evil. Hannah knew this. It was part of her adversity, that the nation had been deprived of their appointed means of approach to God through the blessing of priesthood. This was one of the very things that she sought for in seeking another priest that might arise in Israel. And truly, the answer of God in the provision of Samuel, and her subsequent visits after he had been dedicated, only confirmed everything she had ever thought. The only difference was, that now she could bear with equanimity the wickedness of that place, she could suffer the evil of their priesthood, in the knowledge that the Lord of hosts was at work, and that a foundation for change had already been laid.

Eli's proverb was chilling in its implications, and cautionary indeed, but it utterly failed in its effect. The problem was that their evil was imbedded. These were not occasional lapses in the behaviour of his sons, but the marks of a deliberate and habitual pattern of conduct. Their characters were so bad, that the remedy lay beyond words. Action was needed, both resolute and decisive, but Eli would not act to remove them from office. This was his besetting sin, and his sons, aware of his weakness, were scornful of his rebuke and despised his warning.

His proverb became a prophecy as his admonition fell on deaf ears, and his sons sealed their own fate by their refusal to take his warning. So stubborn was their attitude, and so recalcitrant their spirit that it was the desire of the Lord Himself to kill them. [56] How terrifying to contemplate an attitude so obnoxious to God, that He Himself desired to terminate their lives. It was not He that prevented them from hearing their father's warning, but their own attitude. A spirit of continual

---

[56] The Hebrew is much stronger than the KJV. ASV – "because Yahweh was minded to slay them", GLT – "because Yahweh desired to execute them", YLT – "Yahweh hath delighted to put them to death".

and wilful disobedience had now hardened into that obstinate impenitence that could only lead to punishment. [57]

Hannah had understood all this, for she discerned what Eli did not or could not see. She saw that their spirit was unchangeable, and that their overthrow was inevitable. As the faithful Handmaid of the Highest she had correctly discerned His will and wish in the matter. How was it that she knew God's view with such clarity? It was because she saw the entire matter through His eyes and His only. Her attitude towards Hophni and Phinehas was not based upon her personal feelings, but upon His teaching. The law of her God furnished Hannah with her spiritual standards and her scriptural principles. She looked to the law, and recognised an earlier event which told only too clearly what God's view was on unfaithful priests.

The house of Aaron had been chosen for the priesthood, but his two oldest sons disgraced their office. The story of those unfaithful sons, and their swift and terrible overthrow, gave Hannah cause to believe that God would act in this matter also. [58] If the strange fire and strong drink of Nadab and Abihu brought the fire of the Lord down upon them, [59] then what might Hophni

---

[57] The apparent conflict between human free will and divine foreknowledge is reconciled in the sovereign ability of God to move in the affairs of men without subverting the former, and yet recognising the latter. Hence – "for it was of the LORD to harden their hearts" (Joshua 11:20), "it was of the LORD that he sought an occasion" (Judges 14:4), "for the cause was from the LORD that he might perform his saying" (1 Kings 12:15), "for it came of God, that he might deliver them into the hand of their enemies" (2 Chronicles 25:20). In each instance, God acted only after the attitude of refusal to hear was self-evident. So likewise, here – "Notwithstanding they hearkened not unto the voice of their father, because the LORD would slay them" (1 Samuel 2:25).

[58] The history of Aaron and his family would become the very theme of the prophecy of the Man of God which follows (1 Samuel 2:27-29). Given that his words would give strong endorsement to Hannah, it is more than likely that Hannah herself had thought about the lessons from Aaron's own family, and especially from his two oldest sons, and seen the implications of that judgment which awaited Hophni and Phinehas.

[59] The strange fire of Nadab and Abihu (Leviticus 10:1) offered whilst intoxicated (Leviticus 10:9), resulted in their instant death (Leviticus 10:2), and a principle for priests set down as the basis of their approach before the Lord, "This is it that the

and Phinehas receive whose sins were so much the worse? Hannah already knew the answer, with prophetic insight before it was come – "out of heaven shall he thunder upon them". [60]

And now, God Himself had endorsed her song, and would soon act to bring it all to pass. What she did not know yet, but soon would, was that the judgment ordained of God was very close, for the day of the Lord was near and hasted greatly. The nation stood on the edge of tremendous change, a change brought about by one woman and her faith. Hannah was not the determiner of that change, for that rested in God's sovereign control. But she had been His instrument to effect the change, and now, with Samuel in his appointed place, the Lord was ready to work the work which His Handmaid had sought. Her son was the key, and so crucial was the presence of the child to the advancing of God's plan, that His special care lay upon him whilst in Shiloh.

The mysterious guardian of the child

> "And the child Samuel grew on, and was in favour both with the LORD and also with men." (1 Samuel 2:26)

Hophni and Phinehas might have been on the verge of divine rejection, but already it was seen that Samuel stood in their place. Still only at the end of childhood, he was old beyond his years, as his integrity and faithfulness became evident. There was a paradox here, for the priests in this place were evil to their core. The honour of the sacrifices was corrupted by greed, and the worship of the sanctuary was defiled by immorality. Shiloh was a place of spiritual desolation, and its iniquity had come to the point of no return. And yet, Samuel walked through the midst of all this, and appeared to live a charmed life. He was surrounded by wickedness, yet seemed to be beyond its power, for no evil touched him, and no harm reached him. How came it so, that the little Levite trod in such safety?

LORD spake, saying, I will be sanctified in them that come nigh unto me, and before all the people I will be glorified" (Leviticus 10:3).

60 Her own song had spoken of it – "heaven" here signifying God's personal, direct and sovereign response (1 Samuel 2:10).

There was something more than Eli's hand at work here, for despite his assurance to Hannah concerning the care of her son, much more was needed than what the aged priest could provide. What after all was the greatest need of the child, still so very young, and separated from the warmth and safety of his home, a child who was still in need of care and nurture? This little one still needed help to eat and drink, to sleep and rise, to wash and dress, to speak and read, to sing and pray, to learn and grow. What one thing did he truly need, more than anything else? Why the guardian care of a mother in Israel. And the Lord in His goodness provided such a woman, a virgin at the tabernacle who was ready, so ready to be a mother to the child. [61]

There were signs here of a woman, who as his guardian angel watched his every step, her fierce determination to shield the child, the equal of his mother's. Time after time, the boy was shepherded away from sights and scenes that would trouble his pure and innocent mind. The providence of God provided shelter and shadow, as He has always done for His own. But that providence was manifested in the instrument of God's special choice, and that choice had been made before Samuel had even been conceived. The ways of God are far above our own, for He works in realms of space and time beyond our comprehension. Before Hannah besought the Lord of hosts for a man child, Jephthah's daughter had been dedicated at the sanctuary. She had no idea when submitting willingly to her father's vow, what the consequences of her faithfulness would be. But God did, and was even then preparing for the next stage of His purpose.

There is both wisdom and economy in all the arrangements of God. Here, in one moment of time, God brought the needs of three people into focus. In one action, so glorious in its simplicity, Samuel was protected, Hannah was comforted, and Jephthah's daughter was fulfilled. Never, never could she have dreamed of such a possibility at the time she bewailed her virginity. Never, never could she have known, that even then, the Almighty was

---

[61] See Appendix 6 – "Who was the guardian of Hannah's firstborn son?" on page 228.

shaping events so that she might be the right person in the right place at the right time. The ways of the Lord are inscrutable in their wisdom. Ours is to bow before His prescience with thankful hearts that He knows all.

Hannah, having met this faithful woman, saw in her the divine answer as to how God would care for the child she had loaned to Him. She had always believed, with implicit trust, that He would, but to know how He would do it was a mother's special need. And God who knew the end from the beginning had already prepared the way before Hannah first made request. If she fulfilled her vow and gave her child to Him, He had made ready to receive him. It is humbling to contemplate that the same principle is true in our lives. In our prayers to the Father, what we might imagine is the postponement of His response, is but the adjustment of our timetable to His, until the circumstances are right. If His answer to our request is affirmative, then with it, we may have confidence that the means will already be to hand.

Under this divinely provided canopy of care, Samuel grew in favour both with God and also with men. The result was a child who stirred the heart of his people. They were gladdened at the sign of one who took the worship of the tabernacle so seriously, and already the faithful saw in him the hope of the future. [62] The divine answer to the wickedness of the age lay in a little child who slept peacefully at the house of the Lord.

Hannah and her hope

It would seem unnecessary to report that the child grew. And yet the record would state with threefold emphasis that Samuel did so. [63] His development was noted, for this was Hannah's hope. She hoped that her son would grow into the one through whom God would work. She hoped that her son would be the priest through whom the nation could approach. But for her hope to be realised, it needed him to grow into manhood and into priesthood. Only

---

[62] 1 Samuel 3:20,21.
[63] 1 Samuel 2:21,26; 3:19.

in maturity could he begin to confront the wrong and establish the right. Only as a man could he bring about the dramatic change that would redirect the nation, and until that man arose, the evil of Hophni and Phinehas would continue.

Hannah understood the reality. These men showed no spirit of remorse and even less of repentance. The only way forward lay in their replacement, and this was what she sought. Others saw the influence of Hophni and Phinehas as the present reality. They might have sorrowed at the wrong, yet never once thought about how it might be reversed. People were divided into those who despaired and those who did not care. But none of these saw beyond the problem to its resolution. Hannah did, and in recognising that the nation's only hope lay in the removal and the replacement of these men, she made that her hope, and directed her prayers unto the Lord of hosts to that end. Her capacity to discern the need and then to act for its accomplishment was what made her unique.

How easy it would have been, having petitioned heaven for the man who could bring about this revolution, to be completely focused on him and his immediate work. After all, the man in question was her beloved son, who had been granted in answer to her prayers. But Hannah's vision was not restricted to the changes that Samuel might bring. This woman, whose mind could ascend to higher things, had already anticipated one to come after the order of Melchizedek, and in the same breath had spoken of the resurrection. Only later would it be revealed that the priest of that order must be immortal in nature. Both psalm and epistle would speak as one concerning that priest whose office was only secured by his resurrection to an endless life. [64]

Yet, before these had been written, Hannah had seen him already, spoken of him, hoped for him, and believed in him. To

---

[64] "From the womb of the morning: thou hast the dew of thy youth" (Psalm 110:3,4). "Who is made, not after the law of a carnal commandment, but after the power of an endless life. For he testifieth, Thou art a priest forever after the order of Melchisedec" (Hebrews 7:16,17).

see beyond Samuel from the outset, was something that virtually no one else would have done. But what Hannah envisaged, and how she thought, left an example that could only astonish and humble. She believed that her child was but a figure of one still to come, and saw far enough ahead to contemplate the true. What else might she have known about the meaning of Messiah's future work? What else did she see, reaching forward into the mysteries of Melchizedek? Surely, she stood as a separated one in Israel in this time of spiritual darkness, alone in the breadth of her understanding, and in the depth of her yearning.

Samuel, her Shiloh child, was followed by three brothers and two sisters, giving Hannah a total of six children. The blessing of but one more would have given her a quiver full. But in the divine wisdom, the Lord left her short of the fulness of that number, one short of the seventh, that she might live in hope. Hannah herself would have to wait, as she looked for the one whose coming she believed in. But when he did come, he would be the fulness of all that she had spoken of, the completion of all that Samuel could but faintly foreshadow. This one would not be her child, but he would be begotten by the same principle of divine visitation that produced Hannah's first. In a way, he would be counted as Hannah's seventh, since in him, all her prayers as the Handmaid of the Highest would be made complete.

She would not see him in her mortal life, but had she been in Israel when he that should come, did come, it is certain that she would have been among those who cried out in wonder – "For unto *us* a child is born, unto *us* a son is given". In that child, in that son, Hannah's hope would be realised, and she would be satisfied.

7 |

Hannah and her priest

(1 Samuel 2:27-36)

SAMUEL was still quite young when Eli was visited by a man of God.[1] The visitation was unexpected, as were many such appearances from divine spokesmen,[2] and the occasion remarkable, for only once before in all the times of the judges had such a man been sent to warn his people.[3] This man however, came not to warn the nation, but to utter a prophecy that directly concerned Eli and his sons. Despite his message being delivered in person, his words would neither exonerate nor excuse the old priest. His speech instead was stern and uncompromising, as he proclaimed the impending judgment of God upon Eli's household. Although his words were directed to the priest of Israel, all that he said confirmed the deep concern and righteous indignation that Hannah herself had felt.[4]

In keeping with the spirit of divine intervention which

---

1   The timing of the narrative, following on immediately after the report of Samuel's childhood growth suggests this (1 Samuel 2:26).
2   1 Kings 13:1,2; 20:38-43, etc.
3   The episode in Judges 6:7-10 appears to be the only other occasion of an earthly messenger during this epoch, in contrast to angelic visitations (Judges 2:1-5; 6:11-21; 13:3,9,13; etc.).
4   The focus of 1 Samuel 1,2 is centred on the life and story of Hannah. That the account of the man of God comes at the end of her story is not accidental. Its placement in the narrative indicates that his message represented the culmination of Hannah's work and purpose. Read with that proper perspective, the message was God's endorsement of His Handmaid, who had always sought to serve her Master's cause.

he symbolised, the man of God appeared from parts unknown, and when his message was delivered, disappeared without trace. He was but a stranger passing through, sent by God, but his appearance confirmed that within the nation, there were still those who were part of a faithful remnant. How significant then, that the man of God should appear in the way that he did. At a time when all seemed lost, here was the evidence that there were still others who shared Hannah's love of the Truth, others who did not approve of the iniquity of the priests, others through whom the Lord was at work for the benefit of His people. It taught her that her mission was but one part of the sovereign purpose of the Lord, and this faithful man of God was the proof. That detail would not be lost on Hannah, when she subsequently heard of this dramatic event but a short while later, as heard she did.

Eli received the message in private, which given its harsh denunciation might have been counted as a blessing. But with it came the terrible burden of living in silence with the knowledge of impending judgment, ready so soon to fall upon his household. To arise each day, where to be awake was again to be aware, yet unable to tell anyone, left Eli in the pit of despondency. He longed to converse with somebody on the matter, since a problem shared, is, if not halved, at least diminished. There would have been some comfort to the old man, in knowing that at least someone else knew.

But who could he speak with? It certainly could not be his two sons, Hophni and Phinehas, whose own doom was declared in the message. Scornful and profane, there would only be truculence from that quarter, and their defiance would but add to his despair. He could not share with them, for they had already shown themselves to be beyond correction. They would revile both the message and himself. He had only the lad, but he surely, was too young to be involved in so terrible a matter. So, he bore the burden alone, and aged further under its strain. But then a circumstance arose which altered everything. God shared the matter with Samuel. He knew! Here was the moment for Eli to pluck up the courage and share it with his young protégé.

The fact that the Lord had seen fit to communicate directly with the child concerning the overthrow of his household, [5] was reason enough for Eli to share his own visitation from the man of God. Although the man had spoken with Eli alone, he chose now to reveal the details to young Samuel, after the child had received his own angelic message. [6] Despite the terrible finality of the judgment, Eli accepted the words of the man as being indeed from the Lord, and had bowed before it. And if Samuel already knew of this judgment, then there was no point in hiding from him the words which the man of God had spoken. This was the right occasion for Eli to charge Samuel with the guardianship of all that he himself had failed to safeguard in his own sons. Despite his evident weakness, there was still a love of the Truth in Eli, and the pure and holy spirit of the child who ministered before him, touched him with sadness for the past and hope for the future.

Samuel in turn, and no doubt at the first opportunity, spoke of these matters with his mother. All his life, she had guided him towards his priestly role, and these messages, he knew, would be of compelling interest to his mother. At the time of her next yearly visit to the sanctuary, he was anxious to share them with her. When Hannah heard the startling news, she, like her son, was astonished and amazed at these words from God. It was fitting that Hannah be informed by the Lord concerning the next part of His plan. It was He who had answered her first heartfelt plea by granting her a son, and it was He who had accepted the charge of caring for the child when she brought

---

5   1 Samuel 3:11-14.
6   It is unlikely that Eli would have shared the message of the man of God with his two sons, for they had proved themselves to be beyond correction. But there was every reason for him to share it with Samuel (whom he loved), at some point before his death. Although the Spirit could have revealed the conversation directly to the author of 1 Samuel, it could just as easily have been received from Samuel himself, who had become privy to the details from Eli. Perhaps Eli did this after the angel's message to Samuel, which the little boy had shared with the old priest, upon his solemn adjuration to tell him all. At that moment, Eli was certain that the work of God would be continued through Samuel. Here was the time to tell him of the words of the man of God, and to urge him to uphold the Truth, which Eli's own sons had so terribly disgraced.

him in faith to the sanctuary. But now, she learned, through the unequivocal words of the man of God, that He intended to raise up for Himself a faithful priest.

Even more striking was the message of the angel. Since until that moment, Eli, as High Priest wearing the ephod had been the medium of divine communication in Israel, what could be made of the news that the Lord had called the child, [7] but to recognise that here was an intimation that the faithful priest God had in mind was Samuel himself. Hannah learned thereby of the purpose of the Lord to work through her son. Only later would all Israel know that Samuel was established to be the spokesman of God, but his mother would be made privy to his work and destiny much earlier. It was a just reward for the sacrifice she had made, and a privilege she was thankful to know.

And, far from being dissatisfied that God had not spoken with her directly, her heart rejoiced to hear the matter from Samuel himself. He was still too young perhaps to understand the dreadful fulness of these messages, but Hannah swiftly understood how absolute the judgments were. And to receive them from the mouth of Samuel, confirmed for her that God had already begun to use him as His channel of communication. When she heard these words of the man of God, and still further those of the angel of the Lord, she felt again that surge of fierce joy in her heart. Her son's priestly work was already in motion. God had answered her, and even now was preparing that succession of events that would sweep away the household of Eli from the priesthood.

The choosing of the priestly house

"And there came a man of God unto Eli, and said unto him, Thus saith the LORD, Did I plainly appear unto the house of thy father, when they were in Egypt in Pharaoh's house? And did I choose him out of all the tribes of Israel to be my priest, to

---

[7] After the threefold calling of Samuel, the proper emphasis should be – "And Eli perceived that the LORD had called the child" (1 Samuel 3:8).

offer upon mine altar, to burn incense, to wear an ephod before me? and did I give unto the house of thy father all the offerings made by fire of the children of Israel?" (1 Samuel 2:27,28)

The stranger who approached Eli on that fateful day immediately declared his calling. "Thus saith the LORD" he began, and Eli knew that he was in the presence of God's spokesman. It mattered not where he had come from, he spoke with divine authority, and as his message unfolded, Eli doubted not that it was so. He began with a series of questions which reminded Eli of the wonderful privileges attached to his household. They were not intended to be answered aloud, but rhetorical though they were, Eli knew full well what they conveyed. In three short phrases, the fulness of the priestly office was gathered up. "Did I plainly appear unto the house of thy father? Did I choose him ... to be my priest? Did I give unto the house of thy father all the offerings?" From the outset, there was divine grace and divine choice at work when God called his father's house to the charge of higher things within the nation. [8] Whilst still in Egypt, in the land of sin and darkness, Aaron had been appointed as God's interlocutor, [9] jointly responsible with Moses for observance of the Passover which commemorated their redemption. [10] From the very beginning therefore, Aaron was involved with their national deliverance, and his subsequent appointment to priesthood was connected to that imperative. Priesthood was related to the work of salvation.

After the exodus had brought the children of Israel to Sinai, God chose them to be a "kingdom of priests and an holy nation" unto Himself, and it was then that the family of Aaron within the tribe of Levi was appointed to the High Priesthood by divine decree. [11] His appointment was not because of intrinsic worthiness, for shortly afterwards he behaved unwisely. [12] Any

---

[8] The phrase "the house of thy father (1 Samuel 2:27) relates not to Ithamar, but to Aaron, from whom Eli was descended through Ithamar (1 Chronicles 24:3).

[9] Exodus 4:14,27.

[10] Exodus 12:1,43.

[11] Exodus 28:1-3; Numbers 18:1,7.

[12] Exodus 32:21-25,35.

position therefore that Aaron held was because of grace and not of works, lest either he or his family should boast. The decree which granted to his family the priest's office for a perpetual statute, [13] was still conditional upon continued obedience.

Three things marked out the High Priestly role which Aaron held. To be the priest was to ascend God's altar to offer sacrifice for expiation. To be the priest was to burn the daily incense in the spirit of intercession. To be the priest was to wear an ephod as intermediary between God and His people for communication. These were high honours indeed, and not to be taken lightly by those who held the office. They all required the spirit of one whose greater concern was for the spiritual well-being of his people, on whose behalf he ministered.

To high responsibility, the law added high privilege. For the office of High Priest was granted special entitlements on the basis that those that wait at the altar are partakers with the altar. Apart from the burnt offering (where the entire animal was consumed upon the altar) all other altar offerings made by fire provided a portion to the High Priest and his family. [14] The finest of both field and flock belonged to Eli and his household, as the law of God furnished the family with a comfortable and generous livelihood from the nation whom they served. [15]

But these very portions, and especially of the peace offering, were designed to remind the High Priest and his family that they shared in the blessing of fellowship with both God and His people. The priest's portion was granted to him on the basis that he represented God. When he ate his portion as the offerer ate

---

13 Exodus 29:9.
14 Rotherham – "I gave unto the house of thy father all the altar-flames of the sons of Israel" (1 Samuel 2:28). In fact, even in the case of the burnt offering, the skin was still gifted to the officiating priest (Leviticus 7:8).
15 To the High Priest and his family belonged portions of the meal, sin, trespass, and peace offerings, as well as the heave and wave offerings (Numbers 18:8-11). In addition to these, they also received the best of the oil, wine, wheat, and first ripe fruits (Numbers 18:12,13), the devoted things (Numbers 18:14) and the firstborn of household animals (Numbers 18:15-18).

his, he ate on behalf of God in fellowship with His people. It was a rare moment, this memorial meal, eaten with the Lord, and with all the exalted thoughts that accompanied it. It was this holy meal, and this sacred association that Eli and his sons had so despised.

Wherefore kick ye at my sacrifice

> "Wherefore kick ye at my sacrifice and at mine offering, which I have commanded in my habitation; and honourest thy sons above me, to make yourselves fat with the chiefest of all the offerings of Israel my people?" (1 Samuel 2:29)

In the word of judgment from the man of God, the Spirit gave echo to the stern warning of the lawgiver. Moses had spoken of Israel's disobedience, but who could doubt that in Eli was seen an exhibition of the very words which Moses had uttered?[16] How dreadful that the High Priest of Israel had become the very figure of the worst spirit of rebellion against God. Of course, it was his sons who committed the crime of robbery, and who kicked at the sacrifices commanded in God's habitation. But it was not just Hophni and Phinehas who were made fat by their appropriation of the offerings. Eli was unwilling to censure his sons in a matter where he himself stood to gain, and in permitting their excess for his own benefit, he honoured his sons above God. The office of the priesthood brought with it a lucrative opportunity to add to their wealth beyond the perquisites already theirs by divine provision. That wealth enriched them to the point of fatness, a condition which Eli shared, complicit in his acquiescence.[17] Eli's weakness lay in his love for the best things in life, and the opportunity to enjoy them came through enabling the greed of his sons without rebuke. Sin comes when weakness meets opportunity.

---

[16] The words of Moses were – "But Jeshurun waxed fat, and kicked: thou art waxen fat, thou art grown thick, thou art covered with fatness; then he forsook God which made him, and lightly esteemed the Rock of his salvation" (Deuteronomy 32:15). The word 'kicked' (*ba'at*) is only used here and in the words of the man of God (1 Samuel 2:29).

[17] The final comment on Eli being witness – "he fell from off the seat backward, by the side of the gate, and his neck break, and he died: for he was an old man and heavy" (1 Samuel 4:18).

Hannah's prayer had told of those who were full in the abundance of their wealth, and she had spoken in truth of Eli and his family.[18] The evil eye that hasted to be rich, was also the eye that would never be satisfied. Not content with the provision of God, these sons seized the best of the offerings that belonged to the people,[19] and in so doing betrayed the spirit of their office.

The basis of Eli's judgment then was that knowledge brought responsibility. He knew of the role of the priesthood, but failed to uphold it, and permitted his sons to disgrace it. Such a spirit would inevitably incur divine judgment, and the principle has ever been the same with every generation of God's people. He has graciously revealed His mind and His purpose, but He will hold us accountable for that knowledge which we bear.

The law prescribed that every feast of the Lord must include both sacrifice and offering,[20] and Hannah's life had centred on these holy convocations at the sanctuary. Attendance at such a feast was a spiritual highlight for those assembled at the only place where the LORD would permit such offerings to be put upon His altar. Leading them in the climax of that worship were the priests who were charged with the sacred task of preparing the offerings, and distributing the portions as the law required. Yet it was here, at this sacred place and in this sacred moment, that both God's sacrifice,[21] and God's offering,[22] were so wilfully violated. To kick against God's sacrifice and offering was to repudiate the laws which governed their

---

[18] Her prayer mentioned "they that were full have hired themselves out for bread" (1 Samuel 2:5).

[19] The word "chiefest" (*re'shiyth*) is the same as the "firstfruits" that were already theirs by divine appointment (Numbers 18:12). But the reference here is to the best of the offerer's own portion which they stole.

[20] "These are the feasts of the LORD, which ye shall proclaim to be holy convocations, to offer an offering made by fire unto the LORD, a burnt offering, a meat offering [*minchah*], a sacrifice [*zebach*], and drink offerings, every thing upon his day" (Leviticus 23:37).

[21] "When any man offered sacrifice [*zebach*], the priest's servant came ... all that the fleshhook brought up the priest took for himself" (1 Samuel 2:13,14).

[22] "Wherefore the sin of the young men was very great before the LORD: for men abhorred the offering [*minchah*] of the LORD" (1 Samuel 2:17).

apportionment. [23] In the process, Hophni and Phinehas profaned their office, and all for nothing more than carnal greed.

If their sin was to scorn the Lord's altar, then in the absolute justice of God the penalty would fit the crime, and the punishment would follow the perversion. For when God's judgments came by the mouth of the man of God, these vile men might finally have wished to offer for their own atonement. Alas, it was not to be. Their end, as revealed to Samuel, would make that impossible. At the last, when their own need for sacrifice and offering was desperate, God would not accept it at their hands. [24] These priests who had refused to seek reconciliation for others, would find heaven closed to their own entreaties, and shut to their own altar petitions. Their priesthood would be made void, rendered invalid by their own corruption of it.

For them that honour me I will honour

> "Wherefore the LORD God of Israel saith, I said indeed that thy house, and the house of thy father, should walk before me for ever: but now the LORD saith, Be it far from me; for them that honour me I will honour, and they that despise me shall be lightly esteemed." (1 Samuel 2:30)

The priesthood which they rested upon had never been theirs by absolute right. Its continuance depended on obedience, and their disobedience would terminate their office. The intention of God was that their house, once privileged to walk before him in priestly service, would be overthrown. God would replace them with a new priesthood, seen in another house and another priest, who would stand to serve in their place. [25] How

---

23 The words of indictment centred on their disregard for that which God Himself had ordered in His house – "Wherefore kick ye at my sacrifice [*zebach*] and at mine offering [*minchah*] which I have commanded in my habitation" (1 Samuel 2:29).

24 "I have sworn unto the house of Eli, that the iniquity of Eli's house shall not be purged with sacrifice [*zebach*] nor offering [*minchah*] for ever" (1 Samuel 3:14).

25 The repeated phrases of 1 Samuel 2:30,35 make this clear. "I said indeed that thy house ... should walk before me for ever", is followed by, "I will build him a sure house, and he shall walk before my anointed for ever".

far reaching these words of judgment would prove to be, was yet to unfold, but Hannah's son would be bound into the drama of its outworking.

The words which followed were the climax of the man's message, the focal point of all that he would say. Terse in their brevity, they would become a proverb of the great rule which has ever underpinned all of God's interactions – "them that honour me, I will honour", but "they that despise me shall be lightly esteemed". [26] Here was a divine principle. Our destiny is linked to our attitude to God. And in this simple choice of whether to honour or to despise Him, the proverb declared that He would respond to us in a spirit consistent with our own.

When the man of God spoke his words, there was an immediate and evident application to Hophni and Phinehas who, having despised God in their actions, would in turn be lightly esteemed by Him. But the obvious truth of that fulfilment argued for just as immediate an outworking with Hannah, who in contrast would be honoured by God as she had honoured Him, and she the first example of that truth, once pronounced. Who should have received more honour than her, in the outworking of this story, even though she sought no honour for herself, but for her Lord? She was honoured when God enabled her to bear Samuel in response to her prayer. She was honoured when God exalted her son, by raising him to the leadership of the nation. [27] She was honoured when God chose her as His instrument to begin the next great stage of His purpose with His people. But this only occurred because she first honoured God, by placing Him first in her life, before her child. Eli had honoured his sons above God, but Hannah had honoured God above her son. She was the living demonstration of the proverb, both in her spirit and in God's response. But she was also the antithesis of the

---

[26] In the Hebrew, the entire expression is but four words, but they marvellously summarise the basis of all God's dealings with mankind which all rest upon His sovereign majesty.

[27] Even the impending role of Samuel was an elevation of his mother (Proverbs 23:24,25).

High Priest, more spiritual than he in her commitment, more faithful than he in her dedication.

And, given her remarkable faith, why might she not also be honoured in some special capacity in the kingdom? "Them that honour me I will honour" was not necessarily a promise limited to this present mortal life, for God's honouring of his servants reaches into their future status with Him. He might honour them by present blessing, by involvement in His purpose, or by commission in His service. But He might extend that honour by future redemption, by an adoption into His family, and by participation in His glory. If to be lightly esteemed for Hophni and Phinehas related to their premature death, what might it be for Hannah to be honoured? If for Eli's sons there impended a death with no future, then surely for Samuel's mother there awaited a future without death.

All those who hold office in the household of faith must ponder the path of true service, to know whether they honour God or serve themselves. It matters not whether the task is large or small, spiritual or mundane. In every work, we likewise must learn that the privilege of service brings with it a duty to seek God's honour as paramount in that labour. The proverb of the man of God will hold true for all, that there will be a strict correspondence between character and consequence. God will best be honoured, when in whatever office we hold, we work to discharge its responsibilities faithfully, we strive to reach its highest ideal, and we seek to hold ourselves accountable to its best and noblest spirit. To honour God is to work for the triumph of His principles and not our own. When we do, we will know somewhat of the spirit of Hannah, who lived her life at the centre of the truth, and found no fellowship with those who lived at its circumference. Hers was a life that God would honour indeed.

There shall not be an old man in thine house

"Behold, the days come, that I will cut off thine arm, and the arm of thy father's house, that there shall not be an old man

in thine house. And thou shalt see an enemy in my habitation, in all the wealth that God shall give Israel: and there shall not be an old man in thine house for ever. And the man of thine whom I shall not cut off from mine altar, shall be to consume thine eyes, and to grieve thine heart: and all the increase of thine house shall die in the flower of their age. And this shall be a sign unto thee, that shall come upon thy two sons, on Hophni and Phinehas; in one day they shall die both of them."
(1 Samuel 2:31-34)

Eli and his sons had not honoured the Lord, but despised Him, and the sentence now pronounced was the consequence of their spirit and behaviour. The strength of Eli's house was to be cut off, beginning with the dramatic death of his two sons. [28] Their death, occurring as it did in Eli's lifetime, [29] became the sign which confirmed that all the words of the judgment would come to pass. In one blow the immediate offspring of Eli were to be removed as offending limbs, their death as sudden and as brutal as the severing of an arm. Disastrous as this was to the house of Eli, the indictment also brought disgrace upon the house of Aaron, its strength and reputation diminished by such summary judgment upon one of the family branches. As the prophecy was outworked, the influence and authority of the house of Eli was progressively removed, and once God's judgments began, they would not end until every word had been fulfilled.

The divine retribution was to be dreadful: successive calamities that would strike down Eli's offspring in the vigour of their manhood, so that none would reach the dignity of becoming old and full of days. [30] More than once, those of his house were to

---

28 The arm was the symbol of a man's strength, the outstretching of it signifying the reach of his power. Its cutting off here symbolised the dramatic loss of authority and influence that would befall Eli's house (Ezekiel 30:21,22; Zechariah 11:17).

29 The death of Hophni and Phinehas fulfilled the words of 1 Samuel 2:34.

30 The history of the family would be marked by such premature ends – "there shall not be an old man in thine house", "there shall not be an old man in thine house for ever", all the increase of thine house shall die in the flower of their age" (1 Samuel 2:31-33).

experience tragedy which took them away in the flower of their age, as strong men were removed in the prime of life. Potential elders were denied the role that time might have brought, and those that could have risen to prominence were prevented by death from doing so.

The family would experience both distress and decline, linked to the gradual diminishing of the prestige of the tabernacle system to which Eli's house had stood so closely related. "Thou shalt see the affliction of the tabernacle" came the words, and with them the promise that Eli would witness the beginning of those calamities which would decrease the tabernacle's role in the nation, until it was set aside. [31] The distress of the tabernacle began with the capture of the ark, and its removal from the sanctuary. The ark as the focal point of the tabernacle system was the place of the Lord's presence among His people, and its loss represented the greatest blow to the tabernacle ritual which ever occurred. [32]

Despite that loss, the rest of the tabernacle was safely removed from Shiloh, before that place was destroyed by the Philistines. Whether the transfer occurred under the supervision of Samuel or not, the tabernacle was set up again at Nob, and with it the routine of tabernacle worship was resumed. [33] Here again the family of the priests were to be found, [34] but significantly, the priesthood remained as yet with a descendant of Ithamar through the family of Eli, in the person of Ahimelech the son of Ahitub.

---

31 Note KJV margin. Cp. ASV – "thou shalt behold the affliction of my habitation"; *Cambridge Bible for Schools and Colleges* – "thou shalt behold the distress of my habitation" (1 Samuel 2:32). The term "my habitation" should be understood here as relating to the tabernacle, consistent with its earlier use (1 Samuel 2:29).

32 The loss of the ark was deemed a worse catastrophe than the death of Hophni and Phinehas, or of Eli himself (1 Samuel 4:19-22). It marked the beginning of the decline of the tabernacle service, since the ark was never returned there, and the power of the tabernacle system was irrevocably diminished. This was the "distress of God's habitation" indeed.

33 The mention of the shewbread (1 Samuel 21:6) which was placed on the table of shewbread in the holy place (Leviticus 24:5-9), is evidence that the tabernacle was standing and in operation in Nob at that time.

34 Note the phrase, "Nob, the city of the priests" (1 Samuel 22:19).

During Samuel's tenure as leader, there was no mention of the tabernacle system, or of the priestly family. What few indications there were of priestly sacrifice and intercession, came from the hands of Samuel himself. The sudden reappearance of the house of Eli at the place of the tabernacle was therefore unusual, and there was every reason to suppose that this appointment was not of Samuel's making. Given that the prophecy of the man of God tasked him with the preserving of the house of Ithamar but in a subordinate capacity, [35] why would Samuel have reinstated them to the High Priestly role? The very strictures enjoined upon Eli's house in the angelic revelation to Samuel, must have forever forbidden him from promoting their advancement. [36]

The reappointment of the line of Ithamar came about, more probably, at Saul's instigation. His attitude to the role of priests was at best casual, [37] but Samuel's reproof may have been the cause of his decision to retain his own priestly adviser. [38] Had he consulted with Samuel, he would have been advised that the house of Ithamar lay under the severest of divine curses, and that no priest of Eli's house should be appointed. But, as was his wont, Saul, who was not among the prophets, made his own decision without proper thought, and whether by artifice or coincidence, a priest of Ithamar stood ready to join him and to take up priestly honours.

How remarkably then, was the judgment of God outworked against Eli's house. The very act that appeared to hold the key to their family's revival became the basis for their demise. Saul,

---

[35] 1 Samuel 2:36.

[36] The words, "I will judge his house for ever", and "Eli's house shall not be purged with sacrifice nor offering for ever" (1 Samuel 3:13,14) would seem to deny them a further High Priestly role.

[37] His assumption of the role himself without qualm (1 Samuel 13:9-12) being evidence.

[38] The notice, shortly after, of Ahiah being in his entourage suggests that he wanted a priest on hand, with whom he could consult (1 Samuel 14:3). But, in common with other actions of Saul, this appointment was not driven by deep scriptural principles, but for the sake of appearance.

capricious and fickle, [39] unwisely promoted them to officiate again at the tabernacle, and then, in like manner, turned and ordered their subsequent execution. The terrible act of vengeance wrought upon the priests at Nob in the days of Saul, was thereby perpetrated against the line of Ithamar. [40] In the providence of God, the words of the prophecy came to pass with astonishing accuracy. [41]

One man of the line of Ithamar escaped, as young Abiathar, the son of Ahimelech joined David's band, bringing with him the High Priest's ephod. [42] Yet this survivor was also caught within the measure of the curse, and his end would not escape the reach of the divine judgment. Although he laboured with David, circumstances brought about a disengagement between the two men, which in the course of time led to a rupture of trust, and a revealing of the spirit of treachery in Abiathar. The final degradation of Eli's house was made complete in the decision of Solomon to thrust out Abiathar from being priest before the Lord. Solomon's action, in response to Abiathar's betrayal of David in supporting the rebellion of Adonijah, led to his exile in disgrace to Anathoth. [43] With this final banishment, the judgment against the house of Eli was made complete, in a man who although not initially cut off from the altar, would only serve to cause grief to Eli (had he been alive to see it), and shame to Abiathar who was alive to know it. [44]

---

39 He was prepared to appoint a priest, bearing an ephod to accompany him, but equally prepared to interrupt that priest's enquiring of the LORD, when it suited him (1 Samuel 14:18,19, LXX).
40 The record is explicit that the catastrophe fell upon Ahimelech's family even "all thy father's house" (1 Samuel 22:11,16,22). The term "father's house" relates to the line of Ithamar which Ahimelech stood related to.
41 The death of the family of Ahitub and Ahimelech fulfilled the words of 1 Samuel 2:31,32.
42 David being much more inclined to enquire of God than his predecessor (1 Samuel 23:6,9-11; 30:7,8).
43 The divine comment expressly linked Solomon's action to the words of the man of God, thus – "So Solomon thrust out Abiathar from being priest unto the LORD; that he might fulfil the word of the LORD, which he spake concerning the house of Eli in Shiloh" (1 Kings 2:26,27).
44 The demise of Abiathar fulfilled the words of 1 Samuel 2:33.

And, lest Eli thought that the force of these judgments lay far off into the future, he was told by what means he would recognise their harsh reality, and brutal certainty. It was a terrible sign for a father to receive. The sudden and violent death of Hophni and Phinehas, struck down together on the same day, would be a calamity which he would witness in his own lifetime. And despite his age, this immediate outworking was to be the pledge of the future fulfilment of all that was prophesied against his house. Nothing would be left undone of all that the man of God had spoken.

The severity of the judgment could only be explained by the grievousness of the sin. The judgment was so terrible, and the terms so final, that the sins of Eli and his sons must have been heinous indeed. They were. His sons were vile beyond compare, and God would not permit this outrage upon His sanctuary and His holiness to pass unchallenged. He who is merciful and gracious, is also a jealous God and a consuming fire. There has always been a flaw in human nature which is deluded by the notion that evil, if not at the first requited, will never be so. [45] But God is not mocked. He will bring every work into judgment, whether it be good or whether it be evil. That day of accountability had fallen upon the house of Eli now.

Even in this pronouncement of doom, there was a merciful omission. For what the man of God did not divulge, was that the day in which Eli's sons would die, would also be the day when the ark of God was captured by the Philistines. Their sudden death would be as nothing compared to the catastrophe of the day of Ichabod, and it was the shock of this news which finally killed Eli. As well then that he did not know this final part of the story. When it came, it would be the death of him.

And I will raise me up a faithful priest

"And I will raise me up a faithful priest, that shall do according to that which is in mine heart and in my mind: and I will build

---

[45] Ecclesiastes 8:11.

him a sure house; and he shall walk before mine anointed for ever." (1 Samuel 2:35)

God's character has always been that perfect balance of goodness and severity, mercy and truth. But God's mercy would not be seen in granting reprieve to those whose spirit remained unrepentant to the end. For them there would be nothing but removal. His mercy would instead be shown in raising up a faithful priest through whom His work with Israel as an holy priesthood might be resumed. The principle of accountability would not be set aside for Eli's sons, and even now it was God's avowed intention to replace them.

With the death of Hophni and Phinehas, God set in motion the cascade of events that would remove the house of Ithamar and restore the house of Eleazar. But during this priestly interregnum, He provided His people with a faithful priest who would restore their confidence in the office, and lead them back to the true worship of their God. Samuel, marked out from birth, and already resident at the sanctuary was God's choice. But Samuel deserved his appointment, since he had shown himself to be worthy of the role from an extremely young age. [46]

His mother had always believed in his destiny, but the words of the man of God had confirmed it. "I will raise me up a faithful priest" was the promise that God would intervene, but the seeds of that promise had already been sown in the birth of Samuel, and in Hannah's giving him to God. It was her spirit which had made all this possible, the spirit of personal sacrifice, offered at enormous cost, but in absolute confidence that God could work a work though her child. Whatever further aspects of the promise there might have been, the faithful priest who first appeared in answer to the word, was Samuel himself. And as one specially raised in the providence of God, Samuel fulfilled the priestly role in the very details noted.

---

[46] Remarkably, the very term used to describe God's faithful priest whom He would raise (*aman*), was attested of Samuel shortly afterwards – "and all Israel from Dan to Beersheba knew that Samuel was faithful [*aman*]" (1 Samuel 3:20).

He would do all that Hophni and Phinehas did not. He was faithful to offer sacrifice. [47] He was faithful to burn incense. [48] He was faithful to wear an ephod. [49] Samuel was a priest all his life, the spiritual guide and mentor of the nation. Indeed, in all of Israel's subsequent history, Hannah's son was the one person who approached the high rank of Moses. Like Moses he was at once the civil leader, and their priestly intercessor, the like of which would never be seen again. [50] In him the kingly and priestly roles would be combined, in a foreshadowing of future things yet to be revealed in Messiah, [51] but which Hannah had already seen.

And whence this faithful spirit? Why from his mother Hannah! In Samuel would be found an example of faithfulness, so marked, that God could say of him that he would do according to all that was in His heart and mind. At last, there would be found in Israel a faithful priest whose sole interest and highest cause was to set forth the counsel and mind of God before the nation. This was the priest Hannah had sought for, and now recognised in her own son.

Such was the esteem in which Samuel would be held, that God promised to build him a sure house. [52] The promise did not concern his flesh and blood descendants, for his own sons

---

[47] The priestly work of expiation (1 Samuel 7:9,10; 10:8). Note that on these occasions, Samuel did not seek a priest to offer on his behalf but assumed the role instead.

[48] The priestly work of intercession, the burning of incense being but the outward symbol of priestly prayer (1 Samuel 7:9; 12:18; 15:11).

[49] The priestly work of communication, in being the channel of divine counsel from God. From a child, Samuel had worn an ephod (1 Samuel 2:18), but in leading the nation, he became the appointed intermediary of heaven (1 Samuel 3:21). He rehearsed the words of the people in the ear of the Lord (1 Samuel 8:21), who in turn revealed His will in the ear of Samuel (1 Samuel 9:15). Here was divine communication at the highest level!

[50] Hence the outstanding testimony of scripture concerning him (Psalm 99:6; Jeremiah 15:1).

[51] See Appendix 7 – "What was the story of Hannah's faithful priest?" on page 232.

[52] The word "sure" (*aman*) is the same word as "faithful". Samuel's faithful spirit would elicit a faithful response from God, who is the embodiment of faithfulness (Deuteronomy 7:9). The root idea of the word relates to certainty.

disgraced their office, **53** and were removed by Samuel himself. **54** The sure house referred to was a spiritual household that would be associated with him in the kingdom. **55** And their relationship with Samuel would be of a priestly character. It was to Samuel as a faithful priest that a sure house would be built, not to Samuel as a judge or a prophet, although he would be both of these. What was to be perpetuated was the spirit of his faithful priesthood, in a company of priests who would take their example from him, their right to service found not in Aaronic authority, but through some higher priestly line.

That line, related to the order of Melchizedek, was revealed in Samuel, whose own priesthood stood more related to his Nazarite vow than his Levitical descent. How could his sure house be anything other than a future family, when Samuel was promised that he would execute the priestly office in the presence of the anointed of the Lord for ever. **56** To act as priest before the Lord's anointed was one thing. To do so for ever, moved the promise into the realm of the kingdom, and the prospect of future exaltation. And the anointed one before whom he would serve, was the same anointed man with kingly and priestly rights Hannah had seen in her song. **57** The words of the man of God again confirmed Hannah's prophetic expectation of this one who should come, but now added the promise that her own son would be associated with he whose right it was.

How astonished must Hannah have been to know this prophecy. How must her mother's love have overflowed at

---

53 1 Samuel 8:1-3.

54 1 Samuel 12:2.

55 Note the similarity of language with the promise to David (2 Samuel 7:11; 1 Kings 11:38).

56 RSV – "and he shall go in and out before mine anointed". The phrase is an echo of the teaching of the law concerning the work of the priest – "And it shall be upon Aaron to minister, and his sound shall be heard when he goeth in unto the holy place before the Lord, and when he cometh out" (Exodus 28:35). The term "walk" in this context therefore, relates to the fulfilment of Samuel's priestly labours.

57 Her song had concluded with this very thought – "and he shall give strength unto his king, and exalt the horn of his anointed" (1 Samuel 2:10).

such gracious words. To know that her son, the son that she had borne, would be granted the special honour of fulfilling his priestly duties before Christ in the kingdom! It was enough to fill her heart with joy. How marvellous was the thought that he should be so exalted to this degree of privilege. And yet, it was no more than she had intended in her giving. Her offering had always been with the spirit of the kingdom in mind, and the Lord had accepted her gift, that the child might abide before Him for ever. **58** That promise reaching forward into Messiah's day, was surely the ultimate accolade of heaven bestowed upon His Handmaid, in recognition of one whose mind was always focused on higher things.

Shall come and crouch to him for a piece of silver

> And it shall come to pass, that everyone that is left in thine house shall come and crouch to him for a piece of silver and a morsel of bread, and shall say, Put me I pray thee, into one of the priest's offices, that I may eat a piece of bread."
>
> (1 Samuel 2:36)

Whatever future role Samuel was to have in the kingdom, his ascension to influence in Israel would bring immediate repercussions upon the house of Eli, for its survivors were to be brought so low by the removal of the tabernacle, that they would suffer penury. Gathered around the sanctuary at Shiloh, the source and centre of their power, they were the chief sufferers by its overthrow. Their humble request to be granted lowly tasks in the priesthood, **59** was for no higher reason than to preserve their life. What was sought was but a subsistence, such would be

---

58 Notice the permanent spirit of Samuel's priestly role. Hannah's desire – "that he may appear before the LORD for ever (1 Samuel 1:22), was now matched by God's assurance – "and he shall walk before mine anointed for ever" (1 Samuel 2:35). It stands in studied contrast to the permanent overthrow of Eli's house – "there shall not be an old man in thine house for ever" (1 Samuel 2:32), "I will judge his house for ever", "Eli's house shall not be purged with sacrifice nor offering for ever" (1 Samuel 3:13,14).

59 Note KJV margin which captures the idea – "Join me, I pray thee, somewhat about the priesthood" (1 Samuel 2:36).

their reduced circumstances, the mark of their extreme poverty. And poverty indeed it must have been, for the piece of silver they would seek so assiduously was but the smallest of coins. [60] To crouch in obeisance to Samuel whilst pleading for so little, was a righteous retribution upon a family who had acted so imperiously toward others, including Hannah, in vaunting the power of their office.

The words were a direct condemnation of Eli's two sons, who had abused the priesthood to enrich themselves. Hannah's song had spoken of those who though full would be so humbled as to "hire themselves out for bread", [61] and now came the stunning endorsement of her words. Not only would the family be forced to beg for a morsel of bread as the hire of their menial service, but her son, her priest would decide the outcome of such petitions, since his authority would be supreme. In these closing words, Hannah was exalted by God with the promise that Samuel would determine the future of Eli's house. Their very survival was to be dependent on his mercy and provision. It was an astounding reversal of circumstance. If the Lord could bring low and lift up, then He had done so right here in the life of His Handmaid, through this amazing prophecy.

Hannah and her priest

When Hannah learned of the final words of the man of God, her desire was realised to the full. She had no doubt that the promise of a faithful priest concerned her son, [62] but it was humility that filled her heart, and not pride. What moved her the most was

---

60   The phrase "piece of silver" (*agorath keseph*) is translated by the Targum as *mea* and is thought to be connected in thought and etymology with the *gerah*, the smallest silver coin, equal to the twentieth part of a shekel. This smallest of silver coins would be the reward of beggars, and indicated the poverty of the asker.
61   1 Samuel 2:5.
62   Notice that the promise of the faithful priest (1 Samuel 2:27-36), is bookmarked before and behind by references to the role of Samuel. "And the child Samuel grew on, and was in favour both with the LORD, and also with men" (1 Samuel 2:26). "And the child Samuel ministered unto the LORD before Eli" (1 Samuel 3:1). The obvious inference is that Samuel was the faithful priest referred to in the prophecy.

the knowledge that she had set all this in motion. She, a woman, without importance, without rank, without influence, had become the vehicle for the divine purpose. For all our endeavours, we can only ever be but an instrument for the Lord, and it is His sovereign prerogative to decide who or what His instrumentality might be. But God responded to one who pleaded that she might be used to accomplish His purpose. She understood what it meant to be but the Handmaid of the Highest, yet what honour and joy it had brought her at the end. The words of the man of God were so astounding in their magnitude, that she could but rejoice in her part.

There was deep wisdom in the spirit of Hannah, for during the darkness of her trial, not once did she make request for her own sake, or for her own satisfaction. Her desire was always for a priest that would do according to all that was in His heart and His mind, and the Lord heard her request, and approved of her spirit. The startling message of the man of God showed that her cries of despair had been acknowledged, and her fervent pleas answered. It was as if God had said – "Hannah, I have heard you. All that you have grieved over will be removed. All that you have sought for will be performed. All that you have hoped for will be fulfilled".

Hannah mourned over the peace offerings, [63] filled with despair at their desecration by the brazen disregard of Hophni and Phinehas. [64] God's answer condemned Eli's sons in that very sin, [65] and promised that no sacrifice or offering would ever be efficacious on their behalf. [66] In that judgment, Hannah's spiritual grief was vindicated.

Hannah knew that only a better priest could lead the nation to holiness, and she sought to be the bearer of the priestly child, [67] and dedicated him to appear before the Lord for

---

63 1 Samuel 1:3-7.
64 1 Samuel 2:12-17.
65 1 Samuel 2:29.
66 1 Samuel 3:14.
67 1 Samuel 1:11.

ever, [68] clear in her vow that his was a lifetime service of priestly leadership. God's answer promised to raise up the very priest she sought, whose service would indeed be before God's anointed for ever. [69] In that promise, Hannah's godly desire was approved.

Hannah felt the ancient enmity of the seed of the woman against the seed of the serpent from the moment she first met Hophni and Phinehas. [70] That controversy led to her desire to rescue the nation, and her song of thanksgiving saw ahead to the Lord's power to defeat His enemies by sudden and violent overthrow. [71] God's answer revealed His determination, [72] deliberate and terrible, to execute that very penalty upon Hophni and Phinehas. [73] In that verdict, Hannah's divine perspective was endorsed.

Hannah saw that the sin of Hophni and Phinehas was linked to a life made rich by a misuse of priestly privileges. She saw how that wealth corrupted their behaviour, but she firmly believed in God's power to turn their fulness into poverty. [74] God's answer brought that very poverty upon Eli's family, in a reversal announced in Hannah's own words. [75] In that sentence, Hannah's righteous request was fulfilled.

How appropriate it was then, that this testimony from God be heard by Hannah in conversation with her own son. For who better to inform her, than the one in whom the promise of the faithful priest would first be seen? And who, apart from Eli to whom it was spoken, deserved more to hear its stern and sacred words than Hannah herself? Its substance was as much if not more an endorsement of Hannah, as it was an indictment of Eli. In all that the man of God said, his words were at once

---

[68] 1 Samuel 1:22.
[69] 1 Samuel 2:35.
[70] 1 Samuel 1:3,6.
[71] 1 Samuel 2:10.
[72] 1 Samuel 2:25.
[73] 1 Samuel 2:34.
[74] 1 Samuel 2:5.
[75] 1 Samuel 2:36.

the condemnation of Hophni and Phinehas, and the vindication of Hannah His Handmaid. In this promise, all that Hannah had yearned for, and all that Hannah had believed in was realised. It was the vindication of her vision, and the fulfilment of her dream. No finer endorsement of Hannah's burning purpose could be found than in this expression of God's own resolute intention, which Hannah's heart chimed so perfectly with. This was her priest indeed!

It was her spirit of faith which enabled her to see beyond herself to the viewpoint of heaven. The voice of the man of God was heaven's reply, and in heaven's answer, Hannah would be comforted. Whatever might happen, and however it might unfold, she was content to rest in the wonder of this promise. It mattered not now whether she would see its full outworking, or whether she would witness the greatness of her son's spiritual leadership. What mattered was that God had spoken, and she was ready to surrender the future to Him. He would permit her to see whatever His purpose required, for to be His Handmaid was to believe that He would do best. She needed no more, for in these words, she knew all.

8 |

Hannah and her Lord

(Luke 1:46-56)

IT was the strangest thing. More than a millennium had passed since the time of Hannah, and in most cases, the story of one who had gone to the land of darkness and the shadow of death, would long since have been extinguished in the night. Yet a thousand years were but as yesterday when the gospel record began, for at its opening, a woman would appear in whom the spirit of Hannah was seen. It was as if time had stood still, for the account of Christ's birth and childhood was written in such a way, as to bid us see in Mary another Hannah, and in Christ another Samuel.

There was nothing accidental about the likeness, for it was portrayed by the Spirit with such deliberate care as to be unmistakable. But to the curious reader, it invited the question as to why the Old Testament portrait of Hannah and her son was redrawn in the New Testament. Even more puzzling, was the fact that only one gospel would paint this picture. Why then would that gospel, and that gospel exclusively, bring together everyone involved in the drama of Hannah and her son's early life, by presenting an exact counterpart in the story of Mary and her firstborn son?

First to recognise this gospel portrait, and then seek to know why it was painted, begins a journey of discovery and wonder at the ways of God. For there was a reason, the best of reasons, why such a picture was drawn. The answer would be found in knowing who drew it, and why the picture was revealed. Only then would its purpose be clear.

That picture was found in the Gospel of Luke, who alone would record Gabriel's meeting with Zacharias, and then his subsequent appearance to Mary, her song of praise at the promise of a son, his nativity in Bethlehem, his presentation at the temple, his infancy in Nazareth, his meeting with the priests in Jerusalem, and the ponderings of his mother's heart. Unique in all these details, Luke's Gospel would then weave the story of Hannah and Samuel into these events, and in doing so make plain the reason for them all. They served to bring the purpose of that gospel to life, and every word, every phrase was overshadowed by the Spirit to that end.

A special forerunner and a Nazarite vow

The work of Samuel, Hannah's son, had been preceded by another, in whom the Spirit of the Lord would also be seen. Samson was a special child, marked out by God for a special role. His mother and father received an angelic visitation concerning the birth of the child, made more memorable by the fact that the woman was barren and bare not, the studied superfluity of the record emphasising what pain her barrenness had caused.[1] Imagine then, what cause there was for rejoicing when the angel warned her to abstain from wine and strong drink, in preparation for the birth of a son who would be a Nazarite unto God from the womb.[2] From the moment of his birth, this child was set to begin a work that someone else would complete.[3] From childhood, he grew under the divine care, until the spirit of God moved him in the camp.[4]

Like Manoah's wife, Elizabeth, the wife of Zacharias was barren, and furthermore, she was well stricken in years. It was

---

[1] Judges 13:2.
[2] Judges 13:3-5.
[3] Notice the import of the phrase, "he shall begin to deliver Israel" (Judges 13:5). What Samson began, was in fact completed by Samuel (1 Samuel 7:10-13). Samson became the harbinger of Samuel.
[4] Judges 13:24,25.

because of her impediment that they had no child,[5] and this couple knew the same sadness as Manoah and his wife. But they were also to know the same joy, as they received an angelic assurance of the birth of their son – John. Like the story of Samson, the matter of abstention from wine and strong drink was referred to, but this time the restriction would lie upon the child rather than the mother. And like Samson, who was to be a Nazarite from the womb, John was to be filled with the Holy Spirit, even from his mother's womb.[6] The spirit of Nazarite dedication could not be clearer. Like Samson, John's early childhood was overshadowed by God, as he waxed strong in the spirit.[7] And like Samson, John would begin a work, which would be completed by another.[8] How marvellous that the gospel record should begin with the story of a mother and a son who came before Mary and her son. In John and his mother who preceded Jesus, was seen again the story of Samson and his mother who preceded Samuel.

A holy handmaid and her spiritual mind

In every age, there were godly women who sought to serve the Lord, and who uttered their prayer of thanksgiving at the evidence of His mighty hand in their lives.[9] These all revealed a spirit of faithful obedience to the cause of heaven which they engaged in. And there were other women, who in their spirit of humility referred to themselves as an handmaid in declaring their loyalty to the one they were committed to.[10] But there

---

5   Luke 1:7.
6   Luke 1:15.
7   Luke 1:80.
8   The terms, "he shall go before him", "to make ready a people prepared for the Lord" (Luke 1:17) echo the spirit of Samson's labours. John became the forerunner of Jesus.
9   Sarah gave thanks for the birth of Isaac (Genesis 21:6), Miriam gave thanks for deliverance at the Red Sea (Exodus 15:21), and Deborah gave thanks for the overthrow of Sisera (Judges 5:2).
10 Ruth called herself the handmaid of Boaz (Ruth 3:9), Abigail called herself the handmaid of David (1 Samuel 25:24), and Bathsheba also called herself the handmaid of David (1 Kings 1:17).

was only one woman who described herself as the Handmaid of the Lord. That woman was Hannah. [11] None before and none after her in the Old Testament would use this expression. She stood apart and alone in this respect, the one woman whose sense of purpose before her God was so strong, that nothing but this phrase could do justice to the depth of her commitment. The woman whose life revealed her to be the Handmaid of the Highest, chose her word of vow with deliberate intent. She was fully alive to its meaning.

From the beginning, Hannah nurtured a spiritual mind deep within her. That she did so was evident from her conduct, and above all from her prayers. She spoke the truth in her heart, which was only possible because she permitted the law of God to dwell there. [12] One cannot offer prayer, rich in scriptural language and full of spiritual thinking, unless that law has been the meditation of the heart. [13] Our reverent assimilation of the oracles of God reveals itself in our prayers. When the heart is cleansed by the counsels of the word, our prayers are not only God directed, but God focused. This was Hannah's secret strength. In her prayer of anguish, her whole heart was engaged in its outpouring, for her lips but shaped the words which her heart uttered. [14] And in her prayer of praise, it was her heart which rejoiced at the realisation of how God had graciously involved her in His purpose. [15]

Whatever Hannah brought forth in earnest entreaty had already been stored in her heart. This was how she really thought, this was who she truly was. It resided deep within,

---

[11] The reference is made more dramatic by the threefold use of the term – "if thou wilt indeed look on the affliction of thine handmaid, and remember me, and not forget thine handmaid, but will give unto thine handmaid a man child" (1 Samuel 1:11).

[12] Psalm 15:2; 40:8.

[13] Psalm 19:7,11,14.

[14] For so is the description of her prayer – "Now Hannah, she spake in her heart; only her lips moved, but her voice was not heard" (1 Samuel 1:13).

[15] The phrase – "My heart rejoiceth in the LORD" (1 Samuel 2:1) was expressive of her God-centred mind.

for her heart had been made the repository of sacred thoughts and sacred words. There, within the recesses of her private reflections, she dwelt upon the greatness of the divine purpose, and contemplated holy things. The quintessence of who Hannah was, lay within, for hers was a holy heart, and hers a spiritual mind. This was why she burst forth into thanksgiving at the honour done to her as the Handmaid of the Lord. It was in her being to praise Him, since she walked in full awareness of His hand. She prayed so naturally, and yet in so exalted a tone, that her prayers were as if one was talking with God as well as walking with Him. There would be few prayers to match hers for God-centred intensity and God-focused fervency.

Time rolled onward to an age which lay far beyond Hannah's own, yet stood so closely related to hers in the crisis of the moment. When the sun went down over the prophets, when the word of the Lord again was precious, when the priests polluted the sanctuary, another woman arose for the deliverance of her people. Gabriel spoke with Mary, and promised not only a child, but a son born by divine intervention. His words, that "with God nothing shall be impossible", called to mind the miraculous conception and birth of Isaac, [16] who was the firstborn of his barren mother. Yet Mary, in a response both brief yet profound said – "Behold the handmaid of the Lord". Her answer did not recall Sarah, but rather, with a single word, evoked the memory of Hannah, as she bowed in submission to the divine will. [17] Her choice of word was quite intentional, since it would be repeated in her prayer. "For he hath regarded the low estate of his handmaiden" she would cry, and the voice of Hannah was

---

16 The phrase echoed the words of the angel to Abraham – "Is any thing too hard for the LORD?" (Genesis 18:14).

17 Gabriel, in speaking with Mary had described her as "much graced" (Luke 1:28, margin). This was of course the meaning of Hannah's name, whose circumstance so matched Mary's at this moment. But such was the quickness of Mary's mind that she framed her reply to the angel, "Behold the handmaid of the Lord; be it unto me according to thy word" (Luke 1:38), in the beautiful words of Hannah's own response to Eli, "Let thine handmaid find grace in thy sight" (1 Samuel 1:18). Mary was another Hannah!

thereby heard again [18] from the mouth of Mary. In all the New Testament, only Mary would refer to herself as the Handmaid of the Lord, and the special place held by Hannah in the Old, would be claimed by Mary in the New. The spirit of Mary was so wonderfully alike to Hannah, for when Mary prayed, it was immediately evident that she prayed with equal fervency and eloquence. But her prayer, from the beginning was more than just a counterpart of Hannah's. It was Hannah's prayer, as she referred repeatedly to the words of the one who had gone before her. She did so, because she was inspired by Hannah's example. She already knew that her circumstances were strangely similar. And she shared Hannah's sense of privilege in being selected by God to outwork His purpose. She felt exactly like her, as the angel affirmed that the power of the Highest would overshadow her for the bearing of the anointed one of whom Hannah had spoken. Filled with trembling hope and wonder, her mind sought solace in the comforting words of the one who had trodden this path before her, and knew what it felt like. Never were two women more strongly linked than these two, on the day when Mary gave voice to the feelings of her heart. And there was little surprise therefore that when she opened her mouth, the words of Hannah were heard. [19]

What then was the source of Mary's spiritual mind? It came from the same place as Hannah's, for Mary also from the earliest age had begun to fill her own treasury of spiritual thoughts, to be stored safely in her heart. [20] Although the birth of her son quickened her interest even further in a myriad of matters she sought so eagerly to understand, her storehouse was already full of scriptural passages and godly ideas, as her prayer

---

[18] Mary's phrase (Luke 1:48) is a direct quotation from Hannah's prayer – "if thou wilt look on the humiliation of thine handmaid" (1 Samuel 1:11, LXX).

[19] See Appendix 4 – "What was the import of Hannah's special song?" on page 221 for a comparison of the Song of Hannah and the Prayer of Mary.

[20] Luke's Gospel carefully records that – "Mary kept all these things and pondered them in her heart" (Luke 2:19). The statement completed a parallel, for Hannah is the first woman of whom the term "in her heart" is used, and Mary will be the last.

so amply proved. Matters of the divine plan which she knew and loved, stories which excited her curiosity and wonder, events and people which inspired and delighted her: all these were kept, pondered and weighed in the meditations of her heart. Nor was her devotion to collecting and considering such things a passing phase, but her settled way of life. [21] Mary's treasury was a witness to her spiritual mind, a woman of deep understanding, and a pure heart. Not without reason had she been selected by God to be His Handmaid in bringing forth a special son. And neither without reason had Hannah been chosen, to bring forth another son in whom God's work would be seen. How remarkably did these two women of holy faith and spiritual mind resemble each other.

A faithful husband and his yearly pilgrimage

Elkanah, like his wife, was a godly person in an ungodly age, yet despite the wickedness of his times, he sought to lead his family in spiritual ways. In his careful distribution of the portions of the peace offerings, [22] and his awareness of the principles concerning vows, [23] he displayed a knowledge of the commandments of Moses, that was exemplary in his day. Not only did he know the law of God, but he sought to uphold it in his life. But there was one aspect of his faithfulness that especially marked out Elkanah from those around him. In his days, the ordinances of God concerning regular assembly at the place which God had chosen, were largely in abeyance. Instead, people sought to fashion their

---

[21] The doubled account of Hannah, who "spake in her heart" (1 Samuel 1:13), and "rejoiced in her heart" (1 Samuel 2:1), will be matched by the double account of Mary, who "pondered in her heart" (Luke 2:19), and "kept in her heart" (Luke 2:51). Only when the story of Hannah is seen in Luke is the fulness of the parallel seen! The term "kept" here (*diatereo*) means to keep both carefully and continually.

[22] The record is careful to note this – "and when the time was that Elkanah offered, he gave ... portions" (1 Samuel 1:4; cp. Leviticus 7:15,16; Deuteronomy 12:17,18).

[23] The mention of his own vow, and his allusion to the law of vows again illustrated both his knowledge and observance of the teaching of Moses (1 Samuel 1:21,23; cp. Numbers 30:2,14).

own worship activities and locations, [24] since every man did that which was right in his own eyes. Not so Elkanah. He was committed to the practice of going up to the temple in Shiloh every year to worship and to sacrifice. [25]

It was easy to maintain such a standard when his family was smaller in number. But part of Elkanah's faithfulness lay in his continued visits to Shiloh, even when his family continued to increase in number, and the journey was made more difficult. [26] There was a price to pay to sustain this commitment, and to meet the obligations that such a journey brought, but Elkanah willingly did so because of the spiritual benefits it brought to his family. This then, was the spirit and standard of his household, and it was faithful Elkanah who led his family on this journey every year. The very pattern of their spiritual life was marked by the rhythm of their yearly pilgrimage. [27] Luke would record the faithfulness of Joseph in a remarkably similar manner. Their visit to the temple at the dedication of Jesus was strictly in accordance with the law of God, and evidently Joseph was diligent in his observance of the statutes of Moses. [28] In fact, they were anxious that every aspect of the child's life, from his very beginning be in accordance with the law of the Lord. [29]

---

[24] As witnessed by such episodes as the idolatry of Micah (Judges 17:5,6), and the apostasy of the Danites (Judges 18:30,31).

[25] 1 Samuel 1:3.

[26] It is to be supposed that at the first, Elkanah and Hannah made the journey alone. Later, when Elkanah had taken Peninnah as his second wife, and she bore him several children (1 Samuel 1:4), the journey would become more difficult. And after the birth and dedication of Samuel, the family grew in number again, with the blessing of another five offspring which Hannah would bear to her husband (1 Samuel 2:21).

[27] Notice how marked the record is in describing this aspect of Elkanah – "this man went up out of his city yearly to worship and to sacrifice ... in Shiloh" (1 Samuel 1:3), "And the man Elkanah, and all his house, went up to offer unto the LORD the yearly sacrifice" (1 Samuel 1:21), "when she came up with her husband to offer the yearly sacrifice" (1 Samuel 2:19,20).

[28] Note the references to "the days of purification" (Luke 2:22), "as it is written ... every male shall be holy" (Luke 2:23), "to offer a sacrifice ... a pair of turtledoves" (Luke 2:24).

[29] The record will emphasise this spirit – "according to the law" (Luke 2:22), "they brought him to Jerusalem, to present him to the Lord; as it is written in the law

But the visit to the temple in Jerusalem at the birth of Christ, although for a special purpose was not an unusual journey. It was but one incident in the life of a family, who already knew the holy city and the holy place very well. Their commitment to an annual pilgrimage was already an established practice in the household of Joseph, for they went to Jerusalem every year at the feast. [30] They spent sufficient time at the sanctuary to fulfil the days, and then returned afterwards to their home city of Nazareth, in the identical cycle followed by Elkanah and Hannah in an earlier age. [31]

Nor did the journey become any easier over time. Jesus was the firstborn son, born by the direct intervention of the Spirit. But subsequently, Joseph's own household, with the blessing of God, expanded to a total of at least seven children, all of whom accompanied their parents on the yearly journey. [32] Yet despite this additional burden of responsibility, Joseph was steadfast in continuing to take his entire family to Jerusalem, because of the spiritual blessings they could share together in that place. Here was Elkanah's faithfulness manifested in Joseph. The time and circumstances were different, and yet the spirit of the man was the same. The story of Shiloh was to be retold.

An evil priesthood and their violent deeds

And who were the opponents of godly Hannah and faithful Elkanah? Why Hophni and Phinehas, the sons of Eli. These

---

of the Lord" (Luke 2:22,23), "the parents brought in the child Jesus, to do for him after the custom of the law" (Luke 2:27), "and when they had performed all things according to the law of the Lord" (Luke 2:39).

30 In the relevant passage (Luke 2:41,42) the phrase "every year" is rendered "year by year" (GLT), and "yearly" (Rotherham). The language is the exact counterpart of Elkanah's practice (1 Samuel 1:3).

31 The expressions – "they returned into Galilee, to their own city Nazareth, "when they had fulfilled the days, as they returned" (Luke 2:39,43), capture the very cycle of travel to Shiloh, seen in the life of Elkanah and Hannah – "And they worshipped before the LORD, and returned, and came to their house to Ramah" (1 Samuel 1:19).

32 Just as Elkanah's household grew (1 Samuel 1:4; 2:21), so Joseph's family increased to at least seven offspring in the mercy of God (Mark 6:3).

sons of Belial were the worst of men, infamous for their aggressive deeds, [33] and notorious for their arrogant words. [34] They were driven by the spirit of greed, [35] as they sought to enrich themselves, not only at the expense of the people, but at the desecration of their worship. Worse still, their absolute dominance of the priesthood made it impossible for any to challenge them. In such a time of spiritual barrenness all sense of holiness and sacredness was lost. Indeed, it was this very state of affairs which pierced Hannah to her soul, and brought about the birth of her son whom she dedicated to the temple.

His arrival must have been a cause for surprise, for none before had ever dedicated a child so young as he. No one knew what Hophni and Phinehas thought about the little boy who walked within the temple precinct. They may have noticed his godly disposition, but given that he was but a child, they were unaware that in him they beheld their nemesis. God was already at work with Hannah's son, whose destiny was linked to their downfall.

Their example had already incurred the divine displeasure, but Samuel's own example was the antithesis of theirs. [36] His personal integrity was irreproachable, as he eschewed every form of greed or personal enrichment from bribes or oppression. Samuel's personal conviction doubtless sprang from the hand of his mother, who had instilled into her son from the earliest moment a hatred of such corruption and an awareness of the terrible effect it would have upon the worship of the people. When he came to fulness of maturity, his own spiritual standards would be the guide to return Israel to the proper worship of their God. His example would both inspire and direct the nation. Christ would do the same, and the spirit of Samuel would be seen in the child of Nazareth.

---

[33] 1 Samuel 2:13,14.
[34] 1 Samuel 2:15,16.
[35] 1 Samuel 2:29.
[36] 1 Samuel 12:3-5.

At the time of Christ, the priesthood at the sanctuary was just as corrupt and just as evil as it was in Hannah's day. Annas had come to power as High Priest when Christ was still a young child.[37] Although his own tenure lasted for but nine years, he remained a powerful figure, and through bribery and corruption kept his family dominant in the priesthood for the next six decades.[38] When Christ came to the temple as a boy of twelve, he deliberately engaged in discussion with the priests.[39] Even then, he showed such spiritual promise in his earnest questions and discerning answers, that the first stirrings of unease and the first inklings of a future hostility prickled in the air.[40] The priests had beheld the man who would rise to supersede them. And in contrast to their own spirit of avarice and hypocrisy, Jesus would reveal the same standard of personal integrity that was manifest in Samuel in an earlier age.[41]

The House of Annas was extremely rich, and they held a strong grip on the priesthood. The key source of the family's wealth came from the temple market which they operated in the Court of the Gentiles. Known as the "Bazaars of the Sons of Annas", these market stalls controlled the temple activities related to the offerings of the worshippers. Through these, they held a monopoly on the sale of sacrificial animals, and on the exchanging of money into the temple coins needed for the purchase of sacrifices. Their position of power enabled them to amass enormous wealth from these activities, and they enforced their rights without compunction. The dedication of those who

---

[37] Annas was appointed High Priest by Quirinius, governor of Syria in AD 6, and subsequently deposed by the Roman governor Valerius Gratus in AD 15.

[38] A passage in the Talmud illustrates the character of the House of Annas – "Woe to the house of Annas! Woe to their serpent's hiss! They are high priests; their sons are keepers of the treasury, their sons-in-law are guardians of the temple, and their servants beat people with staves" (Pesahim 57a).

[39] For such were the doctors of the law (Luke 2:46). Members of the House of Annas might well have been there at this first meeting, for Annas was already in power at the time.

[40] Rotherham – "Now all who heard him were beside themselves, because of his understanding and his answers" (Luke 2:47).

[41] The words of Christ – "Which of you convinceth me of sin?" (John 8:46), were a clear echo of Samuel's own asseveration (1 Samuel 12:3).

came to worship was the lever which Annas and his family used to enrich themselves. **⁴²** What the Sons of Eli did with the peace offerings at the door of the tabernacle, the Sons of Annas did with all the sacrifices, in their vast market which sprawled across the temple courts. The wickedness present in Shiloh, was as nothing to the corruption seen in the Jerusalem of Annas.

Nor did they hesitate to resort to violence and extortion to achieve their ends. The last of the Sons of Annas to hold the office of High Priest was his namesake, Annas II. His capacity for violence and corruption was typical of the family who had dominated the spiritual life of the nation for sixty years. Of him, it would be recorded that nothing would stop his greed. **⁴³** What chance was there, for the godly in Israel to worship the God of their Fathers in spirit and truth, with such scoundrels in charge? Who could doubt that the priesthood in the day of Christ made worship impossible. Here then, in the time of Christ was the exact counterpart of the rapacious robbery of Hophni and Phinehas. The aggressive actions and arrogant words of the "Sons of Eli" would be seen again in the unrighteous priesthood of the "Sons of Annas". So blatant was their spirit, that the Rabbis of the time described them in this very way. **⁴⁴**

The appearance of another Hophni and Phinehas class called for another Samuel to confront them, and the Lord did

---

42   So influential was the House of Annas, that about the time of Christ, the Sanhedrin transferred its meeting place from the Hall of Hewn Stones in the temple, to the Bazaars of the Sons of Annas (*Life and Times of Jesus the Messiah*, volume 1, book 3, chapter 5, pages 371,372, Alfred Edersheim).

43   The account of his influence is given by Josephus thus – "as for the high priest Annas, he increased in glory every day, and this to a great degree ... for he was a great hoarder of money ... he also had servants who were very wicked, who joined themselves to the boldest of the people, went to the threshing-floors, and took away the tithes that belonged to the priest by violence, and did not refrain from beating such as would not give these tithes to them" (Josephus, *Antiquities of the Jews*, book 20, chapter 9.2).

44   The Talmud recorded – "Our Rabbis taught: Four cries did the Temple Court cry out. The first – 'Go hence, ye sons of Eli', ye defile the temple of the LORD" (Pesahim 57a). In this remarkable statement, the priesthood of Christ's day was considered to possess the very spirit of Hophni and Phinehas in their wickedness.

exactly that in challenging their unrighteous behaviour. He denounced them in the words of the prophets – "It is written, My house is the house of prayer, but ye have made it a den of thieves". **45**

An old man and his priestly blessing

Eli was already full of days by the time Samuel was born, and the Spirit depicted him in old age, as being distinctively associated with the temple. He was sitting on "a seat by a post of the temple" when Hannah first prayed in the desperation of her grief. **46** He was still to be found there several years later when she returned with her son "to present him to the Lord". **47** He was at the temple in subsequent years, when he blessed the child's parents as they came to that place in pilgrimage. **48** Small though Samuel was, Eli saw something in the lad that stirred the spirit of hope, and in his blessing, he focused on the significance of the child who had been lent to the Lord by his mother. **49** Rendered powerless as he was by the dominance of his evil sons, Eli found the presence of Samuel, in all his innocence and truth, to be a gift of joy. Yet even then, Eli had not fully understood the future of the young boy who lived with him at the sanctuary.

But one night when the old priest was asleep, Samuel was addressed thrice, until finally "Eli perceived that the LORD had called the child". **50** In the morning, he ordered Samuel to tell

---

45 The words of Christ (Luke 19:45-48) envisaged a future temple accessible by both Jew and Gentile (Isaiah 56:7), and lamented a past temple which was destroyed because the spirit of Hophni and Phinehas was seen there (Jeremiah 7:9-12).
46 It seems that this throne (*kicce*) was his customary position (1 Samuel 1:9).
47 Hannah would no doubt have returned to the very spot where she had previously encountered Eli, and not surprisingly he still sat there at the temple entrance (1 Samuel 1:24,25).
48 1 Samuel 2:20.
49 The phrase – "for the loan which is lent to the LORD" showed Eli's appreciation of Samuel even at the earliest moments of Samuel's life (1 Samuel 2:20).
50 This occasion must have affected Eli powerfully. As the priest of Israel, and he who wore an ephod before God, he was the appointed channel of divine communication. Yet on this fateful night, the Lord bypassed his priest, and spoke instead with the

him all, and the words which the child uttered, convinced him that Samuel had received a revelation from God himself. [51] Eli recognised, in a blinding flash of insight, what all Israel would soon know, namely that Samuel was chosen of the Lord. [52] With an awareness which must have astonished and thrilled him, he realised that here was the faithful priest of God's own appointing. Whatever might be the fate of his own household, whose wickedness he knew, the purpose of God with Israel would be continued though Samuel. The old man saw it now, in that morning at the temple, and at a time when his own course was run, the knowledge brought comfort. God had never left His people without witness or help, and He would not do so now.

Shortly afterwards, in a catastrophic battle, the ark of God was taken, and in the same tragedy, Eli's two sons, Hophni and Phinehas, were also killed. The judgment of God had come with final and irrevocable force upon his household, and it was no doubt a mercy that Eli lost his life shortly afterwards, in the shock of hearing the news. But it was also a blessing, that before he died, he had seen and recognised this one to come, through whom the divine purpose would be outworked in a new and better priesthood.

In Mary's time, a remarkable meeting occurred in the temple between herself as she brought in her child, and an old man who waited in that place for her arrival. [53] When she and Joseph appeared with Jesus, the old man stepped forward to intercept them. He was a devoted attendant at the temple, and whether of the priesthood or not, he certainly acted in a priestly role. This man, Simeon, had been warned by the Holy

---

little child. The implication, not lost on Eli, was that God had already made choice of the priest through whom he would now work.

[51] Hence Eli's words – "It is the LORD: let him do what seemeth him good" (1 Samuel 3:18).

[52] The expression – "Samuel was established to be a prophet of the LORD" indicates his special selection (1 Samuel 3:20).

[53] The record suggests that he was there before them awaiting their arrival. RSV – "And inspired by the Spirit he came into the temple, and when the parents brought in the child Jesus" (Luke 2:27).

Spirit, that he would not see death before he had seen the Lord's anointed". [54] There could be little doubt, in this gospel of all gospels, that the anointed one whom he was to meet, would be as much a promised priest as a future king.

It was unusual for an old man to see the future written in the face of a little child. It was too early to know what the unfolding of life would bring, for there to be any certainty as to what the babe might accomplish. The old especially, know how the sweep of time and years can change a life that once looked so promising, into a story of sorrow and failure. But, warned of God as he had been, he gazed upon this child and knew that this was he.

Simeon felt compelled to hold the babe, and reaching out his arms, he lifted up the child and held him close. He knew deep within that he was cradling the most precious thing he had ever held, and felt the same trembling sense of realisation as Eli, that he had indeed looked upon the Lord's anointed. Filled with a happiness beyond his experience, Simeon expressed his deepest gratitude for such a privilege. It left him, so thankful for this gift of joy, that he could now die in peace. "Lord, now lettest thou thy servant depart in peace, according to thy word: For mine eyes have seen thy salvation."

He was an old man when at the temple, he saw him whom the Lord had chosen. [55] It was a mercy afforded to one who was "waiting for the consolation of Israel", that God gave him this glimpse of the one through whom that consolation was to come. And it was destined then, that Simeon should also perform the gracious act of blessing the parents of the child as they came to the temple. Just as Eli had encouraged Elkanah and Hannah

---

54 The term – "revealed" (*chrematizo*) means more properly to be warned (Luke 1:26).
55 This is the clear inference of the narrative – "he should not see death, before", "now lettest thou thy servant depart in peace" (Luke 2:26,29). His expression in this latter verse, was in turn a quotation from the words of Jacob in his old age, when seeing the face of his special son Joseph before he died (Genesis 46:30). It was Simeon in his old age who was the counterpart of Eli, himself an old man when Samuel's future priestly work was revealed to him.

with a priestly benediction at the sanctuary in Shiloh, so Simeon bestowed the same upon Joseph and Mary, who had visited the temple at Jerusalem. [56] And just as Eli had focused on the significance of the child lent, so now Simeon made comment on the importance of Jesus, and the impact this child would have upon the nation of Israel. [57] The story of Eli was to become the story of Simeon, as the Spirit overshadowed this writing.

A virgin attendant and her temple service

Samuel was still so very little when first presented at Shiloh. Someone at the temple must have cared for him, for such an important responsibility could not be left to chance. Because God had claim upon the child, in the outworking of Hannah's vow, He also held responsibility for the child's safe nurture. In an amazing display of divine providence, the child's temple guardian had been selected well before the child was even born. [58] That there were women at the temple was undoubted, for there were many activities associated with the temple worship which required the voluntary labour of faithful women. Those who served were provided for by the temple, and found their place within its buildings. Jephthah's daughter was one of the women associated with the temple worship, who lived at the sanctuary, [59] and came under the jurisdiction of the High Priest of the time. Her example was already famed in Israel, celebrated for her faithfulness and holiness. At the time of Samuel's presentation, she had already been dedicated to temple service in her virginity. But here at hand was one so well suited to pour her love and devotion into the most wonderful task she would ever be asked to perform.

---

56 The phrase – "And Simeon blessed them, and said unto Mary his mother" (Luke 2:34) is an obvious and satisfying echo of the earlier account in Hannah's time – "And Eli blessed Elkanah and his wife and said" (1 Samuel 2:20).

57 The words of Simeon were evidently a Spirit inspired comment on the work of Christ – "Behold, this child is set for the fall and rise of many in Israel, and for a sign" (Luke 2:34).

58 See Appendix 6 – "Who was the guardian of Hannah's firstborn son?" on page 228

59 Judges 11:39,40.

Her love of the lad, her commitment to his cause, her recognition of his role, were without question. Blessed by God with this precious charge, she rejoiced to be given in her unmarried state, the task of loving and guarding Hannah's firstborn son.

Indeed, there was a sign of her involvement in the child's life soon after his arrival at the place of the sanctuary. For Samuel was immediately given small tasks, which he undertook with so serious a heart, that even in these he ministered unto the Lord. [60] From the outset, he was a priest in the making, and someone girded him with a linen ephod in recognition of his priestly spirit. [61] Wise hearted women had spun the fine linen for the ephods at the sanctuary. [62] But there were no such garments which would fit a three year old boy. Who then made this little ephod? Not Eli, whose eyes had begun to wax dim that he could not see. Who might it have been other than the guardian who watched so fiercely and so well over his every need. Jephthah's daughter made her own mark on the child, but it was a mark which Hannah must have rejoiced in. The little ephod conveyed a woman's touch, and was the sign of a woman's care: a woman who shared his mother's conviction concerning the destiny of the child – his priestly destiny. As the climax of her sanctuary service, Jephthah's daughter watched over the one in whom God's priestly work amidst His people would be preserved. She would never forget the privilege.

In Luke's portrait, another dedicated woman suddenly appeared at the temple when the child Jesus was presented. But her presence at the temple was not in itself unusual, for she was so devoted as to be in constant attendance, serving God with fastings and prayers night and day. Anna, married

---

60 His labours even as a child were described this way (1 Samuel 2:11,18; 3:1). This term itself (ministered) carried priestly overtones.

61 The juxtaposition of the statement concerning his linen ephod (1 Samuel 2:18) against the comment concerning another garment which his mother brought up (1 Samuel 2:19), suggests that the ephod was provided by someone at the sanctuary.

62 As the law recorded (Exodus 28:3; 35:25).

but seven years from her virginity, had been devoted now to the sanctuary for eighty-four years, a period so long that her temple covenant now exceeded her marriage covenant by twelve times. Counted against the total sum, her dedication to the service of the sanctuary represented by far the substance of her life. She was a virgin attendant at the temple after the spirit of old. [63] So committed was she, that a place of lodging had been found for her within the temple buildings. [64] Like Jephthah's daughter she was resident at the sanctuary.

Samuel met his guardian carer on his first visit to the temple. Luke was careful to record that Jesus would also encounter a dedicated woman on the occasion of his first visit to the temple. How thrilled Anna was to meet the Christ. For like Simeon, she also waited, [65] and like him she offered thanks at the moment of the meeting. Surely it was in the providence of God that both she and Simeon were present at the sanctuary at that time, for their mutual song would fulfil the words of the prophet – "Thy watchmen shall lift up the voice; with the voice together shall they sing: for they shall see eye to eye, when the LORD shall bring again Zion. Break forth into joy, sing together, ye waste places of Jerusalem: for the LORD hath comforted his people, he hath redeemed Jerusalem". [66] But Anna's song was no general outpouring of praise. She saw in Jesus the promise of redemption for the nation. She spoke of him because she believed in the destiny of the child – his priestly destiny. After a lifetime of temple service, Phanuel's daughter

---

63 Why did Luke (guided by the Spirit) use such an extremely rare and unusual form of expression in describing the dignity of Anna's temple service? The phrase – "from her virginity" was not only unnecessary, but very arresting in its association. For there are only two women in all of scripture whose state of virginity is specifically commented on: the virginity of Jephthah's daughter (Judges 11:34,35), and the virginity of Phanuel's daughter (Luke 2:36). Why otherwise would the Spirit in Luke have used this phrase concerning "virginity", if not to draw attention to the parallel?

64 The phrase – "she departed not from the temple" (Luke 2:37) is suggestive of this idea.

65 The word "looked for" (Luke 2:38) is the same word as "waited" used of Simeon (Luke 2:25).

66 Isaiah 52:8,9.

reached the fulfilment of her service in witnessing to the child she met. In Anna, [67] the story of another virgin attendant who served at the sanctuary would be seen, in an astonishing counterpart, that only providence could have ordained.

A little child and his godly growth

The final character in the scene was the little boy himself. It was certainly remarkable that in the midst of all the evil present at the sanctuary, Samuel grew up straight and true, and evidently untouched by the wickedness around him. In the early life of every child, growth was dependent on the care of a mother. [68] In Samuel's case however, he was already weaned before being brought to the sanctuary, and once settled there, could no longer depend upon his mother for his needs. And yet, it was at Shiloh that the record would chronicle the stages by which he moved to maturity of mind, and strength of body.

"And the child Samuel grew before the LORD", "And the child Samuel grew on, and was in favour", "And Samuel grew and the LORD was with him." [69]

Here was the lovely description of the steady progress of Hannah's son into the one who would become God's faithful priest. But given his mother's absence from that place, this report was the diary of his development under his Father's nurture. Almighty God has ever nursed His household thus. [70] Beyond the physical nourishment and growth which he experienced, Samuel received that sustenance which strengthened him spiritually towards manhood. God was at work in his life.

---

[67] How appropriate that the old woman bears the name of Hannah, the mother of Samuel (Anna being but the Greek form). It is yet another striking link in the two stories.

[68] The word "grew" is frequently connected with the nourishment received from the mother's nursing (Genesis 21:8; Exodus 2:9,10; 1 Peter 2:2).

[69] 1 Samuel 2:21,26; 3:19.

[70] Even the title *Ail Shaddai*, is expressive of God's power to be a nursing father to his offspring. God bears, and carries all his children (Deuteronomy 1:31; 32:10-12; Isaiah 46:3,4; Acts 13:18).

And there was one further aspect of Samuel's formative years. He grew "in favour both with the LORD and with men". [71] The two are very different. To grow in favour with God is to be recognised by Him, and this recognition is the result of a heart set on observing His principles. [72] To such a person, God extends the favour of His blessing, and Samuel from infancy stood in this special relationship with the Lord. But to be in favour with men, is to be respected by them because of an integrity of character which commands admiration, and offers no basis for rebuke, or disobedience. [73] Something in Samuel, sincere and godly, produced this reaction among those who observed him.

Luke alone would record the early childhood of Jesus, for it was a crucial part of his gospel. Even so, his account would give but a single verse to summarise those early years. But brief though his comment was, the words would immediately recall that sanctuary child of long ago, whose life and times foreshadowed the Lord's so precisely. "And the child grew, and waxed strong in spirit, filled with wisdom, and the grace of God was upon him". [74]

With that one word "grew", Luke led his readers back to Shiloh, and to the little Levite who fulfilled his priestly ministrations with such care. And like Samuel, Jesus in infancy grew in steady stages distinguished by the Spirit. [75] The Lord's childhood was marked by his vigorous and healthy growth. And as his limbs lengthened, and his bones grew strong, so also his mind expanded, and his wisdom increased. But it was this latter development that was so clearly overshadowed by his Father, for "the grace of God was upon him". In Samuel's case, the grace of

---

[71] 1 Samuel 2:26.
[72] The counsel in Proverbs (3:1-4) is evidently an allusion to this earlier passage.
[73] Samuel himself depicted this principle (1 Samuel 12:2-5). He was blameless in character.
[74] It is important to notice that this verse (Luke 2:40) is indeed the only one which comments on the early years of Jesus, for it relates to his development up until the age of twelve (Luke 2:42).
[75] The sense of the Greek in Luke 2:40 is captured by Rotherham – "And, the child, went on growing, and waxing strong, becoming filled with wisdom".

his mother was upon him, for so was the meaning of her name. But with Jesus, whatever Mary brought to the child as a mother's gift, was enhanced by the Father's favour which was superadded. The result was a child, so endowed with spiritual attributes, that at twelve he could debate the priests of the nation and confound them with his thinking and his answers.

And as with the child, so with the man. For of Christ's growth to fulness of maturity, Luke would state, "And Jesus increased in wisdom and stature, and in favour with God and man". [76] No other gospel writer would record this detail, where, like Samuel, who was both approved of God and accepted by men, Jesus also would receive this twofold testimony. There could not be a plainer parallel. But the one who found favour with God and man was thereby able to be "ordained for men in things pertaining to God". [77] The essence of his priesthood lay in being able to comprehend the claims of the one, yet understand the needs of the other. Jesus would be a priest, after the spirit of Samuel, who led the nation in sacrifice and prayer.

And just as there was another Samuel, so there was another Hannah. The veil would be drawn over the life of the Lord, from the age of twelve, until the age of thirty, but during those years in the home at Nazareth, Christ received an imprint of his mother's heart, just as Samuel had in his home at Ramah.

A Gospel writer and his portrait of Christ

Why then did Luke alone paint this picture, and illustrate it with such breathtaking detail in his gospel? The answer lay in knowing why there were four gospels at all. Each account of the ministry of Christ presented a portrait that answered to one of the four faces of the cherubim. And each of those faces in turn depicted a special aspect of Christ, as the manifestation of the Father. Only

---

[76] This later statement (Luke 2:52) must refer to the time between twelve and thirty, when he began his ministry. It was an obvious allusion to Samuel's life (1 Samuel 2:26).

[77] Hebrews 5:1.

when that aspect was known would the inner secrets of each gospel be seen. Each face was remarkably different, yet they all revealed such strong and unmistakeable characteristics, that all who looked upon them had no doubt what they had seen, and what it told them of the Son of God. Of course, in the life of Christ was the sum of all the cherubic figures, the complete revelation of his Father's glory. But through the power of the Spirit, each gospel writer provided those subtle touches and special details which brought one face into prominence in their portrait of the Lord. Each gospel was enriched because of this focus, as the overshadowing of inspiration fashioned a fourfold picture of the one in whom the fulness of God would be seen. Whatever might be discovered by combining the gospel records, their singularity was to be preserved, that each face might be more clearly seen.

Matthew's Gospel depicted the face of the lion, who with its fierce and gleaming eyes, its expression of maned majesty, and its terrifying roar revealed the face of kingship. The lion was known in scripture for its strength of leadership, [78] its spirit of courage, [79] and its voice of power. [80] Matthew's account would highlight the majesty of Christ's royal leadership, the power of his public discourse, and the greatness of his tender mercy. In his gospel, he would reveal Christ as the perfect king, in whom would be seen that mercy which rules.

Mark's Gospel depicted the face of the ox, who with its soft and bovine eyes, its expression of placid docility, and its gentle lowing revealed the face of service. The ox was known in scripture for its strength to labour, [81] its willingness to serve, [82] and its spirit of sacrifice. [83] Mark's account would highlight the humility of Christ's loyal service, the exhaustion of his faithful work, and the dedication of his complete sacrifice. In his gospel,

---

[78] Proverbs 30:3; Judges 14:18.
[79] 2 Samuel 17:10; Proverbs 28:1.
[80] Proverbs 19:2; Amos 3:8.
[81] Psalm 144:14; Proverbs 14:4.
[82] Deuteronomy 25:4; Isaiah 32:20.
[83] Leviticus 1:5; Jeremiah 11:19.

he would reveal Christ as the perfect servant, in whom would be seen that humility which serves.

John's Gospel depicted the face of the eagle, who with its intense and piercing eyes, its expression of powerful severity, and its harsh cry revealed the face of judgment. The eagle was known in scripture for its power of flight, [84] its extraordinary vision, [85] and its speed of attack. [86] John's account would highlight the spirit of Christ's unerring discernment, the clarity of his divine judgment, and the excellence of his personal integrity. In his gospel, he would reveal Christ as the perfect judge, in whom would be seen that spirit which discerns.

Luke's Gospel depicted the face of the man, who with his bright and understanding eyes, his expression of intelligent sympathy, and his spiritual speech revealed the face of priesthood. The man was known in scripture for his spirit of wisdom, [87] his warmth of friendship, [88] and his sympathy of care. [89] Luke's account would highlight the power of Christ's universal compassion, his blessing of personal fellowship, and the example of his constant prayer. In his gospel, he would reveal Christ as the perfect priest, [90] in whom would be seen that compassion which saves.

Hannah and her Lord

But Luke wrote also to present Christ as a priest according to a different order to that of Aaron, since it was evident that our

---

[84] Proverbs 23:5; 30:19.
[85] Job 39:29; Habakkuk 1:8.
[86] Job 9:26; Lamentations 4:19.
[87] Ecclesiastes 8:1; Acts 6:15.
[88] Exodus 33:11; Proverbs 27:9.
[89] Philippians 2:20; Hebrews 5:1,2.
[90] Each cherubic figure was a symbol of divine manifestation. In Luke, the face of the man signified the perfect priest. The relationship of the humanity of Christ and his priesthood is considered at length by the writer to the Hebrews, where it is evident that a priest taken from among men, was a man endowed with necessary sympathy for his ministrations (Hebrews 2:17,18; 4:15; 5:1-5). It is this man who is declared in the gospel of Luke, whose priestly work was to seek and to save those who were lost (Luke 19:10).

Lord sprang out of Judah. This was why the Spirit overshadowed the writing of his gospel page, and imbedded into his account the story of Hannah, and the promise of Samuel who arose as a faithful priest to supersede the Aaronic order of the day, rejected by God because of their spiritual wickedness. Samuel acted as a priest of God's own appointing to replace Hophni and Phinehas, but his priesthood was based upon his Nazarite status, a different and yet higher priesthood than the Aaronic order. And in this role, Samuel prefigured the Lord whose priesthood would also be of a different order. This was why Hannah and those around her were gathered into Luke's Gospel. Could there be a better foreshadowing of an impending change of priesthood than the story of this remarkable woman and her beloved son? And could there be a better story with which to commence the gospel of the perfect priest than that of Hannah, who sought to provide such a priest for her people?

Where then was Peninnah in this cast of characters? What part did she fulfil in this gospel assemblage of those involved in Mary's day? In truth, she was not to be found. She was never the real source of Hannah's adversity, nor was she the centre of Hannah's controversy. Hannah's work would unfold in Shiloh, where her son had been sent, and where every year, she would add her part. And her controversy would reach its climax when Samuel, grown to maturity, would confront the spirit of the age, and the priesthood who had defiled it. It was fitting therefore, that whilst every other person crucial to that controversy was to be seen in Luke's account, no parallel would be found for Peninnah. The absence, from the Lord's nativity, of one who might be her counterpart, was evidence that Peninnah was not the focus of Hannah's grief, or the key to Hannah's purpose.

How telling that Luke's Gospel began with a priest after the order of Aaron, who could neither lift up hands to petition for others, nor utter for them the words of benediction.[91] It was

---

[91] The inability of Zacharias to fulfil his priestly responsibility in blessing the people, marks the opening scene of the gospel (Luke 1:5,8-10,21,22)!

as if from the outset, his gospel would reveal the inadequacy of the Aaronic order as the prelude to the introduction of a new priest who stood related to a better covenant.

And how wonderful that his gospel ended with a priest after the order of Melchizedek, close by the king's dale, [92] who could both raise his hands in priestly intercession for others, and offer for them the words of priestly blessing. [93]

The faithful priest that Hannah yearned for had appeared. This was his moment. This was his gospel. When the fulness of time was come, God sent forth his Son, born of a woman, and in that birth the story of Hannah came to its conclusion. She would be seen in Mary who shared her spirit and revered her example. Luke revealed the life and times of that new and better priest begun in the birth of another firstborn son. Mary's first, and Hannah's seventh. Mary's son and Hannah's Lord. We read the record and rest content. For in seeing the woman of Ramah in the face of the woman of Nazareth, we know of a certainty that Hannah also was blessed indeed among women.

---

[92] Genesis 14:17.
[93] In leading his disciples to Bethany, the Lord probably led them past the king's dale (on the valley road), the very place where Melchizedek had blessed Abraham of old. And the ability of Christ to bestow that blessing on his disciples, marks the closing scene of the gospel (Luke 24:50-53)!

Epilogue

WHEN the story of the mother and child was inscribed in the gospel of the perfect priest, the Spirit's portrait of Hannah was also completed. In looking upon it, we sense that spirit of holiness that marked her life, so luminous in her love of the sacred before her God. Her character stood out bold and vivid against the darker background of her times. Yet, seen in a wider setting, her life was a cameo of all God's saints. The experiences of all God's people are set within the same framework of light and dark, and good and evil that characterised her age. The trials which befell her, and the truths which upheld her, touch us all. The details may differ, but the principles do not, for our faith also must be worked out within the setting of our own time. Whether we see its darkness and its danger, to challenge it as Hannah confronted hers, is a question that we alone can answer.

In every age, the vast majority accept the prevailing conditions as normal, for they have known nothing else. Their common, shared experience makes them blind to the deficiencies of the age. Only those who view the world through the lens of divine principle perceive its flaws, but such people are special and even unique in their awareness. Hannah was such a person. She recognised the weakness of her time, discerned its deepest need, and saw her vital role in meeting it. Her portrait revealed a woman who had fully known her purpose and manner of life. What then could our part be in the purpose of the Father, and how might we open ourselves to that possibility before Him? It is one of the deepest questions that every saint must ask, for in its answer lies the future focus of our life. It is a question best asked in our youth, when time stretches forward for the Father to show the way. [1] It is evident that Hannah had done so as a young woman, for her life was already shaped by a sense of destiny from the first moment her features were drawn.

The power of Hannah's example teaches us to examine every part of our age, with an eye to scriptural principle. When we do, we are smitten with the realisation that many aspects of the world in which we live are not just different to the Truth, but actively hostile to it. The challenge is to live in awareness of the divine standard, and remain separate from a world which on every side ignores God. Part of our service with reason is to give ourselves to the Truth with deliberate intention from the outset. Knowing what our abilities are, and how we might use them is no small decision. Prayer to God to be guided into those ways where we might best serve Him, is not a prayer of personal importance. It is the very reverse. It is a prayer to set our will aside, that we might advance the Father's cause instead. Even when we do, there will be difficulties in the way. A commitment to serve Him will not come without challenges in the path. The Father tests our resolve, to see whether we will abandon our efforts, or keep them in the spirit of proper dedication. Hannah understood the enormous obstacles that blocked her path, but she had found the right spirit with which to face them.

For one of the most important lessons of life to learn is that we should not dwell upon that which we cannot control. [2] To fret about things which we cannot alter has only ever brought despair. The way of wisdom has always been to focus on those things which we can change, and to let go of the rest, leaving them all in the Father's hands. [3] It was a measure of Hannah's

---

1 Ecclesiastes 12:1; Lamentations 3:27.
2 Ecclesiastes 11:3.
3 This is the essence of the so called Serenity Prayer – "God, grant me the serenity to accept the things I cannot change, Courage to change the things I can, And wisdom to know the difference".

depth that she knew the wisdom of this precept. The grief she felt did concern things which lay beyond her power to change. But, fully aware of what she could and could not do, she focused instead upon the one thing she could do, the one thing that mattered. She sought to be in harmony with the thinking of the Lord of hosts, and committed herself unto Him. Since, with God all things are possible, the secret to change lay in His hands.

That idea, so profound, moved the impetus from that which could not be done, to that which could. For there is nothing that cannot be achieved when the deliberate intent of a person is firmly aligned with the workings of their God. Hannah's story reveals that the spirit of such purpose in a person's life can accomplish things far above the scope of their usual capacity, and far beyond the limits of their normal ability. "Do not forget thine handmaid" was both the watchword and the waymark of her burning purpose. It was not just a term of becoming humility, but an idea conveying the very spirit of Hannah's whole desire. To be His Handmaid was to know the power of surrender to the fulness of the Divine will. By that spirit she petitioned, with that spirit she pleaded, in that spirit she prayed. She sought to be God's channel, God's medium, God's agency, God's means through which His purpose could be effected. The only way her grand objective could be realised was to place it unreservedly in the Father's hands, and be led into the wonder of what it might mean truly to be His Handmaid.

And wondrously indeed did the Almighty work through her. His purpose, which has always been unconstrained and uncontrolled by human agency, was nevertheless set in motion with Hannah at the centre, because her prayer reflected His plan. So closely did her thinking match the perspective of heaven that her own words were echoed by God's spokesman. This is the secret of God manifestation. It is to be so absorbed and so committed to the Divine purpose, that we seek to be the very means of its expression. The glorious thing was that she did not think for a moment about her own importance or rank. Instead she gave herself unreservedly to a cause greater than her own, but within which her own hope was also realised. When our spiritual objectives lie within the overarching purpose of God, there are always possibilities to grow into. For Hannah, the knowledge that God had involved her in His purpose, and had used her as His instrument was almost too wonderful for her heart to bear. The thought of being so identified with the work of God, and the privilege of being so honoured to be His Handmaid, overwhelmed her with a sense of blessedness that lifted her high above the mundane. It was possible, she found, to shed tears of happiness, that spoke what words could not.

Confessing sin, vowing devotion, and sharing fellowship was the threefold experience of the faithful, when they came to the sanctuary to meet their God.[4] The first brought the calm of forgiveness for the past, the second brought the focus of direction for the future, but the third brought the peace of harmony for the present. For Hannah, these were the stepping stones which marked the journey of her whole life. Hannah felt the pull of their teaching, and sought to reach the pinnacle which they promised. But all three depended on a faithful priest, and when Hannah's part was done, that priest was seen, and the smoke of the peace offerings arose afresh. Fellowship with God, in all its mystery and majesty was again made possible for the faithful.

That fellowship, and an abiding sense of living in His presence, was the spirit of this one who was the Handmaid of the Highest. And through the work of her son, as a faithful priest, that hope was made possible. The Lord who could make poor, had made her rich. And with this divine reversal of circumstances, this lifting up of what had been brought low, Hannah's life was made whole. There was restoration for this one who found her destiny in offering the sacrifice of praise. The wonder of fellowship with God which her peace offering signified, exalted her being, for it brought a sense of unity with Him as real as if one had entered

---

4 These answer to the significance of the sin, burnt and peace offerings which the offerer brought.

the Most Holy. Here was the place where principle and practice met, a state of mind only made possible because Hannah was so completely identified with the Lord's purpose as to be subsumed into it. With this disposition, even amidst the evil, she could ascend privately into the presence of God, to be in fellowship with Him, and there, finally, the light would always triumph over the darkness. The deepest desire of this wonderful woman of God is heard in the words of a well-beloved hymn, in a song of such yearning, that we can almost hear the voice of Hannah herself:

"Fill thou my life, O Lord, my God,
   In every part with praise,
That my whole being may proclaim
   Thy being and Thy ways.

Fill every part of me with praise,
   Let all my being speak
Of Thee, and of Thy love, O Lord,
   Poor though I be, and weak.

So shall no part of day or night
   From sacredness be free;
But all my life in every step
   Be fellowship with thee."

Her story gives us hope that we too might know that same sense of reverence for the sacredness of the Truth, and satisfy that same sense of yearning to find fellowship with our God. Both will be found when we share the same spirit of surrender to being God's instrument, and when in seeking to manifest Him, we pray that He might use us for His purpose to the honour of His name. In her calling as the Handmaid of the Highest, Hannah finally found that place and knew that peace, and the fulfilment it brought, graced her entire being with the glow of its spiritual contentment. May the wonder of her life touch ours with its radiance, for hers was a spirit so rare, as to be precious.

Appendices

Appendix 1 |

What was the setting for Hannah's troublous times?

The three appendices of the Judges

THE story of Hannah began in the context of the book of Judges. The final chapters of that book and the book of Ruth form a set of appendices to the judges era, in a threefold summary which captured the character and the failure of this period.

Appendix 1 (Judges 17,18). This section was about apostasy of doctrine found in the tribe of Dan. But it would be dated by the appearance of Jonathan, the grandson of Moses (Judges 18:30). If this episode occurred at the time of Moses' grandson, then it was very early in the epoch of the judges.

Appendix 2 (Judges 19-21). This section was about corruption of practice found in the tribe of Benjamin. But it would be dated by the appearance of Phinehas, the grandson of Aaron (Judges 20:27,28). The Phinehas of this story, was obviously of the same generation as the Jonathan of the previous episode.

Appendix 3 (Ruth 1-4). This section was about faithfulness of spirit found in the tribe of Judah. But it would be dated by the appearance of Boaz, the grandson of Nahshon (Ruth 4:13,20,21). Nahshon however was the prince of Judah at the time of the exodus (Numbers 10:14), and was therefore the contemporary of Moses and Aaron.

All three appendices therefore were set at the beginning of that epoch when the Lord raised them up judges. Their collective lesson was that apostasy of doctrine will inevitably lead to corruption of practice, and that faithfulness of spirit will only ever be seen in a remnant. But what is also clear is that the last episode historically in the book of Judges was the story of Samson (Judges 13-16). The story of Hannah (1 Samuel 1,2) would follow on immediately, and be set in the time of Eli, who was also a judge and an old man by the time Hannah's story began (1 Samuel 1:9; 4:18).

The chronology of the period

Whilst the chronology of the Judges is both complex and difficult, there is sound Biblical evidence to accept that the broad sweep of its latter part moved in sequence from Eli to Samson, and from Samson to Samuel. The Philistine oppression of forty years (Judges 13:1) most probably spanned the last twenty years of Eli's judgeship (1 Samuel 4:18), and the subsequent twenty years of Samson's work.[1] Despite Samson coming before Eli in the Biblical account, it is evident that he judged afterwards. The battle of Eben-ezer when the ark of God was taken and Eli died (1 Samuel 4:10-18), began an interregnum in Israel. That period (1 Samuel 5-6) recorded the journeying of the ark of God in Philistia, and its eventual return to rest in Kirjath-jearim. It was in those crucial years that Samson judged, and the record would provide evidence of his work at that time.[2]

When the ark was captured, it was taken into three cities of the Philistines, each of which were judged by God. In sequence Ashdod (1 Samuel 5:1-7), Gath (1 Samuel 5:8,9), and Ekron (1 Samuel 5:10-12) came under the divine punishment.

---

1 This sequence has been dealt with at reasonable length in both *Samuel the Seer* (pages 49-54, Michael Ashton), and in *Samson Revisited* (pages 5-12, Michael Storey). The writer concurs with the essence of the chronology suggested in these books.
2 The history of the nation written in Psalm 78 indicated this sequence. There, the psalmist reported the loss of the ark (verses 60-62), and the death of Hophni and Phinehas (verses 63,64), followed by the exploits of Samson (verse 65), and the judgment of the emerods (verse 66). The psalm thereby placed Samson's work after the death of Eli.

But there was an undesigned coincidence, which linked the work of Samson to this moment in history. He visited Ashkelon and executed judgment (Judges 14:19), and entered Gaza to show his power (Judges 16:1-3). But he was never recorded as coming against Ashdod, Gath, or Ekron. God had already visited His judgment upon those places, yet Samson did judge the other cities of the Philistines where the ark of God had not come. Samson's controversy was against the five "lords of the Philistines" (Judges 16:5,8,18×2,23,27,30 – seven times). But this was also the burden of the Samuel record (1 Samuel 5:8,11; 6:4,12,16,18; 7:7 – seven times).

The two passages (Judges 14-16, 1 Samuel 5,6) were obviously about the same epoch of time. When Eli died, it was Samson who stepped forward to lead the nation. And there was a special circumstance which energised Samson in his labours. His spirit was stirred in Mahaneh Dan (Judges 13:25), which stood to the immediate west of Kirjath-jearim (Judges 18:12). But this was the town where the ark of God had been returned from the Philistines (1 Samuel 7:1). Samson was excited by the sign of God's presence back among His people. His exploits and his judgeship lasted for twenty years (Judges 16:31), concluding with his untimely death, and the lamentation of the nation (1 Samuel 7:2).

And just as Samson had been ready to lead the nation at the death of Eli, so now Samuel was ready to lead the nation at the death of Samson (1 Samuel 7:3). His work would be the focus of the narrative from this point. His signal victory at Ebenezer at the start of his recorded work as judge, effectively subdued the Philistines to bring a period of peace (1 Samuel 7:13), and his own work as a judge continued throughout the rest of his lifetime (1 Samuel 7:15). The succession of Samuel to the leadership of the nation paved the way for the introduction of the monarchy, and before Samuel died, he had anointed both Saul (1 Samuel 10:1) and David (1 Samuel 16:13) respectively to the office of king.

It is also of interest however, to consider the proximity of earlier judges to the time of Eli's priesthood. Jephthah, Ibzan, Elon, and Abdon all followed each other in succession (Judges 12:7-15), their combined judgeship covering a total of thirty-one years. It is generally assumed that Eli took office after the death of Abdon, but there are several reasons why this might not have been the case, and that these judges might instead have been contemporary with Eli. The KJV margin suggests a geographical aspect. It notes that Jephthah (Judges 11:29), Ibzan (Judges 12:8), Elon (Judges 12:11), and Abdon (Judges 12:13) were all judges in the north-east of Israel, while Eli (1 Samuel 4:16), judged in the south-west. Operating in quite different locations, these northern judges might therefore have been judging in their region at the same time Eli was High Priest and judge in Shiloh.

Chronologically, the record places Jephthah to Abdon immediately before the forty years of Philistine oppression began (Judges 12:7–13:1). Eli's years as a judge can be divided into two parts of twenty years. But if his last twenty years were set in the Philistine oppression, as suggested earlier, then his first twenty years must have been immediately before that time. His judgeship did therefore, in all likelihood, overlap with some if not all of these north-eastern judges. At the least, this detail brings the time of Jephthah much closer to the time of Hannah, whose life would unfold during Eli's term of office.

The twin stories of dedication

That overlap between contemporaries with Eli was significant in the light of two events which would stand out in their respective epochs. There was a close juxtaposition between the story of Jephthah's daughter, and the story of Hannah's son. Both were committed to the Lord in vows of dedication by a parent, a father with his daughter, and a mother with her son. Here were two exceptional stories of dedication, closely set in the divine record together, and yet without parallel in any other epoch of time.

Jephthah's Vow (Judges 11)	Hannah's Vow (1 Samuel 1)
Jephthah vowed a vow in faithfulness (verse 30).	Hannah vowed a vow in faithfulness (verse 11).
If thou shalt without fail deliver the children of Ammon into mine hands (verse 30).	If thou wilt indeed look on the affliction of thine handmaid (verse 11).
Jephthah promised to dedicate a person to the Lord (verse 31). [3]	Hannah promised to dedicate a person to the Lord (verse 11).
The sacredness of the vow which proceeded out of his mouth was upheld (verse 35).	The sacredness of the vow which proceeded out of her mouth was upheld (verse 23, LXX).
His only daughter was thus dedicated to the sanctuary (verse 39).	Her only son was thus dedicated to the sanctuary (verse 28).
Her dedication was also accompanied by a whole burnt offering (verse 31). [4]	His dedication was also accompanied by a whole burnt offering (verse 24).

---

[3] The word "whatsoever" (*aser*) in the phrase "whatsoever cometh forth from the doors of my house" (Judges 11:31) is better rendered "whosoever". Hence Rotherham / RV – "whoever cometh forth out of the doors of my house". The word *aser* is likewise rendered "whoever" in the only other passage with the same phrase – *aser ye-se mid-dal-te* (Joshua 2:19). The context of the passage suggests that Jephthah intended to devote a person from the outset. He was not intending to offer an animal, but to dedicate a person.

[4] The phrase "and I will offer it up for a burnt offering" (Judges 11:31) is expressed by only two words in the Hebrew. The English word "for" does not appear in the Hebrew. It would require a prepositional prefix to represent "for", but it is not there in the text. The following comment is helpful – "*we-ha-let-hu olah*, and I will offer him [or to him, i.e., Yahweh] a burnt offering, for *hu* may with much more propriety be referred to the person to whom the sacrifice was to be made, than to the thing to be sacrificed" (*Treasury of Scriptural Knowledge* on Judges 11:31, page 177). The import of this, is that in addition to devoting a person without right of redemption, Jephthah also offered a corresponding burnt offering to symbolise the complete dedication of the person devoted. That Hannah followed the identical procedure (1 Samuel 1:25-28) is corroborative evidence of how Jephthah's vow should be interpreted.

Jephthah's Vow (Judges 11)	Hannah's Vow (1 Samuel 1)
The faithful visited the sanctuary to meet and converse with her (verse 40).	The faithful visited the sanctuary to meet and converse with him (verse 19).

There were no other examples in scripture of a personal vow which involved such amazing commitment between a faithful parent and an obedient child for its fulfilment. In both cases the child entered into the vow of their parent with such zeal as to sanctify its sacred intent. But most remarkable is the fact that the two occasions were very close in time. Indeed, the uniqueness of these two episodes, found in such proximity in the divine record, argues that the one was in fact the catalyst for the other.

The dedication of Jephthah's only daughter, occurred not simply before the dedication of Hannah's only son, but probably preceded him by just a few years. It helps to explain why Jephthah's action not only inspired Hannah, but why the presence of his daughter at the sanctuary gave Hannah the hope she needed to dedicate her son in that place. The timing of the dedication of Jephthah's daughter meant that, far from being an old woman when Hannah brought Samuel, her age was probably much more akin to Hannah's herself. That her placement at Shiloh prior to Samuel was a providential arrangement in the overarching wisdom of God, is not an unreasonable conclusion![5]

---

5   See Appendix 6 – "Who was the guardian of Hannah's firstborn son?" on page 228 for further detail on the reasons why Jephthah's daughter would have been the ideal guardian for Samuel when he was presented at Shiloh.

Appendix 2 |

Who were the enemies of Hannah's holy cause?

THAT Hannah had an enemy is not in dispute. But the identity of her enemy requires more careful Bible scrutiny. The general view of most commentators is that Peninnah was Hannah's enemy, based upon the so-called 'adversary passage' (1 Samuel 1:6). Evidence for a reassessment of this passage is given in Appendix 3. [1] Here however, the objective is to permit a contextual examination to resolve the identity of Hannah's real enemies. Three matters are reviewed which contribute to our understanding.

The flow of the narrative

The strongest argument in favour of recognising Hophni and Phinehas as the real enemies of Hannah, lies in the flow of the entire narrative. As it unfolds, from beginning to end, the overwhelming focus is on Hannah's controversy with these two men. The magnitude of that controversy is inescapable. Time and time again, the record will present her in conflict with the two sons of Eli. Consider the sequence:

- 1 Samuel 1:3 – The sons of Eli officiate over the temple offerings.
  - 1 Samuel 1:6,7 – Hannah is provoked by her adversity at the temple.

---

1 See Appendix 3 – "What was the source of Hannah's great adversity?" on page 216.

Appendix 2 – Who were the enemies of Hannah's holy cause?

- – 1 Samuel 1:10-13 – Hannah vows to give her child for temple service.
- 1 Samuel 1:14-16 – Eli rebukes Hannah in error.
  - – 1 Samuel 1:23-28 – Hannah dedicates her son before Eli at the temple.
  - – 1 Samuel 2:1-11 – Hannah's song and Samuel's service at the temple.
- 1 Samuel 2:12-17 – The sons of Eli sin grievously with the offerings at the temple.
  - – 1 Samuel 2:18,19 – Hannah encourages her son at the temple.
  - – 1 Samuel 2:20,21 – Hannah is blessed by Eli at the temple.
- 1 Samuel 2:22,23 – The sons of Eli exhibit complete corruption.
- 1 Samuel 2:24,25 – The sons of Eli are threatened with death.
  - – 1 Samuel 2:26 – Hannah's son prospers and grows at the temple.
- 1 Samuel 2:27-34 – The sons of Eli to be overthrown by God.
  - – 1 Samuel 2:35,36 – Hannah's son to be exalted at the temple.

Who could doubt that the centre of this story was the controversy between Hannah and the sons of Eli? Any interpretation as to the real identity of Hannah's enemies which fails to recognise this pattern is inconsistent with the evidence. The record provides its own interpretation.

The evidence of Hannah's song

When Hannah offered her song of thanksgiving, she was in Shiloh at the sanctuary. And since she had just brought a bullock unto the priests to be offered (1 Samuel 1:24,25), there can be little doubt that she had been in contact with Hophni and Phinehas on that very day (1 Samuel 1:3). Whether they were in earshot of her when her song began mattered not. She was acutely aware of their presence. And, significantly, her song began with the thought that her mouth was enlarged "over her *enemies*" (1 Samuel 2:1). The plural term immediately forbids its application to Peninnah. Whoever Hannah's enemy was, it could not be Elkanah's second wife. And whilst we have no knowledge whether Peninnah was even there, we can be much more certain that Hophni and Phinehas were.

The use of the plural then was not accidental on Hannah's part. And there can be no mistake about its intentional use by her, for towards the close of her song, she referred to the "*adversaries* of the LORD" (1 Samuel 2:10). Again, the plural term is unambiguous, and, even more remarkably, Hannah's phrase implied that those who were her enemies, were also God's enemies. Their destiny, in Hannah's words, was to be "broken in pieces", implying their deliberate death at God's hand. Now, whatever troubles Peninnah might have caused in Hannah's life, it would have been unjust in the extreme for her to hope that Peninnah would be slain by God. Many saints have suffered at the hand of others in the Truth, and have endured trials of jealousy, malice, envy, slander, and even hatred. Such trials can be deeply painful, wounding the soul. None of them justify our wishing for the death of those who have wronged us.

But what Hannah could not have suggested of Peninnah, she could and did of Hophni and Phinehas with the greatest of justification. They *were* the adversaries of God, as well as being the enemies of Hannah. And her prophetic insight that they would meet a sudden and violent death by the judgment of God which would thunder upon them (1 Samuel 2:10), was precisely the intention of God Himself (1 Samuel 2:25). Hannah's song was not preserved to record her unjust condemnation of another, but to commemorate the righteous prayer of a woman whose very spirit matched the thinking of God Himself. There was no room in Hannah's song to see Peninnah as her real enemy, but every reason to be convinced that Hophni and Phinehas were.

The opening and the close of the story

When the above theme is recognised, the opening and the close of the story suddenly take on fresh meaning. The story begins with Hannah who has no child, the wickedness of Hophni and Phinehas at the temple, and their corruption of the priesthood. Notice the key ideas:

> "*Hannah had no children. And this man went up out of his city yearly to sacrifice unto the* LORD *of hosts in Shiloh. And the two sons of Eli,* **Hophni and Phinehas**, *were priests* of the LORD *there.*" (1 Samuel 1:2,3)

The record closes with the promise of the sudden death of Hophni and Phinehas, and the provision by God of a better priest, who self-evidently in the record is Hannah's child:

> "And this shall be a sign unto thee, that shall come upon *thy two sons*, on **Hophni and Phinehas**; in one day they shall die both of them. And I will raise unto me *a faithful priest* [who would be *Hannah's child*]." (1 Samuel 2:34,35)

The juxtaposition of word and phrase suggests a sense of chiasmus here. The words of the man of God are indeed the resolution and the climax of the story of Hannah. And in that resolution lies the confirmation that the real enemies of Hannah were Hophni and Phinehas.

Appendix 3 |

What was the source of Hannah's great adversity?

THE most common interpretation of the reference to Hannah's adversary (1 Samuel 1:6) is to identify it with an assumed rivalry between Hannah and Peninnah. After all, the differing status and circumstance of the two wives is mentioned just before the adversary reference (1 Samuel 1:4,5). Here then, it is suggested, is the basis for the conflict that wrought so much pain in Hannah's life. And here was the person to whom the epithet 'adversary' might most reasonably be assigned. There is no doubt that there were tensions in Elkanah's household. How could it have been otherwise when one wife was beloved but still barren, and the other fruitful yet not favoured. Whatever his reasons, Elkanah, in taking to himself a second wife, had departed from the divine ideal.[1]

That departure would not come without consequences, and the family must have known strife and unhappiness because of it. Nor did Elkanah's behaviour help. His evident love for Hannah provided as much pain for Peninnah in her fruitfulness, as Hannah felt in her barrenness. But the nature of their suffering differed. Peninnah sought the love and acceptance of her husband through the bearing of many children. Hannah sought the fulfilment of

---

[1] The divine ideal concerning marriage (one man and one woman for life) was established by God at the foundation of the world (Genesis 2:24). It has never altered since, and has always been the divine standard referred to in the prophets (Malachi 2:15), the gospels (Mark 10:6-9), the epistles (Ephesians 5:31,32), and the Apocalypse (Revelation 19:7).

God's purpose through the bearing of but one son. There is no doubt that Elkanah's home at Ramah bore the strain of these unresolved matters. Nor is there any doubt that there may have been tension between Hannah and Peninnah. But the question here is not whether Peninnah caused difficulties for Hannah, but whether she was the real source of Hannah's adversity.

A question of translation

To begin with, there is a problem with the word 'adversary' itself, and the matter is both a textual and a contextual one. Each will be considered, in arriving at a suggested answer. The word 'adversary' (*tsarah*) is used seventy-three times in the Old Testament. Apart from this one instance (1 Samuel 1:6), it is *never* translated 'adversary' anywhere else. On *every* other occasion, it is translated by words such as adversity, affliction, trouble or distress. Rendering the term as 'adversary' immediately personalises the word to an individual, but this is not the normal use or meaning of the word. The usual meaning, 'adversity', has a quite different connotation, focusing instead on a condition or situation rather than a person. There should be caution about the inference of a personal adversary to Hannah, which depends on a single word in a solitary verse. Even Gesenius (who suggests the term – rival) provides no other scriptural examples to support the term. In his lexicon, the only other passage cited as evidence in support of a rendering of *tsarah* as 'adversary' is from an apocryphal writing (Ecclesiasticus 37:10,11).

But this passage, when examined, provides better evidence to render the term as 'adversity' rather than 'adversary'. The passage concerns those from whom it is unwise to seek counsel, and lists them as follows: "With a wife concerning her [*tsarah*] adversity / adversary, and a rebel concerning battle, with a buyer concerning his strife, and from an acquirer concerning selling, with an evil man concerning loyal dealing, and a cruel one concerning good tidings, a maker of vanity concerning his work, a watcher of vanity concerning coming distress." Every other example in this list concerns either a condition or a situation, and not a person. To translate *tsarah* as 'adversary' here interrupts the pattern of the verse. A rendering of 'adversity' (relating to the condition of a woman troubled by her barrenness) preserves the pattern, and is the better translation.

Consistent with this usage of the word, Young's Literal (YLT) translates the passage as follows: "and her *adversity* hath also provoked her greatly, so as to make her tremble, for the LORD hath shut up her womb. And so he doth year by year, from the time of her going up into the house of the LORD, so it provoketh her, and she weepeth, and doth not eat." In rendering the word *tsarah* as 'adversity', YLT retains the integrity of the word as used elsewhere. It suggests that Hannah certainly had a source of adversity that vexed her greatly, but that it was her condition or circumstance that was the cause of her grief, rather than an individual. YLT in turn is consistent with the LXX rendering – "For the LORD gave her no child in her *affliction*, and according to the despondence of her affliction; and she was dispirited on this account, that the LORD shut up her womb, so as not to give her a child. So she did year by year, and in going up to the house of the LORD; and she was dispirited, and wept, and did not eat". This alternative rendering of the LXX evidently follows a different 'vorlage' to the Masoretic text, and it is relevant to note that the Samuel fragments in the Dead Sea Scrolls, frequently follow the LXX record rather than the Masoretic version in both 1 and 2 Samuel. It is the view of the writer, that in this instance, the LXX translation is to be preferred. The most convincing reasons however, lie not in a textual examination (which must always be subjective), but in the lines of contextual argument which support this reading.

The puzzle of Elkanah's response

The timing of this episode is important for a proper understanding of Hannah's adversity. For if, as the record indicates, this difficulty happened *every year* at the time of their visit to Shiloh, then to suggest that Peninnah's goading of Hannah was the cause of her provocation, is to ignore the evidence of the context. If Peninnah was the problem, why would Elkanah permit her to continue vexing

Hannah, right there in front of him? Why would he not put a stop to it immediately, especially given that they were all there together, at a time of worship before God? What husband loving his wife, would stand by and allow her fellowship meal and joy to be destroyed? Elkanah might not have had his wife's depth of feeling for the sanctuary, but he was not so blind as not to notice his second wife upsetting his first. To propose that Peninnah, at the fellowship meal with Elkanah, taunted Hannah until she broke down in tears every year (1 Samuel 1:7), [2] without Elkanah realising it, is to condemn him as being singularly incapable. And if Peninnah did behave so badly as this, for Elkanah to then ask Hannah why she was crying, is to suggest that he was an ignorant and obtuse man.

Such an interpretation demeans this godly Levite, and is inconsistent with the context. Of all moments when Peninnah might have discouraged Hannah, the last time to choose would have been in full view of Elkanah, and at the sanctuary. When Elkanah was out of range, out of view, out of hearing, Peninnah might have had opportunity to vex Hannah. But these moments were all at home in Ramah. The last place and the last time to do so, would be at the fellowship meal which all the family shared. This was not the moment. And yet the record is insistent that this was when Hannah felt her deepest grief.

The setting of the sanctuary

Why then was her anguish worst at the temple? Because this was where her fellowship meal with her God was eaten, and this was when the horror of a corrupt priesthood was daily evident in the destruction of that fellowship. Hannah's grief was not at home, where Peninnah might have had opportunity to speak and act in a hurtful manner, when Elkanah was absent from the house. No, her

---

2 That this was a yearly episode is a crucial piece of information. Any explanation of her adversity must explain why it happened at the sanctuary, at the fellowship meal of the peace offering, and harmonise it with the key episode in 1 Samuel 2. There, the priests interrupted the fellowship meal of the peace offering until people spurned the offering in despair. When the two chapters are read together, the source of Hannah's great adversity is clear – and it is not Peninnah!

pain, her grief was related to the matters at Shiloh, and the work of the priesthood. How significant then to note, that the record expressly tells us, immediately *before* the matter of her adversity, of the presence and dominance of Hophni and Phinehas at the sanctuary (1 Samuel 3:3). [3] Hannah's adversity was related to the circumstances in which she found herself there. It was in that place that the key to her anguish lay, and her song which followed would confirm the matter. Throughout Hannah's story, we will not only witness her controversy with Hophni and Phinehas, [4] but receive *a detailed description of both the words and the actions of these evil men.*

The role of Peninnah

By contrast, despite the appearance of Peninnah at the beginning of the story (1 Samuel 1:2,4), she will never enter the record again. She appears once (to highlight the contrast between the natural and spiritual seeds, as with Sarah and Hagar of old), but then disappears completely. Whatever role she played, she was not at the centre of this story and was not the real source of Hannah's adversity. To cast her in the role of a goading and spiteful woman, does disservice to Peninnah herself, whose character is impugned in the process. In the divine record (and in contrast to Hophni and Phinehas), we do not have a single word attributed to Peninnah in the narrative. The argument advanced for her adversarial role is by inference only, and that from one word. Recognising Hannah's difficulty as her "adversity", rather than her "adversary" greatly enriches our understanding. Her cause for sorrow was not related to Peninnah's behaviour (whether that had been good or evil). Nor was her anguish simply a reflection of her barrenness. Her adversity lay in her inability to bear the child who might rescue the nation from the wickedness of Hophni and Phinehas, seen at its worst in the sanctuary.

---

3 The mention of these two immediately before the adversity passage is significant in its placement.

4 See Appendix 2 – "Who were the enemies of Hannah's holy cause?" on page 212.

Appendix 4 |

What was the import of Hannah's special song?

Her extensive use of scripture

TO receive and read a letter from a close friend is to have them near. When we read it, we hear them speaking, since it sounds just like them. It is possible however, to read the oracles of God, but never to hear His voice. Yet that Word is the expression of the mind of God. When Hannah heard scripture, she heard the voice of the Lord speaking to her.[1] That relationship with God was deep and real, and her quotations in her song reflected her understanding of His character. However the Spirit overshadowed her utterances, they began in the mind of one who was steeped in holy thoughts from the holy oracles.

It is possible for a prayer to recite scripture in a way which glories in good recollection, and clever phrasing. That is not what the faithful do. But they do seek to draw from the language of scripture to fashion their prayers in deep reverence for the Word, and with deep respect for the honour of God. Learning to think in Biblical terms is the basis of learning to express our thoughts in Biblical terms. Part of the challenge of the age is the decline of speech in prayers to a level which is shallow, worldly, familiar, lacking in dignity, and devoid of the language of scripture.

It is axiomatic that prayer should be earnest and sincere.

---

1 Her deep knowledge of scripture was probably gleaned by her attentive listening at the sanctuary when the priests read the law (Deuteronomy 31:10-13). Hannah's story reveals insights into every book of Moses, and the book of Job.

But sincerity, expressed in language which bears no relationship to the Truth, is deficient in another vital aspect. True sincerity will seek to approach the Father in a manner which will be acceptable to Him. The Deity before whom we come in prayer, has insisted that He will be sanctified in those who draw near unto Him. [2] Part of that separation lies in the reverential use of language which He delights in, language which is found in His Word which he has magnified above His name. [3] Hannah led by example in this respect. She knew her Bible, and drew upon its words to frame her own prayers, that she might offer acceptable incense when seeking to address God. We should do likewise.

The riddle of the battle theme

How strange that a prayer of thanksgiving, centred upon the giving of a little child, should sound like a battle hymn. And yet, there was a definite tone of military conflict throughout Hannah's song. Such phrases as – "enlarged over mine enemies", "the bows of the mighty men are broken", "the wicked shall be silent in darkness", "the adversaries of the LORD shall be broken in pieces", "out of heaven shall he thunder upon them", all conveyed the spirit of the contest. Perhaps this in part was because Hannah in her song drew on the battle songs of Moses (Exodus 15, Deuteronomy 32), and Deborah's war song (Judges 5). But these Spirit inspired allusions might themselves have been deliberate, since Hannah believed she also was in a battle for the Truth.

The result of the conflict that she was engaged in, was to be a catastrophic overthrow of the enemies, whose death was predicted by prophetic insight. Hannah could never have sought such a dreadful destiny against Peninnah, even in her most difficult of times. And her story provides no evidence to apply these terms to the Philistines, despite their presence in the

---

[2] The terrible death of Nadab and Abihu being witness of His requirement (Leviticus 10:3).
[3] Psalm 138:2.

land. Yet any interpretation of her song must account for these battle terms. The most convincing explanation lies in the conflict Hannah had with Hophni and Phinehas, the one dominant controversy that pervaded her entire story. That this was the battle she envisaged was made certain in the prophecy of the man of God which followed shortly after. His sign to Eli, that his two sons would both die in one day (1 Samuel 2:34), was fulfilled by their death on the battlefield (1 Samuel 4:10,11), slain by the sword in the height of the battle (Psalm 78:64).

Her influence on the prayer of Mary

Hannah's song became the basis for Mary's prayer of rejoicing. There was every reason for Mary to feel a kinship with Hannah,[4] but the degree to which she alluded to her song was remarkable. So close was the correspondence, it was clear that Mary had carefully studied Hannah's life, absorbed her spirit, and shared her hope. For the mother of Christ to recognise Hannah as her role model and example was a tribute indeed.

The Prayer of Mary (Luke 1)	The Song of Hannah (1 Samuel 2)
And Mary said, My soul doth magnify the Lord (verse 46).	And Hannah prayed, and said … mine horn is exalted in the LORD (verse 1).
And my spirit hath rejoiced in God my Saviour (verse 47).	My heart rejoiceth in the LORD … because I rejoice in thy salvation (verse 1).
For he hath regarded the low estate of his handmaiden: for, behold, from henceforth all generations shall call me blessed (verse 48).	If thou indeed wilt look on the affliction of thine handmaid, and not forget thine handmaid (1 Samuel 1:11).

---

[4] See Chapter 8 – "Hannah and her Lord" on page 175, under the heading "A holy handmaid and her spiritual mind" for an expansion of this thought.

The Prayer of Mary (Luke 1)	The Song of Hannah (1 Samuel 2)
For he that is mighty hath done to me great things; and holy is his name (verse 49).	There is none holy as the LORD: for there is none beside thee: neither is there any rock like our God (verse 2).
And his mercy is on them that fear him from generation to generation (verse 50).	
He hath shewed strength with his arm; he hath scattered the proud in the imagination of their hearts (verse 51).	Talk no more so exceeding proudly ... the adversaries of the LORD shall be broken to pieces (verses 3,10).
He hath put down the mighty from their seats, and exalted them of low degree (verse 52).	The bows of the mighty men are broken ... the LORD maketh poor, and maketh rich, he bringeth low and lifteth up (verses 4,7).
He hath filled the hungry with good things; and the rich he hath sent empty away (verse 53).	They that were full have hired themselves out for bread; and they that were hungry ceased (verse 5).
He hath holpen his servant Israel, in remembrance of his mercy (verse 54).	
As he spake to our fathers, to Abraham, and to his seed for ever (verse 55).	

Appendix 5 |

What was the lesson of Hannah's little coat?

THE little coat Hannah brought up for Samuel to wear, was indeed like the garment of the High Priest. In fact, on *every* occasion the word *me-iyl* was used before this episode, it referred exclusively to the robe of the ephod worn by the High Priest (Exodus 28:4,31,34; 29:5; 39:22-26; Leviticus 8:7). The robe of the ephod divided the two sets of clothing the High Priest wore. Beneath the robe were the linen garments he wore in common with his sons. But the garments for glory and beauty, which he wore over the robe, were exclusively his. That robe had a special woven collar, so strong that it could not be torn. It symbolised that the High Priest would unite the nation unto himself though his anointing. Only the High Priest then, wore both the linen ephod and the robe of the ephod. They were peculiarly and exclusively his.

These two articles of the High Priest's clothing – the robe of the ephod and the ephod itself were found together in a remarkable episode in David's life. At the time of the bringing of the ark to Zion, David arrayed himself in these articles of clothing normally reserved for the High Priest. In an ecstasy of joy, and under the power of the Holy Spirit, David foreshadowed within himself the future work of Christ, as Messiah King (*mashiyach melech*) and Messiah Priest (*mashiyach kohen*). The record tells us expressly that only David wore the two garments. [1]

---

1   The precise words – "And David was clothed with a robe of fine linen ... David also

Given that he was in Salem, the city of Melchizedek when enacting this parable, it is evident that he clothed himself in full awareness of the significance of his actions, which were prophetic of one still to come. The prophecy was this, that he who was the king of righteousness (the robe of fine linen), would also have the right to enter the presence of God for divine communication (the ephod of linen). Only one man had ever held these rights in unity, and his name was Melchizedek, king of Salem and priest of the Most High God. This man, in his dealing with Abraham had brought forth a fellowship meal of bread and wine for them to share together (Genesis 14:18), and David, in the spirit of his predecessor did the same (1 Chronicles 16:1-3).

This wonderful episode in David's life was probably the very circumstance which prompted the writing of Psalm 110, as he reflected on the events of the day. In the psalm, the Spirit gave utterance through David of another king-priest who would indeed arise after the manner of Melchizedek. But David spoke of one who would be appointed to govern as king (verse 2), and to intercede as priest (verse 4), by virtue of his special anointing according to the spirit of holiness, by the resurrection from the dead (verse 3). David knew that only the Son of God (verse 1) could be both king and priest after the order of Melchizedek forever, but he knew he was coming, and he foreshadowed him.

Now, apart from the reference in the law to the attire of the High Priest, and this singular occasion in the life of David, there was only one other place in scripture where these two garments, the ephod and the robe of the ephod were seen together. They would both be worn by Hannah's son (1 Samuel 2:18,19), and it was his mother who would dress him so. Here was a clear intimation of her firm belief in the priestly role that Samuel was intended to play.

But it also gave proof that she had seen the work of Melchizedek and believed in one to come who would renew that

---

had upon him an ephod of linen" (1 Chronicles 15:27), indicate the deliberateness of David's actions.

role. Her inspired utterance and action (1 Samuel 2:10,19), may well have been pondered by David. He was certainly familiar with Hannah's song, and referred to it in several of his own psalms. [2] How interesting to consider that Hannah's thinking, so in advance of her time, might have inspired David to a similar conclusion, only to be blessed with a similar utterance about the coming order of Melchizedek, which she had seen. If David clothed himself thus in awareness of the story of Melchizedek, then it is equally reasonable to assume that Hannah robed her son with the same acuteness of understanding. She was a woman of extraordinary faith, and spiritual foresight. But then, Hannah's mind had always been on higher things.

---

[2] David saw the controversy of Hannah against Hophni and Phinehas (1 Samuel 2:3-5,9,10) as typical of the conflict between the righteous and the wicked in his own day (Psalm 37:10-15). And her song which envisaged a strong king and an exalted priest set up after the Lord's adversaries were broken to pieces (1 Samuel 2:10), was quoted by David in his psalm about a king set by God upon the hill of His holiness (the sanctuary where the priest officiated) as the anointed of God, whose opponents would be dashed to pieces (Psalm 2:2-9).

Appendix 6 |

Who was the guardian of Hannah's firstborn son?

It was self-evident that Samuel must have been under the care and protection of a guardian, from the moment he was presented to the Lord. That person was not named, and therefore we cannot be certain of their identity. But, given the tremendous responsibility which lay upon this individual, we can be certain that providence overshadowed their selection and their placement. Pondering the unique needs of the little child, we recognise the qualities that his guardian must have possessed, and the possibilities are greatly narrowed as to who that guardian might have been.

A woman who lived at the temple

Given that Samuel was so very young when coming to Shiloh, it is logical to assume that a woman must have had his charge, for the aged Eli would not have been able personally to minister to the child's needs. A woman then was essential, but not any woman might do. To begin with, she needed to be resident at the sanctuary. Only someone who was permanently in attendance could offer the continuing attention necessary for a young child, every single day. Every day he would need to be washed and clothed and fed. Every day he would need the security of her voice, the warmth of her touch, the care of her love, the sense of her presence. She had to be constantly there in his life. As the child grew, her role would change, but she would always need to be visible and accessible to him.

A woman who shared Hannah's spirit

But this woman would be responsible for much more than the feeding and clothing of the child. His spiritual, social and mental development were of paramount importance for the role he was destined to fulfil, and someone was needed who could watch over these with godly care. The households of Hophni and Phinehas would not be suitable. Whatever the spirit of their wives might have been,[1] the presence of Samuel in a home dominated by such men could not have provided the spiritual haven so necessary for his spiritual nurture during his early formative years. In fact, this woman needed to share the faith of Hannah herself, a kindred spirit in her fervent love for the Truth, and like-minded concerning the destiny of the child. She would need to be to the little Levite in Shiloh, what Hannah would have been for him in Ramah. This woman would be the child's mother, in the absence of the mother herself.

A woman who commanded respect

And there was one last but vital quality needed in the woman who might overshadow Samuel's life. She needed to have a personal standing, and a moral authority that was beyond reproach, and beyond rebuke: a woman whose influence was so strong, that she could truly provide the blessing of godly supervision. How else might the evil of Hophni and Phinehas be kept at bay, other than in one whose example could quell even those workers of iniquity. Such a woman would be rare indeed, but only in one who commanded such respect would the ideal of guardian care be realised.

The example of Jephthah's daughter

In the providence of God, there was someone who met all three requirements. A woman who was resident at the sanctuary. A woman who shared Hannah's fervent spirit. A woman whose reputation was formidable enough to silence even Eli's sons.

---

1 The wife of Phinehas was evidently a woman of faith (1 Samuel 4:19-22). But her husband was an evil man, and his house no fit place for the rearing of Samuel in holy ways.

One whose own dedication to the Truth was undoubted, and whose commitment to the spirit of vows and their performance was unquestioned. A woman whose example was celebrated and revered by the daughters of Israel. Jephthah's daughter commanded such fame and respect in the land (Judges 11:40), that even Hophni and Phinehas would have been most reluctant to challenge her. Her reputation for godliness was so well known that she would be the one person at the sanctuary whom they dare not oppose or confront. A woman whose sanctity was beyond compromise or corruption, and who as a living legend would be an ideal protector for the child. She could wrap him in a robe of privacy and conceal the worst excesses of that place from his young eyes and innocent mind. Being under her watchful eye was to be under the chaperonage of one who could nurture Samuel as if she were his guardian angel.

How significant then that the very phrase used to describe the yearly pilgrimage of Elkanah and Hannah in their visits to the sanctuary, was the phrase used earlier to describe the yearly pilgrimage of the daughters of Israel to meet and talk with Jephthah's daughter (1 Samuel 1:3; cp. Judges 11:40). Hannah had probably met this woman, and knew her story. In fact, her example of being dedicated to lifetime service was the most likely source of Hannah's inspiration. Her commitment to the fulfilment of her father's vow (Judges 11:36) convinced Hannah to make her own. Here was an example, still living, of one who was committed for service without remission or redemption, and with a whole burnt offering to accompany the completion of her father's vow (Judges 11:31,39; cp. Psalm 66:13,14). Who better to have inspired Hannah, for would not she also offer her firstborn in perpetual dedication accompanied by a whole burnt offering? (1 Samuel 1:11,22,24,25). The whole story of Samuel's dedication rang with the tones of the dedication of Jephthah's daughter. Her fervency and her faithfulness were the keys which furnished Hannah with the hope that it could be done, the catalyst which stirred Hannah into her own dramatic and decisive action.

At the last, we do not know who this mysterious woman was. And yet, the story of Jephthah's daughter offers by far the strongest Biblical lines of evidence for anyone who could be identified. In every respect, she would have been the ideal choice to offer guardian care to Samuel. It is the view of the writer that Jephthah's daughter was providentially raised up and placed in Shiloh at the very moment she was needed, and this is the view expressed in this book. This woman, whose own prospect of marriage was removed by her dedication, was nevertheless privileged to nurse a child, and not just any child, but one who was set for the deliverance of his people. There could not have been a more wonderful outcome to her life. But her presence in Shiloh was also the perfect answer to the requirements of the mother and child whose lives would intersect with hers at the tabernacle. The heart sings at the thought of such gracious provision to meet Samuel's need, and calm Hannah's fear. But let everyone be fully persuaded in their own mind!

Appendix 7 |

What was the story of Hannah's faithful priest?

NO one knows why the priesthood passed to the line of Ithamar, for scripture is silent concerning the circumstances. Josephus records that the interruption occurred when Zerahiah the son of Uzzi,[1] did not become High Priest, and the High Priesthood was transferred instead to Eli of the line of Ithamar.[2] But in the judgment brought against Eli by the man of God, there was a clear intimation that the line of Ithamar would be removed from that High Priestly honour and the line of Eleazar restored. The earnest of that reversal was seen in the elevation of Samuel himself, who would preside over the epoch of change in the priestly lines. His advent marked the beginning of the end for Eli's house, as the prophecy began to take effect with ever increasing force.

First came the sudden loss of Hophni and Phinehas, slain by the sword on the same day, during the fateful battle against the Philistines (1 Samuel 4:11). Their death, in association with the loss of the ark of God, proved that they had never stood

---

1   He writes – "After High Priest Ozi (Uzzi) of Eleazar, Eli of Ithamar received the priesthood" (Josephus – *Antiquities*, book 5, chapter 11.5).

2   The respective genealogies would seem to corroborate the account of Josephus. For the corresponding lines of descent (from the point of interruption) are: from Eleazar – Zerahiah, Meraioth, Amariah, Ahitub, Zadok (1 Chronicles 6:4-7), and: from Ithamar – Eli, Phinehas, Ahitub, Ahimelech, Abiathar (1 Samuel 14:3; 22:11,20), with the fifth in each line (Zadok and Abiathar) both contemporary with David (2 Samuel 15:35).

related to the things of holiness which the ark taught, but which Hannah so fervently believed. In the history of the times which immediately followed, Samuel (as the faithful priest) held authority to determine who of the house of Eli would play any role at all in the matters of priesthood.

The prophecy of the man of God (1 Samuel 2:27-36), ended with a clear indication of a priesthood which would bear the ultimate authority, and a subordinate priesthood, whose tasks and duties would be subservient to that higher order. That twofold priesthood was revealed in the gradual but irrevocable decline of the line of Ithamar, in favour of the line of Eleazar in whom the principal order of priesthood would be again reaffirmed. The culmination of the reversal came with the dismissal of Abiathar and in his place, Zadok of the line of Eleazar was advanced to the High Priesthood. It would not depart from that line until the Priesthood itself was extinguished in AD 70.

But existence of a higher priesthood and a lesser one, as seen in the lines of Eleazar and Ithamar, foreshadowed the Zadokite and Levitical priesthoods that will officiate in the temple of the future. There, the prince-priest who is after the order of Melchi-Zadok will preside over a priestly order of immortal ones, revered for having kept the charge of their God, and whose right it will be alone to approach near unto Him. To them belongs the primacy of priesthood, for these faithful ones, designated as the Sons of Zadok, who kept the charge when Israel went astray, are privileged to be the ministers of the sanctuary, and the ministers of the table. [3] Below them, and subordinate in rank and responsibility are the Levites, whose priestly tasks are to minister to the people, but not to the Lord, to keep the charge of the house, but not the charge of the altar. These are consistently represented as holding lesser authority, and come under the jurisdiction of the Sons of Zadok. But these Levites, evidently taken from the mortal population, still

---

[3] The different nature of the order and spiritual precedence of the Sons of Zadok is carefully noted in the record (Ezekiel 40:46; 43:19; 44:15,16; 45:4; 48:10,11).

minister in that lesser capacity God has been pleased to permit unto them. **4**

How marvellous that all this was set forth in the work of Samuel, raised by God as a faithful priest to supersede the corrupt priesthood of his day, as seen in Hophni and Phinehas. The gradual decline of the house of Ithamar, the inexorable rise of the house of Eleazar, the final appearance of the king-priest after the order of Melchizedek, the elevation of the Sons of Zadok in the kingdom, and the subordinate role of the Levitical order in that age, were all hidden in the destiny of Hannah's son. His priestly calling, based upon a higher principle, was the true foreshadowing of the Sons of Zadok who will stand before the Lord's anointed for ever in the kingdom. Amongst them, as their great prototype will be Samuel, while those who appear with him will be the constituents of his sure and faithful house.

What great things were set in motion by Hannah, this holy woman of such earnest faith.

---

4   The role of these mortal Levites is more restricted in scope, ranking beneath the Sons of Zadok, since they are forbidden to come near to the Lord (Ezekiel 40:45; 44:10-14,17-22; 45:5; 48:13,14).

Scripture index

Genesis

2:24.................. *216*
11:30................. *131*
14:17................. *199*
  :18............ *98, 226*
  :19,20 .... *98*
  :20.................... *98*
  :22.................... *98*
15:9.................... *72*
16:1,2................. *16*
  :2..................... *131*
  :16................... *132*
17:1.................... *132*
18:14................. *179*
19:26................. *103*
20:17,18 .... *22*
21:1,2................. *131*
  :6..................... *177*
  :8............... *71, 193*
24:12,15,42-45 .... *45*
25:2................... *132*
  :21..................... *22*
29:32-35.............. *64*
30:1-3.................. *16*
  :6...................... *64*
  :22,23 .... *61*
  :23..................... *16*
38:4...................... *64*
46:30................. *189*
49:3...................... *76*
  :10-12 .... *99*

Exodus

2:7-10 .... *68*
  :9,10 .... *193*
4:14,27 .... *155*
6:26.................... *38*
9:28.................... *96*
12:1,43 .... *155*
  :17,41,51 .... *38*
13:10.................... *63*
  :12,13 .... *76*
15:11.................... *84*
  :21..................... *177*
20:13.................... *36*
22:8,9,28 .... *143*
25:21,22 .... *37*
27:3................... *113*
28:1-3 .... *155*
  :3..................... *191*
  :4,31,34 .... *225*
  :33-35 .... *138*
  :35.................... *169*
  :35,43 .... *104*
29:5..................... *225*
  :9..................... *156*
  :38,42 .... *44*
  :39,40 .... *127*
30:6,7.................. *128*
  :8...................... *44*
32:21-25,35........ *155*
33:11................. *197*
34:22.................... *63*
  :23..................... *17*
  :24..................... *17*
35:22-29............. *135*
  :25................... *191*
38:3..................... *113*
  :8............ *135, 136*
39:22-26............. *225*

Leviticus

1:3........................ *73*
  :4,5.................... *73*
  :5..................... *196*
2:3,10 .... *36*
  :11................... *110*
3:3,4,9,10,14,15
  .... *107*

:14-16 .... *107*	**Numbers**	:40,41 .... *136*
:16,17 .... *108*		:47 .... *136*
4:3 .... *73*	**1**:3 .... *38*	**35**:1-5 .... *16*
:3,5,16 .... *98*	**2**:32 .... *38*	:25,28 .... *138*
6:12 .... *107*	**3**:6-12,45 .... *11*	**36**:7-9 .... *8*
:17,25,29 .... *36*	:30-32 .... *12*	:10-12 .... *8*
:22 .... *98*	**4**:3 .... *39*	
7:1,6 .... *36*	:3,23,30 .... *134*	**Deuteronomy**
:8 .... *156*	:4,13-15 .... *113*	
:11,12 .... *109*	:31,32 .... *93*	**1**:31 .... *193*
:13 .... *109*	**5**:2,3 .... *53*	**4**:25 .... *25*
:14 .... *110*	**6**:1-8 .... *52*	:35,39 .... *84*
:15 .... *110*	:2 .... *35*	**6**:7 .... *69*
:15,16 .... *181*	:2,3 .... *48*	**7**:9 .... *168*
:20,21 .... *110*	:3,4 .... *52*	**9**:18 .... *25*
:23-25 .... *108*	:5 .... *52*	**10**:8 .... *45*
:29-31 .... *107*	:5,8 .... *43*	**12**:6,7,12 .... *111*
:30,31,34 .... *108*	:6,7 .... *52*	:17,18 .... *181*
8:7 .... *225*	:8,13 .... *42*	:18 .... *88*
:22-28 .... *108*	:22-27 .... *128*	**16**:16 .... *17*
10:1 .... *145*	:24-27 .... *56*	:16,17 .... *111*
:2 .... *145*	:25 .... *37*	**17**:8-13 .... *143*
:3 .... *146, 222*	**8**:10-13 .... *108*	**18**:5-7 .... *45*
:9 .... *52, 145*	:24,25 .... *41*	**19**:17-19 .... *143*
:12,17 .... *36*	:24-26 .... *134*	**21**:17 .... *21*
14:13 .... *36*	**10**:14 .... *206*	**23**:21-23 .... *34*
21:5,10 .... *52*	:33-36 .... *39*	:23 .... *68, 79*
:10,11 .... *52*	**16**:15 .... *95*	**25**:1 .... *143*
:22 .... *36*	**18**:1,7 .... *155*	:4 .... *196*
22:29,30 .... *111*	:8-11 .... *156*	**27**:7 .... *111*
23:17 .... *110*	:12 .... *107, 158*	**31**:9 .... *141*
:19,20 .... *110*	:12,13 .... *156*	:10-12 .... *141*
:37 .... *158*	:14 .... *36, 156*	:10-13 .... *221*
24:5-9 .... *163*	:15-18 .... *156*	:29 .... *25*
:9 .... *36*	**19**:11-13 .... *53*	**32**:4,5,15,28-31
25:29 .... *63*	**25**:6-13 .... *13*	.... *84*
:32-34 .... *16*	**30**:2 .... *68*	:10-12 .... *193*
27:1-8 .... *35*	:2,14 .... *181*	:15 .... *157*
:2 .... *35*	:6-8 .... *58*	:16,21 .... *25*
:28 .... *36*	:13,14 .... *68*	:39 .... *89*
:28,29 .... *36, 52*	:13-15 .... *59*	
:29 .... *36*	**31**:35 .... *136*	

Scripture index

Joshua

2:19................... 210
5:13-15............... 38
6:17-21................ 36
11:20.................... 145
18:1................ 11, 45
20:6..................... 138
21:20-26................ 10

Judges

2:1-5 151
:12..................... 25
3:9,15,31 41
5:2...................... 177
6:7-10 151
:11-21.............. 151
:12..................... 85
:14..................... 41
10:1........................ 41
11:1........................ 85
:29..................... 209
:30..................... 210
:30,31 37
:31..................... 210
:31,39 230
:34,35 192
:35..................... 210
:36..................... 230
:39..................... 210
:39,40 190
:40..... 17, 211, 230
12:5........................ 10
:7–13:1 209
:7–15 209
:8........................ 209
:11...................... 209
:13....................... 209
13:1....................... 207
:2.................. 7, 176
:3........................ 22

:3-5 176
:3,9,13 151
:4,5,7,13,14 63
:4,7,14 48
:5.......... 41, 43, 176
:24,25 176
:25..................... 208
14:4...................... 145
:18.................... 196
:19.................... 208
16:1-3 208
:5,8,18,23,27,30
.... 208
:17...................... 43
:29..................... 93
17:5,6................... 182
18:12.................... 208
:30..................... 206
:30,31 182
20:27,28 206
21:19............... 17, 63
:19-21 136

Ruth

1:20....................... 32
2:1.......................... 85
3:9....................... 177
4:12,13 130
:13,20,21 206
:15................ 28, 89

1 Samuel

1:1............. 9, 10, 11
:1,2........................ 9
:1,2,5 7
:1-8 7–30
:2......................... 15
:2,3.................... 215
:2,4..................... 220
:2,5,6 131
:3......................... 17,

18, 38, 84, 85,
182, 183, 212,
214, 230
:3,6.................. 173
:3-7 172
:3,7,21 17
:3,21 63
:4....... 44, 181, 182,
183
:4,5............ 20, 216
:4-7 107
:5........................ 15
:5,6............. 22, 23
:6......... 49, 60, 212,
216, 217
:6,7............ 23, 212
:7.......... 31, 44, 219
:7,9,24 15
:8........................ 27, 57
:9........... 18, 31, 51,
138, 187, 207
:9,10 31
:9-18 31–54
:10..................... 32
:10-13 213
:11......... 34, 37, 40,
42, 52, 68, 76,
172, 178, 180,
210, 223
:11,22,24,25
.... 230
:12,13 70
:12-14 43
:13..................... 178
:14-16 213
:15,16 46
:17............... 56, 75
:17,18 50
:17-19 130
:18. 31, 51, 57, 179
:19.... 42, 104, 127,
183, 211
:19,20 55
:19-28 55–78
:20..................... 63
:21.................... 182

:21-23 65
:21,23 .... 59, 181
:22 ..... 78, 170, 173
:23 210
:23-28 213
:24 .... 72, 74, 210
:24,25 ...... 71, 187, 213
:25 74
:25-28 210
:26 129
:26-28 74
:27,28 129
:28 210

2:1 ...... 80, 178, 181, 214, 223
:1,2 81
:1-10 .... 79–102, 120
:1-11 213
:1,19 15
:2 224
:3 .... 84, 86, 95
:3,4 82
:3-5,9,10 227
:3,10 224
:4,5 85
:4,7 224
:5 ...... 86, 158, 171, 173, 224
:6,7 89
:8 91
:9,10 .... 82, 94
:10 ...... 25, 98, 106, 146, 169, 173, 214, 227
:10,19 227
:11 ..... 42, 103, 104
:11,18 ..... 122, 191
:11,18,26 78
:11-19 103–126
:12 .... 49, 105
:12-17 .... 140, 172, 213
:13,14 .... 112, 113, 158, 184
:13-17 107
:14 ..... 20, 119, 159
:15,16 ...... 84, 114, 116, 184
:16 116
:17 .... 116, 141, 158
:17,18 121
:17,24 87
:18 .... 168, 191
:18,19 .... 121, 213, 226
:19 ...... 17, 63, 124, 191
:19,20 182
:20 .... 104, 128, 129, 187, 190
:20,21 ..... 131, 213
:20-26 127–150
:21 .... 131, 182, 183
:21,26 ..... 148, 193
:22 .... 134, 136
:22,23 ..... 140, 213
:23,24 138
:24 140
:24,25 213
:25 .... 96, 142, 145, 173, 214
:26 .... 146, 151, 171, 194, 195, 213
:27 155
:27,28 155
:27-29 145
:27-34 213
:27-36 .... 151–174, 171, 233
:28 .... 122, 156
:29 .... 157, 159, 163, 172, 184
:30 159
:30,35 159
:31,32 165
:31-33 162
:31-34 162
:32 .... 163, 170
:33 165
:34 .... 162, 173, 223
:34,35 215
:35 .... 167, 170, 173
:35,36 213
:36 .... 87, 164, 170, 173

3:1 ..... 122, 171, 191
:1-3 41
:3 220
:8 154
:11-14 153
:13 139
:13,14 ..... 164, 170
:14 172
:15 13
:18 188
:19 .... 148, 193
:20 .... 167, 188
:20,21 148
:21 168

4:4 40
:10,11 223
:10-18 207
:11 232
:13 138
:16 209
:18 ...... 18, 45, 157, 207
:19-22 ..... 163, 229

5:1-7 207
:8,9 207
:8,11 208
:10-12 207

6:4,12,16,18 208

7:1 208
:2 208
:3 208
:7 208
:9 .... 64, 70, 168
:9,10 168

:10-13 .... *176*	**17**:10 .... *196*	**24**:3 .... *155*
:13 .... *208*	:17 .... *136*	
:15 .... *42, 208*		**2 Chronicles**
:17 .... *42*	**1 Kings**	
8:1-3 .... *169*		**5**:5 .... *60*
:21 .... *168*	**1**:17 .... *177*	**6**:41 .... *94*
9:5 .... *11*	**2**:26,27 .... *165*	**20**:19 .... *12*
:15 .... *168*	**7**:15,16 .... *93*	**23**:6 .... *60*
:25 .... *42*	:21 .... *93*	**25**:20 .... *145*
10:1 .... *208*	**8**:38,39 .... *33*	**29**:5 .... *60*
:8 .... *168*	**11**:26 .... *10*	**30**:27 .... *60*
12:2 .... *169*	:38 .... *169*	**31**:16 .... *72*
:2-5 .... *194*	**12**:15 .... *145*	**33**:4,7 .... *11*
:3 .... *185*	**13**:1,2 .... *151*	**34**:12 .... *12*
:3-5 .... *184*	**20**:38-43 .... *151*	**35**:2,3 .... *11*
:18 .... *64, 168*	**22**:19 .... *38*	:3 .... *60*
13:9-12 .... *164*		
14:3 .... *164, 232*	**2 Kings**	**Job**
:18,19 .... *165*		
15:11 .... *70, 168*	**19**:15 .... *37*	**1**:20 .... *91*
:27 .... *126*		:21 .... *90*
16:13 .... *208*	**1 Chronicles**	**2**:8,12,13 .... *91*
21:6 .... *163*		:10 .... *4, 90*
22:11,16,22 .... *165*	**4**:9 .... *64*	**7**:11 .... *32*
:11,20 .... *232*	**6**:4-7 .... *232*	:11,13 .... *49*
:18 .... *122*	:26,35 .... *10*	**9**:6 .... *93*
:19 .... *163*	:33-38 .... *9*	:26 .... *197*
23:6,9-11 .... *165*	:34-36 .... *11*	:27 .... *49*
:9 .... *122*	:66-69 .... *11*	**10**:1 .... *49*
25:1 .... *42*	**7**:16 .... *64*	**16**:15 .... *91*
:24 .... *177*	**9**:19,21 .... *13*	**19**:25-27 .... *90*
:37 .... *46*	:19-27 .... *136*	**21**:4 .... *49*
28:13,14 .... *126*	:20 .... *13*	**23**:2 .... *49*
30:7,8 .... *165*	:22 .... *13*	**30**:19 .... *91*
	:23-33 .... *12*	**37**:4,5 .... *96*
2 Samuel	**15**:2,3,15,26 .... *11*	**38**:4-6 .... *93*
	:16,17 .... *12*	**39**:29 .... *197*
4:6 .... *135*	:27 .... *226*	**40**:9 .... *96*
6:2 .... *40*	**16**:1-3 .... *226*	**42**:6 .... *91*
7:11 .... *169*	**21**:24 .... *35, 79*	
15:35 .... *232*	**23**:26-29 .... *12*	

:10 90

Psalm

2:2-9 227
11:2 86
15:2 178
19:7,11,14 178
24:9,10 40
37:10-15 227
:14,15 86
40:8 178
50:2 37
:23 111
64:3,4 86
66:13,14 230
:13-15 72
75:3 94
:5,7,10 94
:10 81
78:60-62 207
:63,64 207
:64 223
:65 207
:66 207
80:1 37
:1,3,7,19 40
82:1-8 143
84:10 13
86:16 40
92:10 81
99:1 37
:6 .... 64, 168
103:20,21 38
110:1 226
:2 226
:3 226
:3,4 149
:4 226
112:9 .... 81, 130
113:1,2 92
:5,6 92
:7,8 92
:9 92
116:16 40
121:4-8 134
131:2 71
132:9,16 94
138:2 222
139:21,22 119
144:14 196
147:14 107

Proverbs

3:1-4 194
14:4 196
:10 33
16:2 85
19:2 196
:17 130
21:2 85
22:6 68
:9 130
23:5 197
:24,25 160
27:9 197
28:1 196
:27 130
:28 29
29:2 29
30:3 196
:15,16 24
:19 197
31:21 123
:28-31 108

Ecclesiastes

3:4 4

5:1-6 34
8:1 197
:11 166
11:3 201
12:1 201

Isaiah

4:1 16
6:1-3 40
15:5 72
28:9 71
32:20 196
37:15,16 40
38:15 32
45:7 90
46:3,4 193
49:15 127
52:8,9 192
56:7 187
57:15 92

Jeremiah

2:8 142
6:26 77
7:9-12 187
9:3 86
11:19 196
14:21 92
15:1 .... 64, 168
:7-9 88
17:12 92
48:34 72

Lamentations

1:4 137
3:27 201

Scripture index

4:19 197

Ezekiel

21:26,27 99
22:26 142
30:21,22 162
40:45 234
  :46 233
43:19 233
44:10-14,17-22
  234
  :15,16 233
45:4 233
  :5 234
48:10,11 233
  :13,14 234

Daniel

2:22 4

Hosea

4:6,9 142
  :9 117

Amos

3:8 196
8:10 77

Habakkuk

1:8 197

Zephaniah

3:4 142

Haggai

2:7-9 40

Zechariah

6:12,13 98
9:9-11 99
11:17 162
12:10 77

Malachi

2:6,7 84
  :7,8 142
  :15 216

Matthew

21:16 70

Mark

6:3 183
10:6-9 216

Luke

1:5,8-10,21,22
  198
  :7 .... 22, 177
  :15 177
  :17 177
  :25 16
  :26 189
  :28 .... 51, 179
  :38 179
  :46 .... 80, 223
  :46-56 175–199
  :47 223
  :48 .... 180, 223
  :49 224
  :50 224
  :51 224
  :52 .... 88, 224
  :53 224
  :54 224
  :55 224
  :69 81
  :80 177
2:19 .... 180, 181
  :22 182
  :22,23 183
  :23 182
  :24 182
  :25 192
  :26,29 189
  :27 .... 183, 188
  :34 190
  :36 192
  :37 .... 137, 192
  :38 192
  :39 183
  :39,43 183
  :40 194
  :41,42 183
  :42 194
  :46 185
  :47 185
  :49 104
  :51 181
  :52 195
6:21 3
9:62 103
18:1 44
19:10 197
  :45-48 187
23:51 11
24:50-53 199

John

7:2-5 133
8:46 185
11:51 129
18:16,17 135

Acts

1:13,14 44
2:42 44

6:4...... 44	**6**:18...... 44	**5**:1...... 195
:15...... 197		:1,2...... 197
7:20...... 68	**Philippians**	:1-5...... 197
12:13...... 135	**2**:20...... 197	:12-14...... 71
13:18...... 193		**7**:7,8...... 98
	Colossians	:16,17...... 149
Romans	**4**:2...... 44	**11**:23...... 68
4:19...... 131		**13**:7,17,24...... 47
8:32...... 121	**1 Timothy**	
11:29...... 42	**1**:18...... 135	**1 Peter**
12:12...... 44	**2**:1,2...... 47	**2**:2...... 68, 193
13:1-7...... 47	**5**:17-19...... 47	:13-17...... 47
1 Corinthians	**2 Timothy**	**2 Peter**
2:11...... 33	**2**:19...... 95	**2**:7,8...... 25
7:32-35...... 137	**3**:15...... 68	:8...... 60
Galatians	**Hebrews**	**1 John**
4:22-27...... 88	**2**:11,12...... 131	**5**:14...... 56
	:17,18...... 197	
Ephesians	**4**:15...... 197	**Revelation**
5:31,32...... 216		**19**:7...... 216